This Music Leaves Stains

This Music Leaves Stains

The Complete Story of the Misfits

James Greene Jr.

TAYLOR TRADE PUBLISHING
Lanham • Boulder • New York • Toronto • Plymouth, UK

Published by Taylor Trade Publishing
An imprint of Rowman & Littlefield
4501 Forbes Boulevard, Suite 200, Lanham, Maryland 20706
www.rowman.com

10 Thornbury Road, Plymouth PL6 7PP, United Kingdom

Distributed by National Book Network

British Library Cataloguing in Publication Information Available

The hardback edition of this book was previously cataloged by the Library of Congress as
follows:
Greene, James, Jr., 1979–
This music leaves stains : the complete story of the Misfits / James R. Greene Jr.
p. cm.
Includes bibliographical references and index.
1. Misfits (Musical group) 2. Punk rock musicians—United States—Biography. I. Title.
ML421.M576G74 2013
782.421660092'2—dc23
[B] 2012042761

ISBN 978-1-58979-892-2 (paper : alk. paper)
ISBN 978-0-8108-8438-0 (ebook)

∞ ™ The paper used in this publication meets the minimum requirements of American
National Standard for Information Sciences Permanence of Paper for Printed Library
Materials, ANSI/NISO Z39.48-1992.

Printed in the United States of America

For Theodora and James Sr.

Contents

Acknowledgments

A sincere and heartfelt thank-you to every person who agreed to be interviewed for this book. Though some ultimately had to be excised from the final pages, every single one of your stories, knowledge, and remembrances helped shape the narrative considerably. I am greatly indebted to you all.

Thank you also to every person who did not agree to be interviewed for this book but conveyed their response in a polite, mannered way that also expressed support and the best of luck with this project. In an age where it is incredibly easy and generally more convenient to simply ignore e-mails, text messages, and other communication from parties unknown, your etiquette touched me even if you were cranking it out on autopilot.

To the handful of individuals who would only agree to aid me for "a nominal fee," I must say: some of your figures are staggering. If they are indicative of amounts you have received in the past for such projects, bravo. I obviously missed the class on master negotiating you attended.

The following individuals went above and beyond their proverbial calls of duty to help this volume come to fruition: David Adelman, Kathleen Bracken, Chris Bunkley, Ken Chino, Liz Eno, Danny Gamble, Bennett Graff, Christopher Harris, Rollie Hatch, Mark Kennedy, Taylor Knoblock, Brie Koyanagi, Aaron Knowlton, Pete Marshall, Mick Mercer, Rachel Hellion Meyers, Linnéa Olsson, John Piacquadio, Bill Platt, Michael Poley, Lyle Preslar, James Edward Raymond, James Lewis Rumpf, Kevin Salk, Dave Schwartzman, Mike Stax, Bear Steppe, Chopper Steppe, Jim Testa, John L. Welch, Matt Whiting, Joshua Wyatt, and Jay Yuenger.

Thank you of course to the Misfits themselves—even the ones who turned down the opportunity to participate here. Without your fertile subject matter, this book would probably be about something dreadfully boring, like impression-die forging or the history of Quaker Oats.

Extra special thanks to the taco truck at the corner of Stuyvesant Avenue and Broadway in Brooklyn for providing many a platter of pork nachos to help fuel late-night writing sessions. Thank you also to the PepsiCo corporation for the same via their wide variety of Mountain Dew products. Thanks also to the physicians who will help me with the kidney stones I most likely developed from ingesting so much food of this quality.

Preface

The Misfits are a band who have long had a "secret club" aura surrounding them. Like the jaded B-movie criticism vehicle *Mystery Science Theater 3000* or the drug-mad writings of Hunter S. Thompson, fans first stumble across this entity and marvel, "I can't believe something like this exists!" If you feel the connection it is euphoric—finally, a cultural force speaking in a voice previously unheard yet familiar to your own inner monologue. Suddenly you want to know everything about them. You devour information like a rabid dog, swallowing every tidbit you come across.

At fifteen I became aware of the Misfits thanks to an upperclassman in my drawing class named Ed who regularly wore a tattered black shirt bearing the band's famous blaring white skull mascot. It was vintage, Ed claimed, passed down to him from a cousin or a sibling who had known the band and managed to get the image widely known (despite its lack of red hue) as the Crimson Ghost silkscreened directly on his or her own design-free T-shirt. A logo of the Champion brand on the garment's sleeve seemed to support my friend's story ("The Misfits wouldn't *sell* a T-shirt with some company's name on it," Ed offered, reasonably). At the time I had never heard the Misfits but appreciated that I knew someone who owned something someone relatively famous once touched.

A few months out of high school I was killing time between community college courses at the home of a female friend; to give you some idea of the time period, I believe on that particular afternoon we were commiserating over the sudden gruesome death of Phil Hartman. As we conversed, my friend's brother began loudly playing a spate of punk rock from his neighboring room. The rapid thumping, muffled ever so slightly by the home's drywall, was no bother—the Ramones were my bread and butter, after all—but a few minutes in I was struck by the distinct voice cutting through the smashing drums and roaring guitars.

Is that Glenn Danzig?

Like moth to a flame I shuffled into this kid's room. I don't remember our verbal exchange—just the surreal moment I picked up the jewel case for *Collection II* and saw Glenn Danzig's name clear as day on the sepia-toned back cover. Suddenly it dawned on me.

Oh my God. The guy who sang "Mother" was in a punk band. Like, a really good punk band. This sounds like Elvis and the Ramones and there are goddamn skulls and murder all over this thing.

I was beside myself. Danzig's eponymous heavy metal band had danced across MTV for a brief moment just a few years before this, but I never bothered to penetrate beyond the surface radio hits. Glenn Danzig's deal had seemed clear to me: enormous belt buckle, mutton chops, buckets of swagger, deep voice, wanky metal junk. I figured the buck stopped there. Rarely have I ever been so pleased being dead wrong.

The real tipping point was "I Turned into a Martian." Such a massive amount of catharsis flows through that song for anyone who's ever identified with being an outcast or an outsider or on the wrong side of normal. In my late teens I was certainly cognizant of the fact it was okay to be different, but that didn't necessarily always act as a salve when I felt out of place. To hear Danzig just completely own his metamorphosis into an otherworldly creature, to clench it with his fists and turn it around into an anthem of empowerment . . . I mean, that was the most reassuring thing in the world. When he shouts "This world is mine to own!" at the end of the second verse, I always find myself standing up a little straighter.

And the way the Misfits glued the song's melodies to that grinding riff is just astounding. How often to you ever hear something so forceful, so hard-charging—those first three chords just come barreling out at you like cannon blasts—that's also so sweet and romantic and (for lack of a better word) epic? There was just no turning back once that song hit my ears. Nearly every Misfits song is great, but for my money "I Turned into a Martian" is the greatest.

The next several years were spent absorbing the dark greatness of the Misfits—not just their music, not just their image, but their strange and twisted story. Along the way I saw the band a handful of times during the first five years as a reunited entity, when Michale Graves was filling the unenviable position of Glenn Danzig's replacement. They were theatrical, a bit showbizzy, but no more so than Danzig's eponymous band, which I also saw during the same period. I had nothing to judge these experiences against as I was all of four when the Misfits first dissolved in 1983 and I knew no music outside my scratched copy of "Snoopy vs. the Red Baron"; but both experiences offered a fair amount of camp with raw rock n' roll thrills. In one instance I saw the Misfits at a miniscule club in Daytona Beach called Orbit 3000; the space was so cramped that the crash cymbals sitting above Dr. Chud's drum kit (an exaggerated set-up that in reality wasn't that much larger than your average percussion set) were grazing the ceiling. The stage actually collapsed during one of the opening bands that night. Still, the Misfits went on—Michale Graves literally pushing Orbit 3000's owner out of the way so the band could spread out on the sunken structure and play for the sweaty, packed house. Moments before that, as their ominous intro music played, I remember a backstage light illuminating muscular guitarist Doyle in such a way that his massive shadow spread across a neighboring wall like some horrid two-dimensional monster. A more perfect visual couldn't have been scripted by Tobe Hooper himself.

A couple days after that particular show, I heard a rumor that the Misfits and the assaulted club owner got into another tussle once the band left Orbit 3000's stage for the evening, and the end result of that donnybrook was Doyle pitching a security guard through a plate glass window. I tended to believe this story not because Doyle and his brother Jerry were hulking weightlifters with short tempers from New Jersey but because the oppressive heat of central Florida has been known to cause plate glass hurlings before. In 1997 Charles Barkley was arrested in downtown Orlando for chucking some guy through the front window of Phineas Phogg's just because the victim had tossed some ice in Barkley's general direction. And this wasn't even during the regular NBA season—Charles was in town for a friggin' exhibition game. His Greatness was released on $6,000 bond after spending five hours in jail; as for Doyle, I never heard of any charges one way or another, but interestingly enough the Misfits never again played a show in Daytona Beach.

There was definitely no such violence at the Danzig show I attended circa the same era, and there were also no Misfits songs. That's what got me in the door. I mean, aside from the thought process "I should see Glenn Danzig in concert just in case this Y2K thing turns out to be real." Rumors were circulating online that Danzig was closing shows on this particular tour with assorted material from his salad days. Alas, no such luck with the gig I attended. The Internet used to lie a lot more back in the 1990s. It was pretty thrilling to see Glenn nonetheless. His relaxed demeanor between songs conveyed to me that the public image is not always the person and vice versa. For a guy depicted as being so glum all the time he sure was smiling a lot up there (then again, this was the House of Blues, so I'm sure the soup spread backstage was above average).

But I digress. For a long time there was an accepted and set narrative regarding the Misfits, one expertly dug up in the pre-Internet age by devoted historians who understood the aforementioned thirst for knowledge and hoped to quench it. They did a fantastic job, but as the years grew on, this particular fiend needed to know more. Not only because the band was stretching itself in a new form across our new century, but also because so many questions in the oft-repeated tale remained unanswered. It was also stunning that no singular book had yet been devoted to the Misfits, despite the mark they made in punk and the shadow they cast over mainstream rock music. For these reasons, two years ago I decided to buckle down and attempt to author the definitive Misfits tome myself.

Not every mystery regarding this legendary band is solved in the pages that follow (which I suppose is just as well, lest these figures lose their entire sense of intrigue), but light is certainly shed on numerous aspects of the Misfits story that had continued to confuse, and the music is finally given what I hope is considered its full critical shake. It is my sincere hope that my fellow Misfits enthusiasts accept and enjoy this book. It would also be nice if fans of disciple bands took to it as well for any knowledge it imparts.

Hell, so long as this book isn't burned en masse in any town square or witches' coven, I'll be happy. Thank you for your patronage, even if you are only reading this in chunks during occasional visits to the local book store or library.

Chapter One

Stuck in Lodi

I could say some nasty things about New Jersey, but once my darling mother said, "Don't speak unkindly of the dead." —Billy Murray, "Over on the Jersey Side"

Of course the Misfits are from New Jersey. No other state could have bred an outfit so great that was ignored for so long. Pop culture's relative blind eye to the Misfits is very much a microcosm of Jersey itself—despite being perfectly situated between several major metropolitan areas (New York City to the north, Philadelphia and Washington, D.C., to the south), the Garden State has long suffered little brother syndrome. For decades the rest of the country has mercilessly taunted New Jersey for being uncultured, odorous, and of no consequence. Never mind that New Jersey is where Thomas Edison did the lion's share of his groundbreaking scientific and electrical work.[1] Never mind that New Jersey hosts some of our country's most esteemed institutions of higher learning, including Princeton, William Paterson, and Rutgers. Never mind that saltwater taffy and Campbell's Soup were both created in New Jersey.[2] This state, to so many, is simply a retainer for the undesirable.

Jersey may shake that stigma yet, but one facet they can't live down is the number of spooky, ghoulish, and just flat-out bizarre happenings that have occurred within its borders. There was Orson Welles's mania-inspiring *War of the Worlds* prank,[3] the still-debated kidnapping of the Lindbergh baby,[4] the crash of the Hindenburg,[5] and the ferocious shark attacks by the so-called Jersey Man-Eater;[6] a handful of motorways like Clinton Road and Shades of Death Road that are said to be festooned with all manner of angry poltergeists,[7] as are a number of structures with apropos names like the Devil's Tree[8] and the Devil's Tower;[9] one of history's most famous cryptids, the Jersey Devil, has allegedly been raising hell in the Pine Barrens since colonial times;[10] numerous odd conglomerations of societal outsiders like the alleg-

1

edly inbred Jackson Whites[11] and the nature-worshipping Gatherers;[12] and who could forget Suzanne Muldowney, that extremely intense woman who runs around New Jersey performing interpretive dance routines in her home-made Underdog costume.[13] It's understandable how all this might inspire a few outcast kids to start dressing like zombies and write songs about murder.

Speaking of murder: New Jersey is also noted for its rich mafia history, which dates back to America's Prohibition era. The Gambino, Genovese, and Lucchese crime families have all had their fingers buried deep in the Garden State at varying times,[14] and the indigenous DeCavalcante family served as the basis for HBO's wildly popular *Sopranos* television series.[15] In fact, Lodi's own Satin Dolls strip club on Route 17 served as the filming location for Tony Soprano's favorite hangout,[16] the Bada Bing! (Satin Dolls proudly touts this fact in all their current advertising.)[17]

This litany of macabre happenings aside, there is still an all-American charm to New Jersey, thanks to its sprawling, often picturesque suburbs, most of which were first constructed during the 1950s post-war boom. Neighborhood after neighborhood of ranch style homes project safety, comfort, and serenity. Every little borough has its own beloved pizza place, its own quaint town hall, its own ragtag high school football team the whole area gets behind with a fervor. In many ways New Jersey's assorted townships and villages are as close to *Leave It to Beaver* as you can get. To a teenager with dreams of conquering a neighboring metropolis, though, such an environment can be the epitome of boring, regressive, and stifling, breeding a dangerous complacency. Often, the only respite in such a situation is music.

Luckily, New Jersey has a rich and varied musical lineage. Hoboken's native son Frank Sinatra crooned his way to icon status, redefining cool along the way, in the 1940s and 1950s.[18] Belleville's Four Seasons are considered by many to be the greatest pop vocal act of all time (and they have the millions in sales to back that assessment up).[19] Although he is usually associated more closely with Asbury Park, the city of Long Branch can claim Bruce Springsteen and his songwriting genius as their own. Jersey City gave the world soul/funk ambassadors Kool & the Gang.[20] Jersey was also the sight of the first live performance by the Velvet Underground, a 1965 gig at Summit High School (for which the influential assembly charged just $2.50 a ticket).[21] And as if those giants weren't enough, Les Paul, the man who more or less gave birth to rock n' roll by crafting and marketing one of the world's first solid-body electric guitars in the 1940s, settled for years in the township of Mahwah until his death in 2009.[22]

From this frothy stew of cultural activity both great and dubious rose the Misfits, founders and pioneers of what many dub "horror punk," as that strain of music had never been so ghoulish or gothic before. How could it not be, considering their surroundings? Yet, at the same time, for the same reason, their music was accessible, strangely familiar, utterly digestible. It is the living embodiment of where they came from, a strange territory that doesn't get nearly enough credit and is burdened by some dark aura.

Naturally there were larger cultural factors that played into the birth of the Misfits. The principal band members belonged to one of the earliest American generations to mature in the warming glow of television. From the mid-1950s well into the late 1970s TV's vast wasteland was dotted with weekend horror movie syndication packages, wherein classic monster films from years earlier were aired on the small screen, often with humorous commentary by some sort of otherworldly host. The earliest example of such programming was *The Vampira Show*, a critically acclaimed KABC-TV production in 1954 Los Angeles that was hosted by a slinky, sexy female creature of the same name.[23] Four years later, ABC's New York station was invaded by the similarly droll ghoul Zacherley and his *Shock Theater* (which would later move to rival WPIX and become that station's long-running *Chiller Theater*). Imitators sprung up across the country over the next decade like wildfire, and it was because of these creature features and their unusual hosts that cheap, B-grade horror movies became ingrained in American youth culture. If you lived in the so-called sticks and weren't old enough to drive yet, all you could do on a Friday night was hang out at home and watch someone like Zacherley or Ohio's beloved Ghoulardi try to creep you out with fare like *Son of Kong* or *White Zombie*.[24]

Not that you'd necessarily have to stay in your living room to see that kind of thing come the late 1960s or early 1970s. This was the period in which the cinematic practice of midnight movies flourished; movie theaters enticed patronage with late showings of controversial films both new and old, partially in an attempt to steal viewers away from the growing threat of those televised creature features. Similarly, this stretch of time saw drive-in theaters, desperate to retain business as the novelty of watching movies in your car wore off, begin to shift their hosting duties from normal Hollywood material to the seedy waters of exploitation. That seemingly catch-all genre included not only B- but Z-grade horror films, as well as violent outlaw biker epics, titillating flesh-heavy "nudies," arty Italian suspense thrillers, the mondos or "shockumentaries" that attempted to tear the cover off boring everyday life, and wild chop socky kung fu masterpieces imported directly from China. Maximum weirdness was sometimes just a few dollars away.[25]

If there is one specific piece of fringe cinema to single out as most important to the following narrative, it is most definitely George Romero's 1968 zombie nightmare *Night of the Living Dead*. The cult masterpiece follows the plight of five survivors of an unexplained viral disaster who attempt to safeguard themselves in a Pennsylvania farmhouse as legions of corpses rise from the grave, hungry for human flesh. Romero's vision was a stark one, from the low-grade black-and-white visuals of the panicked survivors fighting off their lumbering attackers to the film's semi-surprise ending that is void of hope or relief. *Night of the Living Dead* forever altered the DNA of the horror film, exorcising cheap thrills and camp in favor of complete dread. It eventually became a staple of Americana thanks in part to the film's public domain status (*NOTLD*'s original distributor failed to place copyright notice on original prints of the film, allowing anyone and everyone to release it over the years).[26]

Similarly, the nation's magazine racks were not as sanitized during this era as they are today. Sensational periodicals like *The National Informer* and *The Exploiter* sat next to *Newsweek* and *Time*, routinely splashing gory images on their covers underneath screaming headlines like "KILLER PLAY-BOY DIES IN HAIL OF BULLETS!" and "MAN CUT IN HALF—HE LIVES!" Also mixed in with these tabloids were magazines like *Cinefantastique* and *Famous Monsters of Filmland* that were dedicated to fictional ghouls and murderers. The cult rag market would only grow as the years stretched on, birthing such forgotten classics of murder porn such as *Violent World*, *The Godfathers* (dedicated to mafioso killings), and *True Sex Crimes*.[27]

Popular musicians in the United States had been crafting material with varying supernatural themes since the Great Depression—the same period when Hollywood began offering classic horror movies such as *Dracula* and *Frankenstein*—though not with much regularity. Jazz titan Louis Armstrong famously crafted a spooky swinger called "Skeleton in the Closet" for the 1936 Bing Crosby film *Pennies from Heaven* ("Skeleton" is noted for a spoken word opening by Armstrong that ends on a humorous mispronunciation: "Boy, don't you go in there . . . don't you know that house is ha'nted?")[28] One year later, Mississippi-bred blues guitarist Robert Johnson stoked the embers of a future legend by suggesting he once allowed Satan to tune his instrument at a dusty crossroads (in exchange for Johnson's soul, of course) by recording "Me and the Devil Blues" for Columbia Records.[29] One of the biggest hits of the 1940s big-band era was the Harold Arlen and Johnny Mercer–penned "That Old Black Magic," which, despite being a love song, referenced to witchcraft and vividly described the frigid fingers of the protagonist's paramour.[30]

No one artist fully embodied the term "horror," though, until the sudden 1956 appearance of bellowing bluesman Screamin' Jay Hawkins and his cathartic, unhinged bump "I Put a Spell on You." Hawkins, a World War II vet who began his music career with dreams of conquering the opera world, displayed what many consider the first true shock rock persona. The wild-eyed singer was noted for accenting performances by wearing a fake bone through his nose, carrying around a skull-capped scepter he nicknamed Henry (Henry could often be seen with a lit cigarette clenched between his exposed teeth), and beginning numerous concerts by rising from a rickety coffin. Many fans bought Hawkins's shtick hook, line, and sinker, believing the Ohio native was actually a foreign-born practitioner of voodoo.

With his constant grunting and dips into subject matter as unsavory as cannibalism and constipation, Screamin' Jay ultimately proved too outrageous to sustain a healthy career. "I Put a Spell on You" endured nonetheless, covered over the following decades by a slew of popular and influential artists of varying genre. Artists as diverse as soul legend Ray Charles, jazz great Nina Simone, 1960s roots rockers Creedence Clearwater Revival, and Florida-bred goth shocker Marilyn Manson took on "Spell" in tribute to Hawkins' genius.[31]

Seven years after the release of "I Put a Spell on You," an aspiring actor from Massachusetts co-authored and recorded what is arguably the most popular horror rock anthem of all time. Bobby Pickett, desperately wanting to get in on the Twist dance craze, utilized the keen impression of *Frankenstein* star Boris Karloff he often did merely for his friends' amusement to birth the poppy mad scientist lament "Monster Mash" in 1962. Released that August, Pickett's "Monster Mash" featured an assembly of studio musicians to forever be known as the Crypt-Kickers and rode its goofy waltzing refrain into a number one hit by October, locking Pickett in to a profitable career as one of novelty music's most beloved icons. Bobby "Boris" scored again in 1975 with the "Star Trek" spoof record "Star Drek"; less popular were Pickett's assorted "Mash" sequels, such as the Christmas-themed "Monster's Holiday" from December 1962, a 1985 hip-hop reworking called "Shock the Body," and the 2005 global warming redux "Climate Mash." Still, the original endured, so much so that it was adapted into a feature film in 1995 starring Pickett himself alongside the catch-all likes of *Full House*'s Candace Cameron, Jimmie "Dynomite" Walker, and John Waters accomplice Mink Stole.[32]

There was also, around this time, a spate of macabre pop songs revolving around grizzly automotive deaths of teenagers, a reflection of or reaction to the dangerous youth street racing trends of the period. Beginning with Mark Dinning's 1959 "Teen Angel" and climaxing with the 1964's "Dead Man's Curve" by Jan & Dean and the Shangri-Las' "Leader of the Pack," these entries into the musical canon—which came to be affectionately known as "splatter platters"—dramatically detailed young love cut short by reckless driving (sometimes complete with stomach-churning car crash sound effects). The popularity of the splatter platters proved the American public, despite wanting to appear outwardly normal, had a remarkably wide morbid streak.[33]

Screamin' Jay Hawkins, "Monster Mash," and the splatter platters all paved the way for raspy Detroit singer Vincent Furnier, who adopted the stage name Alice Cooper in 1968 and used his penchants for classically spooky theatrics to transform his rock music into the ultimate shock-laden stage show. By 1971 the Alice Cooper Group, responsible for such creepy entries as "Dead Babies" and "The Ballad of Dwight Fry," were selling out venues across the country with a concert experience that included bloody doll parts, staged fights, and the shaggy-haired mascara-smeared singer's own pretend electrocution. Yet it was a very real act of gore that propelled Alice Cooper into the national spotlight just a few years prior—a 1969 Toronto gig was punctuated by the unexpected arrival of a stray chicken to the stage, which Cooper, an urban youth who had no experience with barnyard fowl, scooped up and tossed into the air under the assumption the bird would simply fly away. It did not. Plummeting to the ground in front of the crowd, the chicken was instantly descended upon by angry fans who began savagely dismembering it (believing it was all part of the show). Newspapers embellished the story the following day by claiming Cooper murdered the chicken onstage and ritualistically drank its blood.

Fellow rocker Frank Zappa, who had signed Cooper's group to his Straight Music record label, immediately phoned the shell-shocked singer regarding the blood-drinking tale and offered the following expert career advice: "Whatever you do, don't tell anyone you didn't do it." The strategy appears to have worked: Of the six albums Alice Cooper released in the succeeding half decade, five went platinum. The singer's raucous 1972 anti-education rant "School's Out" also became a top five hit in several countries despite (or maybe because of) its depiction of an exploding schoolhouse.[34]

A back-to-basics movement happening within the general rock n' roll scene at approximately the same time would simultaneously help set the stage and create a template for the style of music the Misfits would ultimately produce. A handful of bands during this period, eventually to be known as the proto-punks, pushed aggressively against the bloat that was decaying (or at least dulling) the genre into extended instrumental solos and drug-fueled conceptual nightmares; the proto-punks yearned for the brevity and liveliness that encapsulated rock n' roll as it was birthed a decade before and attempted to resuscitate that musical strain before it flatlined. From Detroit came the raucous MC5, whose hard rhythm and blues was based around their pledge to "kick out the jams, motherfuckers"; also from Detroit was the MC5's "little brother" band, the Stooges, who wrote two chord stomps that singer Iggy Pop yelped and groaned over;[35] California offered psychedelic blues pioneers Blue Cheer, who managed to score a Top 20 hit in 1967 with their cover of Eddie Cochran's "Summertime Blues";[36] and in New York City, the aforementioned Velvet Underground experimented with moody guitar jangles[37] while neighboring act the New York Dolls kept their material glittery and upbeat.[38] All of these bands would flame out long before their time but would manage to make their mark of influence on a select and important cross section of minds.

Right in the northeastern corner of New Jersey sits Bergen County, the most populous county in the entire state. In the county's southwest corner, nestled between the more recognized cities of Passaic and Hackensack, is Lodi, a borough of only two-and-a-half square miles comprised of the same serene residential neighborhoods and tiny shopping plazas you'd find so many other places in the state. Long before such bucolic charms existed, Lodi (and most surrounding areas) were inhabited by an Algonquin nation of thousands. Known as the Lenape tribe, [39] these Native Americans were eventually ousted by European settlers in the 1600s. The invading Europeans redubbed the land New Netherland in 1664 before settling later on the moniker New Barbadoes. [40] A couple hundred years went by before New Barbadoes (which gained notoriety in the eighteenth century as a major centerpiece in the lucrative fur trade) was rechristened Lodi Township in the 1820s, in honor of Lodi, Italy. [41] The industrial revolution quickly took hold, and Lodi became a manufacturing hub of grist mills, salt mills, bleaching and dyeing factories, and noxious chemical plants.

This working-class atmosphere stuck with the town into the twentieth century as its numbers grew steadily. The population seemed to quadruple with each passing decade, and the predominant ethnicity was in fact Italian—neighboring areas would come to dismissively joke that Lodi was a mere abbreviation for "Lots of Dumb Italians." Lodi was just like any other small American town, though, in that the men went out and busted their humps at their jobs, the women stayed home to raise the kids, everyone went to church on Sunday, and everyone pulled for the local sports team. By 1950 a cozy community of just over 15,000 resided in Lodi, which, at the time, was probably best known for being the home of WABC-TV's 648-foot-tall transmitting tower (powerful enough to allegedly send its signal across "thirty-eight states and half of Canada" [42]).

It was into this environment that Glenn Allen Anzalone was born on June 23, 1955, the third of four brothers raised in a bucolic neighborhood on MacArthur Avenue near Lodi's easternmost border. Glenn's Protestant father, Richard, was the third of four children himself and grew up in neighboring Hackensack to become a military man, serving his country as a Marine in both World War II and the Korean conflict. Richard Anzalone settled into civilian life thereafter, supporting his family through television repair (with so many sons in his brood, it should come as no surprise that Richard also became active in the Boy Scouts, at one point leading Lodi Troop 117 as well as Cub Scout Pack 102). [43] Glenn's mother, Maretta, was a Catholic two years Richard's junior who had one full sister and several half-siblings from her mother Maretta Mae's second and third marriages. In general Maretta was a homemaker, and early on she realized it was perhaps her job to instill in her four sons the fundamental importance of religion. Mrs. Anzalone dutifully took her brood to church every Sunday, though Glenn would later remark he never felt Catholicism had been "forc[ed] . . . down [his] throat." ("My dad didn't really care [if I went to church]," he said in 1992.)[44]

Later in Glenn's youth, Maretta took a job as a clerk at Stern's department store (the anchor of the then-new Bergen County Mall in nearby Paramus),[45] a job from which she would bring home Beatles and Rolling Stones albums for her sons to enjoy. Glenn, an artistically curious youth, especially appreciated this and eventually discovered more incredible artists via the record collection his elder brothers Bruce and Chris amassed. Although the future singer would take both piano and clarinet lessons during his formative years, his primary interest at this time was comic books. Glenn kept up with all the requisite heroes—Batman, Spider-Man, Captain America—but would later cite loner "anti-heroes" such as bitter Holocaust refugee Magneto and oceanic mutant Namor the Sub-Mariner as his true favorites. He also gravitated toward dinosaurs, spending hours sketching various thunder lizards for his own amusement.[46]

Adolescence for Glenn coincided with the discovery of macabre entries both old (EC Comics' *Tales from the Crypt*) and new (*Night of the Living Dead*). By this time the third Anzalone child had already developed a reputation for being outspoken and difficult despite his diminutive, seemingly non-threatening physical stature. Steve Linder was a year behind Glenn at Thomas Jefferson Middle School and remembers being acutely afraid of this "short [Anzalone] kid" who had a "big mouth." "I was kinda petrified of him," Linder says. "He was a wise guy. He was more this tough metal shop guy than a drama or music club guy. Y'know, typical short Italian guy from Lodi with a temper."

Regardless, Glenn's fascination with music was growing. Through his brothers he was turned on to the mournful wailing of Roy Orbison, who scored a string of Top 40 hits in the early 1960s like "Oh, Pretty Woman" and "Only the Lonely"; the dramatic touch of the Righteous Brothers, whose driving 1965 smash "You've Lost That Lovin' Feeling" would become a heartbreak standard; the weary poetic genius of Bob Dylan's introverted folk anthems; and the strange mystery of psychedelic blues rockers the Doors, led by swaggering baritone sex symbol Jim Morrison. The dalliances of Bruce and Chris in local bands also played a factor in Glenn's development. The younger Anzalone would act as a roadie for his brothers' gigs and subsequently got his first tastes of the raw live rock n' roll scene. He loved it, and it rubbed off on him in more ways than one—Glenn's hair soon became an unruly thicket that hung down far past his shoulders, the standard style of rockers at the time. The wavy locks may have annoyed his conservative ex-

Marine father but they also framed Glenn's steely gaze and prominent jaw rather nicely.

Comic book art remained Glenn's top priority, however, and following his graduation from Lodi High School in 1973 the aspiring artist began focusing on making that dream come true. He dutifully attended art classes in Manhattan, to which Maretta drove her son (who lacked a driver's license for decades).[47] Eventually, Glenn worked up the courage to send drawing samples to his heroes in the bullpen at Marvel Comics. Though he possessed a clear talent for rendering, two years went by with no job offers or advancements. In hindsight this is not surprising: the mid-1970s for the comic book industry was a time marked by shifting economics. Newsstand sales were sliding downward, and companies such as Marvel and DC were canceling more books than they were creating so as to streamline their titles and corresponding revenues. (Marvel even discontinued one of Glenn's favorite, Namor the Sub-Mariner, to try experimenting with less specific pulp genre tales.)[48] Frustrated by his stalled artistic dreams and growing restless in his hometown, Glenn Anzalone took his mind off professional woes by joining a cover band put together by some old high school friends that bore the very 1970s-sounding hard rock name Talus.

Glenn filled out the vocal position alongside bassist Jerry Byers, guitarist Ronnie Damato, and drummer Allen Becker. For Glenn, singing Top 40 rock songs was a fun way to blow off steam, and according to those around at the time there was no question the rich baritone for which he would later gain esteem was already almost fully developed. Talus existed for about a year before various members lost interest. Byers remained passionate about playing, though, so he sought out two other musician friends: Steve Linder, who by this point had become known around Lodi as an accomplished guitarist, and drummer Jim Catania, as cherished for his percussive skills as he was for his valid driver's license and car ("Nobody had wheels back then, so he was the guy!" Linder recalls). When it came time for this youthful trio to find a vocalist, Byers immediately called Glenn Anzalone.

Upon his admission Glenn christened this nascent outfit with a seemingly nonsensical name: Koo-Dot-N-Boo-Jang. His band mates were perplexed by the voodoo-ish moniker but accepted it for its originality. Koo-Dot quickly adopted a serious approach, practicing three nights a week and eschewing all social activities (even their increasingly impatient girlfriends) to perfect their takes on hits by rock n' roll pioneers Chuck Berry and Elvis Presley as well as more contemporary material by the likes of Free, Led Zeppelin, and the J. Geils Band. Glenn in particular tried to be as professional as possible—on the Zeppelin songs, the nascent singer refused to ape Robert Plant's famous carnal screams for fear of damaging his own vocal chords. The young singer also tried to get his Koo-Dot band mates to work on original material, but the creations or ideas he presented were usually labeled as too dark or off-the-wall for the bar band scene (one of the original songs that Koo-Dot did perform, courtesy of bassist Byers, was a tongue-in-cheek testicular ode called "My Nuts or Your Nuts").

Such rejection was not always easy for young Anzalone to hear. "Glenn was very sensitive," says Steve Linder. "You couldn't mess with one of his originals. He took himself very seriously. One time, we were arguing about something related to our band, and he just snapped at me—'The only thing *I have* is my voice!' You know, some shit, he could dish out but he couldn't take it."

During their heyday, Koo-Dot-N-Boo-Jang would play a variety of backyard parties in and around Lodi; the band's shining moment, though, came nearly a year in when they were hired to perform at a function hosted at the local Catholic Youth Organization hall. Although many priests at the venue were perplexed by the band's odd name, which the rockers were not wont to explain, Koo-Dot drew a decent crowd and put on a good enough show that they were invited back for another event. Unfortunately, by that time Byers and Catania had grown bored with the material and had given up on KooDot-N-Boo-Jang.

Linder and Glenn soldiered forward, recruiting bassist Tony Leek, drummer Manny Martinez, and guitarist Charlie Jones for another covers act. Feeling more assured as a singer and front man, Glenn demanded that this new outfit perform more of the fringe proto-punk material he was growing to love. This included such songs as former Roxy Music singer Bryan Ferry's arrangement of the Bob Dylan classic "A Hard Rain's A-Gonna Fall" and "Walk on the Wild Side," a gritty depiction of inner-city life wrapped in an FM-friendly melody and delivered by Velvet Underground figurehead Lou Reed ("We even did those really high 'doo-do-doo' parts!" Linder recalls with an embarrassed laugh). The rest of the band was more interested in sticking with the meat-and-potatoes hard rock they had always loved, but they appeased their talented front man nonetheless.[49] Glenn's foremost allegiance in the area of hard rock and/or heavy metal was to genre founders Black Sabbath. He would later cite Sabbath's 1970 debut as one of the most influential and important records he ever purchased,[50] often citing it as the very first record he purchased of his own accord. Creepy, impenetrable dirges like "The Wizard" and "N.I.B." may have been panned by critics at the time for being too doom-ridden but they certainly opened up a whole new universe for millions of frustrated adolescents at the tail end of the flower power era. Black Sabbath was also the first concert that Glenn ever attended; the dour rockers played New York City a handful of times when Glenn was just fifteen, usually performing at the city's Fillmore East.[51] The future Misfit remembered the show in a 2010 interview: "I remember that me and my friend were at this show and we were the littlest kids there. It was oversold and the crowd was rocking back and forth so we just started punching and kicking people—that's the kind of kids we were."

Musically, Glenn enjoyed his first experience with Sabbath, though was somewhat dismayed that the band were not quite as good live as they had been on record.[52] Unfortunately, Glenn's musician friends did not hold Black Sabbath in the same reverence and could not be convinced to cover any material by the decidedly evil group. Also shot down by his band mates were songs by Glenn's other perennial obsession, Detroit's legendary Stooges.[53] Led by outrageous feral animal Iggy Pop, who would mark live performances by smearing himself with peanut butter and sometimes slashing his chest with broken glass, the Stooges released three albums of brutal, sexually charged rock n' roll before splintering apart amidst a druggy haze in 1974. Primitive freakouts like "Dirt" and "TV Eye" were too raunchy and/or liberated for the general populace at the time; thus, Glenn would have to be content with strumming the handful of chords that made up the Stooges' depraved, subservient 1969 ode "I Wanna Be Your Dog" endlessly at night on his own guitar alone in his bed room.[54]

This third and final cover band featuring Glenn Anzalone would perform a handful of gigs at dive bars around town under a variety of different names. At first, they were known as Orex; later, they became P.O.N.Y. (an acronym for something lost to time); and still later, Prostitutes. In concert the band tried to set themselves apart from other more staid acts by wearing scuba gear or wrapping their bodies in cellophane. Dubious gimmicks and ongoing identity crises aside, Orex/P.O.N.Y./Prostitutes was relatively enjoyable for all involved until a bit of unsavory back-channel gossip broke them apart for good. Linder struck up a friendship with Glenn's younger brother Scott during this third's band's run; one afternoon, Scott revealed that Glenn had said Linder was the worst guitarist he'd ever played with. Naturally, Linder was painfully wounded. "I got so upset," the guitarist says, "that I went [to the practice space] and took my amp and never wanted to talk to [Glenn] again. And I never really did."[55]

Steve Linder's defection and the subsequent dissolve of this name-shifting covers band didn't bother Glenn very much; by March of 1977 the singer had had his fill of performing other people's material. The punk rock movement was beginning to galvanize in his proverbial backyard thanks to a Queens quartet known as the Ramones, who became the toast of Lower Manhattan by dressing in matching leather jackets, pushing their distorted guitars to eleven, and writing twisted two-minute pop nursery rhymes about abusing household toxins ("Now I Wanna Sniff Some Glue") and attacking toddlers ("Beat on the Brat"). The Ramones' fierce gnawing sound and incredible velocity became the sonic template for all punk bands to follow, as would their image of arrested adolescence—the four members made sure the world believed they were real siblings with the surname Ramone (they weren't) who each loved all-American activities like baseball and surfing (in truth, only guitarist Johnny Ramone liked baseball, and only bassist Dee Dee surfed).[56]

Meanwhile, thanks to some cross-pollination between key figures in New York and London, England was seeing a simultaneous (albeit more newsworthy) uprising of raw rock n' roll sounds lead by a controversial band called the Sex Pistols. The Sex Pistols' debut single "Anarchy in the U.K." was a mad waltz celebrating disaster topped off by the ear-clearing caterwaul of singer Johnny Rotten. An expletive-filled appearance on a morning television program in December of 1976 sealed the band's fate as British tabloid fodder for the remainder of their natural existence. Though questions would eventually arise over just how legitimate this band's calls for civil unrest were (they had, after all, assembled in a trendy London clothing shop co-owned by future fashion icon Vivienne Westwood) there's no denying that the Sex Pistols offered a colorful, humorous alternative to mainstream rock with a string of explosive singles that shoehorned lethal amounts of energy back into rock n' roll.[57]

Sensing the right atmosphere, Glenn Anzalone decided to give up his long-term career goal of being a renowned comic book artist so he could focus on forming a wholly original punk rock band that might navigate him away from the Garden State's apparent dead ends. Aside from experience, Glenn had age on his side. Already in his early twenties, the square-jawed singer did not possess the same blind, confused anger that was the hallmark of so many younger punks of the time. He was angry, certainly, about life and Lodi and popular music and movies, but he was also more rational and determined and able to approach things from a more nuanced perspective. Glenn knew his punk band had to stand out, and more importantly, he had the raw talent to make them do so. Other punks mumbled, gurgled, or shrieked; the young Anzalone, in contrast, was discovering he could create rich sounds very much like his vocal heroes the Righteous Brothers, Jim Morrison, and Roy Orbison, with equal tone, sustainability, and range. He could legitimately sing, despite having never taken a lesson in his life. Years of studying pop art had also given him great insight into visual presentation. Glenn was certain whatever he did would be quite different from whatever else was going on—and more macabre.

Chapter Two

Teenagers from Mars

One of the great values of the Misfits is the sound of struggle . . . [it's the sound of] people expressing their art in the middle of artlessness. —JR, Rosemary's Babies[1]

From day one, Glenn Anzalone's new musical project would be called the Misfits, a name borrowed from the final film of his true Hollywood obsession, Marilyn Monroe. It was an apropos choice considering the rocky path this band would eventually go down: Directed in 1961 by John Huston, *The Misfits* has always been known just as much for its troubled production as for the weary desert romance it put on screen. Monroe was in such terrible shape from her drug and alcohol abuse that production had to be halted at least once. A doctor was eventually hired to look out for her as well as co-star and fellow boozehound Montgomery Clift. Huston himself also regularly imbibed while directing *The Misfits*, sometimes falling asleep during shots, sometimes gambling away portions of the budget with the film's extras.[2] Clark Gable, the marquee name of the film, insisted on doing every rigorous stunt scripted for his character despite his questionable condition—Gable was a weak sixty years old, severely damaged inside thanks to years of heavy smoking (the intense hundred-plus degree heat of the Nevada desert did the aged star no favors either).

Clark Gable would just barely survive filming *The Misfits*, suffering severe coronary thrombosis a day after production wrapped on November 4, 1960. The legendary actor died in the hospital eleven days later. The strain of the entire situation fractured Monroe's marriage to *Misfits* screenwriter Arthur Miller; the two divorced right before the film's February premiere. The following summer, Monroe herself died of a drug overdose in her Los Angeles home.[3] Putting a final stamp on the alleged curse of *The Misfits* was Clift's 1966 death from a fatal heart attack mere hours after his personal

13

secretary suggested the two watch a television broadcast of the movie ("Absolutely *not*," was Clift's alleged response). [4]

Not surprisingly, Glenn Anzalone wasn't the first musician who laid claim to the name Misfits (though he would ultimately prove the most successful with it). In 1964 a San Diego garage rock group under that moniker scored a minor hit with a reworking of the Coasters' classic "I'm a Hog for You, Baby" called "This Little Piggy." Said group boasted future Moby Grape singer/bassist Bob Mosley and garnered enough popularity to open for the Rolling Stones on that group's first U.S. tour. [5] Meanwhile, another garage rock assembly in Houston calling itself the Misfits began making the scene around the same time, buddying up to Roky Erickson's highly influential outfit 13th Floor Elevators. Unfortunately, a 1966 LSD bust sullied the reputation of Houston's Misfits enough that the band eventually changed their name to Lost and Found. [6] Also in 1966, a one-off single was released in Scotland by yet another Misfits to support their local school charity campaign. [7] The Scottish Misfits are notable in the grander scheme of things only because one of their drummers, John Wilson, would go on to play in Van Morrison's garage outfit Them. [8]

Several years into the career of New Jersey's Misfits, a female-fronted punk group from Albany, New York, began playing and releasing music under the same name. This upstate contingent, perhaps anticipating the litigious nature that in many ways would come to define Lodi's most notorious sons, renamed themselves the Tragics and faded into history despite their strong 1981 clarion call "Mommi I'm a Misfit." [9]

Immediately after settling on the name, Glenn Anzalone began scouring his neighborhood for musicians willing to back up his fledgling punk rock dreams. Prostitutes drummer Manny Martinez was pulled into the fold and would prove the only musician Glenn deemed worth keeping from the virgin Misfits lineup, which also included a female bassist, Diane DiPiazza, and a mysterious guitarist known only as Jimmy Battle. Martinez, whose drumming style was more rooted in the jazz improv of 1940s big bander Gene Krupa than that of Tommy Ramone, hosted Misfits practices in his parents' garage, the geographic location of which would help the band to acquire their permanent bass player and second-largest personality.

"I used to hang out with friends at a park in town," Gerald Caiafa remarked decades later. "It was like a local hangout, and Manny's house happened to be next door to the park. . . . I would hear them playing and shit and I never thought much about it."

Caiafa, known to friends and family as Jerry, was born April 21, 1959, the eldest of three brothers being raised by a machinist father—Jerry Sr.'s own acclaim came from his founding of the Congruent Machine manufacturing company, creators of the successful X-Acto-style Proedge hobby knife—and his wife on the southern end of Lodi on sleepy Grove Street. A massive

Bowie and Ramones fan also looking for a musical outlet, Jerry had asked for and received a bass guitar in February of 1977 as a belated Christmas gift (following the wisdom of a high school classmate who pointed out a four-string bass would be easier to play than a six-string guitar[10]) but couldn't find much immediate use for the instrument. Curiosity eventually got the better of newly minted rocker when he began dating a girl who lived next door to Manny Martinez; Jerry ventured over to Martinez's garage one afternoon where he found the drummer and Glenn, who was hunched over an electric piano, running through a few numbers.

The gregarious Caiafa, a high school footballer voted "Most Popular" by his fellow graduating classmates that year, quickly bonded with Glenn over the excitement of the burgeoning punk rock scene. They were both particularly enamored of the British punk bands yet to make much of an impact in the United States. There was the Damned, whose fuzz-drenched singles "New Rose" and "Neat Neat Neat" reveled in their own rowdiness; the Adverts, who offered a breathless teenage restlessness the Misfits would soon easily replicate; Generation X, whose singer Billy Idol gleefully conveyed a devil-may-care attitude in his addictive vocal cadence; and, of course, the Sex Pistols, the most notorious of the UK's punk class who burst with the most zeal, color, danger, and playful bile. Glenn deemed the outgoing and personable Caiafa a good fit for the Misfits and invited him to join the band. The trio began regularly rehearsing together, bringing to life the powerful songs that Glenn had kicking around in his head.[11]

The Misfits played their first gig less than a month after Jerry's entry into the band at New York City's on-the-rise Bowery bar CBGBs (Glenn, ever confident and embracing punk's true spirit, is said to have booked the show before the Misfits had a concrete lineup). It was April 18, 1977, the same night President Jimmy Carter addressed the nation to outline his ten-point energy conservation plan to help reduce growing dependence on natural resources—the precursor to Carter's infamous "Crisis of Confidence" speech three years later. There was also a solar eclipse that evening, but of more prescient concern to Glenn was his bassist's choice of attire for their band's public debut. Glenn found himself repulsed by the garish open-toed platform shoes and tight sequined pants glam fan Jerry adorned for this seminal CBGBs appearance, so much so that the singer nearly cancelled the performance. He didn't want to be visually lumped in with the endless New York Dolls imitators clogging the Manhattan punk rock scene at the time. Glenn relented at the last minute, however, taking the stage with Jerry and chalking the episode up to miscommunication regarding the image he wanted the Misfits to put forward.[12]

The irony was that soon Jerry would become the Misfit most entrenched in punk fashion, dying his dark brown hair electric blue, wearing a chain and padlock around his neck, and sporting a leather motorcycle jacket like Bowery favorites the Ramones (except that his had "THE MISFITS" emblazoned on the back; the Ramones weren't quite as shameless in their advertising). In these early years Jerry often looked more countercultural than Glenn, who initially preferred a soft brown leather jacket over an open dress shirt accented by a shaggy just-below-the-ears mane, a look that made him seem like just another two-bit New Jersey street tough. But Jerry was more pedestrian than his bellowing band mate in some ways; immediately after he graduated from high school he started pulling twelve-hour shifts at his father's machine shop in Paterson, New Jersey. Jerry later recalled the grind of staying out all night in Manhattan and then going directly to Paterson to wash his punk rock makeup off in the employee bathroom before the start of his day-long machine work. "It was tough," he told interviewer Daniel Russell. "But if the people back in the day didn't sacrifice, the scene would have never taken off." [13]

A month after their debut gig the Misfits put their costuming issues aside to record their first single, "Cough/Cool," at Manhattan's Rainbow Studio. [14] "Cough/Cool" paints the Misfits as anything but a sequin band—the music is centered around a pit of introversion, atmosphere, and drama. The stream-of-consciousness title track flows like a beat poet's horrifying late night fever dream ("Drench your face in darkness, spit up blood when you cough, cool cool cool cough") set to odd, incessant keyboard bleating and stuttering drums. Glenn's strong vocal is unmistakable on the track; when he holds notes, they triumphantly rise above the rest of the lo-fi din. The two-minute track begins with a sparse arrangement but builds in such intensity that by the end the listener feels enveloped by this humid blanket of electric piano chords and jazzy surf percussion. The final seconds find the Misfits pounding out one chord in succession with Manny's drums, tapping the nightmare right into your forehead until an abrupt stop accented by a tiny cymbal noise. Within an instant, "Cough/Cool" has faded away like a ghost.

The single's more straightforward B-side, "She," retells the Patty Hearst kidnapping scandal with a sense of brimming urgency. Raw and affecting, "She" paints a picture of a girl who loved "naked sin" instead of passing judgment on "Daddy's little girl" with the "machine gun in her hands." The song further sexualizes an already sensational crime story with Jerry's bleating bass and Glenn's naked emotional screams during the chorus. There's so much gusto in the singer's voice you can hear he's on the brink of natural distortion on this recording; luckily, the frequencies hold, keeping one of Glenn's best performances completely intact.

Five hundred copies of "Cough/Cool" were pressed by the Misfits and they released it on their own label, Blank Records, created specifically for the single's release. On the back cover, Glenn accidentally misspelled Jerry's last name as "Caifa." This prompted the bass player to demand he be billed specifically as "Jerry, only Jerry." Glenn wryly transformed this request into the nickname Jerry Only, a stage name that was brilliant in that it did not seem to have much connotation one way or the other (as opposed to those of the Misfits' British heroes Johnny Rotten, Dave Vanian, or Gay Advert).[15] Similarly vague was the surname Glenn Anzalone adopted at this time—Danzig.

The singer has long been cagey on the origin of his alias—for years he insisted Danzig was in fact his real birth name, and even now he will only say he carries some ancestral connection to the coastal Polish city of the same name (now known as Gdansk). The prevailing rumor among those close to the Anzalone family, however, is that Glenn was simply taken with the port of Danzig, a scenic destination comprised of elaborate gothic architecture dating back to the 1300s, during a post-high school trip overseas and decided to adopt its name as his own. Glenn eventually changed his last name legally from Anzalone to Danzig, apparently several years after the Misfits disbanded.

By October of 1977, the Misfits had grown tired of the obtuse sound Glenn's keyboard afforded them and were interested in pursuing a more aggressive punk sound. Danzig's electric piano was abandoned, allowing the singer to focus on his vocals, and the trio invited Jerry's childhood friend Frank LiCata to play guitar for the band. Another Lodi native (the youngest and only boy among his three siblings), LiCata had been playing guitar on and off since childhood and counted David Bowie guitarist Mick Ronson, the Ramones, and blues legends Buddy Guy and Willie Dixon among his major influences. With a slicked back blond coif and wraparound shades, Frank—rechristened Franché Coma by Glenn, an apparent play on France's eastern "Free Region" of Franche-Comté—looked the part of the throwback greaser ruffian, an anachronism in shaggy suburban 1970s America.

LiCata's choppy, violent style of down-stroking (copped from furious axeman Johnny Ramone) helped thrust the Misfits toward the angrier, more visceral area they were looking to inhabit. Despite a minimal equipment setup LiCata was able to pull a fierce gnawing sound out of his instrument, one that seemed to be continually growling as he churned out his chords. When it came to actual songwriting, however, the literal nuts and bolts of putting the music together, Danzig was the main force. The guitarist is firm in his assertion that "Glenn wrote everything, [all] the words and the melodies," though he will admit the two would sometimes work together to hash out a harmony for a particularly tricky composition. "We did an early version of 'Who Killed Marilyn?' that was way different than the [solo] record he put out later," Frank offers. "More background vocals, kinda tradin' off . . . it was pretty wild. But he or we decided not to do anything with it at the time."[16]

Jerry Only remembers the songwriting situation a little differently. In 2003, the bassist stated—as he had many times before—that he and the other

Misfits wrote a least a quarter to a third of the music, creating various introductory guitar riffs and arrangements for the songs, and that they merely ceded credit to Glenn to satisfy his fragile ego ("Glenn was real psyched on having everything in his name and all that kind of stuff"). Only would concede that Danzig, who he deems "an excellent songwriter," composed the lion's share of Misfits lyrics,[17] but not without a little coaching sometimes.

"Every once in a while, I'd give him a line, because he would mumble shit," Only said in 1998. "For example, in 'Devil's Whorehouse,' 'night time for midnight masses'—I thought that's what he said during the practice, and I said, 'What a cool line.' He said, 'Oh," and he wrote it down."[18]

Aside from the requisite roadblocks a punk rock band faced in 1977—lack of money, lack of credibility, an underground network not yet as connected and fluid as it would one day be—the Misfits had other challenges. Toward the beginning of October 1977, a boiler in the Martinez garage exploded into flames between rehearsals, damaging Manny's drum set and the various amplifiers the other band members stored there for practice. Later that month, just hours before his live debut with the band at Eddie's Lounge in neighboring Teaneck, LiCata absent-mindedly placed his flashy Gibson Explorer guitar on one of the club's active kitchen stoves. The instrument was thankfully still in its case, but the accident was frightening enough to the already nerve-racked LiCata, who had never performed publicly before.

But the band made some progress as well. LiCata recalls an early 1978 gig opening for fractured singer Richard Hell, he of *Blank Generation* and *Destiny Street* fame, at the Show Palace in Dover, New Jersey, wherein the Misfits went over like gangbusters ("The place was jam-packed," the guitarist remembers, "And we blew 'em away without a doubt. People were jumpin' on tables . . . everybody was goin' nuts!").[19] Around the same time, the band were presented with an enormous opportunity thanks to an oversight made by one of the country's most prestigious record labels. In November of 1977, Mercury Records—the Chicago label founded in 1945 renowned for releasing records across a wide variety of genres—was preparing to distribute the debut offering from Cleveland art punks Pere Ubu, whose dark experimental caterwaul had already spread itself across a handful of homemade singles. Entitled *The Modern Dance*, Pere Ubu's record was scheduled to be pressed on a Mercury imprint called Blank. The company was completely oblivious to the existence of the Misfits or the fact the band had legally beat them to the name "Blank" by just a few months. When confronted by Danzig during an angry phone call, Mercury agreed to gift the Misfits thirty hours of studio time to record an album (with the option of release) in exchange for permanent ownership of the Blank name.

Ecstatic, the Misfits booked their thirty free hours at New York's C.I. Recording Studios for January.[20] Before the session, however, the band decided to fire Manny Martinez. Aside from accusations that the drummer didn't take the band seriously enough and was often too drunk to play, the Misfits cited creative differences, claiming his love of Santana-style jam sessions interfered with their punk ethos. Brought in to replace Martinez was Koo-Dot graduate Jim Catania. A reserved, easygoing individual with shoulder-length hair and a permanently unaffected expression on his face, Catania's forthright drumming style gave the Misfits the backbone they needed to stand up straight on two legs. Catania played with no frills and an unbreakable meter—though his percussion did have a distinctly loose feel, never crowding the music, simply moving it along. Initially, Catania (dubbed Mr. Jim) joined the Misfits as a lark, but he quickly realized the group's potential. He was impressed by Glenn's "amazing talent," which in turn made the band "want to do as much as we could [and] take on whatever we could take on."[21]

The emboldened quartet entered C.I. that January and laid down seventeen songs (to save time, Jim Catania used the studio's house drum set, an assembly also used at that time by legendary soul session drummer Bernard Purdie for various recordings). Aiding in the production was Mercury Records engineer Dave Achelis, whose previous production credits included work with the New York Dolls, jazz great Dave Brubeck, and a litany of commercial radio jingles. Achelis jumped at the chance to work with the fledgling punk band that the other C.I. engineers had turned down as they seemed so different from the type of material he was used to recording. Any reservations about the unprofessional or rude nature of punk rockers went out the window almost immediately; Achelis found the Misfits to be fun, focused players who were not distracted by drugs and thus managed to get a great deal accomplished for their virgin album outing. He also took note of the band's dynamic. "Glenn was the boss, no doubt about it, " Achelis says. "But he and Jerry were very close . . . they had a Steven Tyler/Joe Perry type of thing. Jerry definitely had a lot of input, and his playing was driving a lot of the actual music itself. He was powering the sound with his bass playing. It was that typical punk rock bass sound, very fast and energetic."[22]

Much of the material the Misfits recorded for their proposed debut album wasn't too far removed from "Cough/Cool," despite their move toward a more conventional rock band instrumentation. Songs like "Static Age" and the pounding "TV Casualty," two tales of cathode tube–based complacency, not to mention the dreary murder narrative "Theme for a Jackal," are brooding drones in the style of the preceding single, built around one or two chords and Danzig's non-rhyming lyrical schemes. Yet the Misfits were also transitioning to a more straightforward songwriting approach at this time. "Some Kinda Hate" (an apparent response to the Velvet Underground's "Some Kinda Love") slams ahead on a firm seesawing riff, tightly moving between its brief verses and syrupy refrains of infectious but non-distinct crooning. Pulse-quickening "Hybrid Moments" owes much of its romantic drama to the touch of Roy Orbison but serves up a swinging rock bravado all its own, finding a great middle ground between a vintage 1950s melodic approach with the weighty sensibilities of Black Sabbath. Similarly, the five-minute ballad "Come Back" props its Elvisy longing on a typical chord progression from the nascent days of the King's given genre.

Though he would always err toward naming Orbison, the Righteous Brothers, and Jim Morrison as his vocal gods, there is no escaping the hard truth that Glenn Danzig's voice, especially at this early stage, was uncannily similar to that of Elvis Aaron Presley, the King of Rock n' Roll, the handsome good ol' boy who used his range-defying voice (and obscene pelvic movements) to change the course of popular music. Certainly Danzig liked Elvis, as he would cover various tunes made famous by Presley throughout his career, but it is easy to understand how the former might dismiss the latter as anyone to admire. After all, Elvis was famous for using outside songwriters, rarely (if ever) composing music on his own. Elvis also transformed into such a shallow and bizarre parody of himself by the mid-1970s that it almost began to hurt what he accomplished years prior. Orbison and the Righteous Brothers were smart enough to keep their heads down and work, avoiding the pitfalls of celebrity. The same can't be said for Morrison, but his premature demise prevented him from becoming a chubby, karate-obsessed weirdo like Elvis. Still, the King made his mark on Danzig in several ways, not merely with his vocals—Glenn would adopt that trademark swagger (though he would twist it into something more sinister), and massive sideburns were only a decade away.

If there is a consistent lyrical theme throughout all this material the Misfits recorded at C.I. in early 1978, it's one that Danzig would return to time and time again: power. His song's protagonists are either arrogantly brandishing it ("We want, we need, we take it!" cries the cold, unfeeling alien leader of "Teenagers from Mars"), struggling to retain it ("Attitude"), or feeling the vacuum that surrounds its loss ("Come Back," which finds a lovelorn Danzig pleading for his love to return and bite his face in lieu of kissing it). The unseemly imagery in some of these songs, including festering maggots and bloated corpses, is not used for comic affect a la the Ramones' "Texas Chainsaw Massacre" or Jim Carroll Band's lurid party anthem "People Who Died." Rather, these visions or situations are described very matter-of-factly, as if they are but a way of life for the Misfits. As far as anyone knew at the time, it was.

In February, the band mixed fourteen of the seventeen songs captured on sixteen-track tape and delivered the finished product, tentatively titled *Static Age*, to Mercury in hopes the label would exercise its release option. The Misfits didn't hear back until June, and the answer was negative: the label would not be releasing their debut record. Though Pere Ubu's *Modern Dance* charmed critics as esteemed as *Village Voice* scribe Robert Christgau with its damaged deconstruction of rock, the album did not meet Mercury's optimistic sales expectations. The storied label, whose bread-and-butter artists included bland pop sensations like Rod Stewart and Bachman-Turner Overdrive, dropped Pere Ubu and made the executive decision not to gamble again on a punk rock band—certainly not a relatively unknown punk rock band from the furthest corners of New Jersey. The Misfits were disappointed (as they would be when more punk-friendly labels such as Seymour Stein's Sire Records and Pere Ubu's new home Chrysalis also turned down the record),[23] but they didn't wallow in despair. "Punk rock was a singles market," says Franché Coma. "So the album not coming out, yeah, it kinda sucked, but we just turned it around and put out the 'Bullet' single [that June]."[24]

"Bullet," one of the last songs the Misfits recorded for *Static Age*, was a stark retelling of the John Kennedy assassination that Glenn had written as a poem in 1974.[25] The song has a crisp sound that hits the ground running, an intense blast from the very first second. Without question it captures madness and mania of the scenario it describes ("President's shattered head hits concrete / ride, Johnny, ride"). The frenzied song becomes a twisted sexual fantasy in its final verse as Glenn informs the widowed Jacqueline Kennedy that his ejaculate is the only substance that will prevent her from becoming "poor and devoid." Again, Danzig's lyrics outline a power play, this time set against one of history's most bloody and shocking incidents. In many ways, "Bullet" is a companion piece to Paul Krasner's infamous 1967 article "The Parts That Were Left Out of the Kennedy Book" in which Lyndon B. Johnson is fictionally posited as sexually penetrating John Kennedy's fresh assassination wounds on the flight home from Dallas—the article a gleeful prank that managed to fool a good portion of naïve Americans; "Bullet" is just a song, yet it equally sexualizes the same gruesome event in its own particular way.

Glenn Danzig wasn't the only member of punk rock's first generation to have been deeply affected by the startling gore of the Kennedy assassination and the insinuation of its visuals into our cultural fabric. Colorado native Eric Boucher counts the Zapruder film as one of his earliest childhood memories; the evil and cynicism of the event——more so than the blunt violence—had informed Boucher's character by young adulthood, leading the nascent artist to San Francisco looking in search of some kind of outlet. Six months before the Misfits released "Bullet" Boucher found a handful of like-minded players with whom he founded the notorious surf-influenced punk band the Dead Kennedys.[26] Although willing to go for shocks as excessive as "Bullet's" bloody cover—their 1981 EP *In God We Trust, Inc.* depicted Jesus's crucifixion on a cross made of dollars[27]—the Dead Kennedys would never be as bloody, nor would they musically revisit the events in Dealey Plaza (when a reporter in 1979 suggested their moniker was in poor taste, DK guitarist East Bay Ray retorted, "The assassinations weren't too tasteful either").[28] The San Francisco group never offered their opinion of the Misfits or the "Bullet" single, but they eventually ran afoul of Glenn Danzig for creative similarities unrelated to America's thirty-fifth president.

Three other songs from the Misfits' C.I. sessions were included on the band's second single: "We Are 138" slows things down to swagger and lets the band breathe as they triumphantly repeat that strange mantra; the caustic "Attitude" finds a cheery melody belaying agitated, violent lyrics concerning Danzig's issues with a challenger, the first hint this band could compete with the Ramones; and "Hollywood Babylon," a song that roots itself in a distinct feeling of Eisenhower-era juvenile delinquency—the guitar rolls along like a motorcycle cruising down a lonely highway, Glenn's sturdy vocal bellow a hard wind in the listener's ear (the singer's Marilyn Monroe obsession is also clearly reflected here, as "Hollywood Babylon" swipes its title from the controversial 1965 Kenneth Anger Tinseltown tell-all that related the seamy details of Monroe's death and placed her cleavage-bearing image on its cover).[29]

"We Are 138" sparked fierce debate about its subject matter and inspiration. The common line of thought suggests the song is a retelling of George Lucas's 1971 doom-laden cinematic forecast *THX 1138* in which an android police state controls the human populace and prevents them from acting on feelings of love and desire. There are enough references in Danzig's lyrics to suggest this link, though the singer himself would prove notoriously coy in discussing or dissecting any of his lines specifically at this or any other point in his career (Glenn preferred the listener interpret his work in their own way and in time would banish lyric sheets from his releases). The other band members recall Danzig creating various buttons for them to wear around the time of *Static Age* that featured a half-man, half-robot with "138" stenciled on his forehead. It seemed clear to them that Glenn was siphoning off *THX 1138*'s cool for his own purposes and would explain "We Are 138" as such over the following decades.

When asked point blank years later about the meaning of "We Are 138," Danzig famously snarled, "They didn't write it, and they don't know what the fuck it's about. It's about violence."[30]

The "Bullet" single's cover was designed to accentuate the strength of its titular song. Quite an artistic leap over the simple black-and-white photo that graced "Cough/Cool," "Bullet" presented a Lichtenstein-esque picture of JFK designed by Glenn wherein the president is smiling in his open convertible in Dealey Plaza, unaware of the comically large streaks of red blood spurting out from the back of his head. Tucked under the president's left arm is an equally bright red Misfits logo scrawled out in Glenn's handwriting that appears to be inked with Kennedy's blood. Initially, "Bullet" was to be distributed by Ork Records, the label belonging to the art punk outfit Television's manager Terry Ork. That partnership collapsed, though, affirming for the Misfits that they should stick to distributing their records themselves (often the DIY ethos of punk bands was born out of necessity rather than preference). Since the Blank name had been traded away to Mercury, the band rechristened their record label Plan 9—a tribute to the comically awful Ed Wood horror movie *Plan 9 from Outer Space.*[31] "Bullet" was sent to the requisite punk-friendly publications and was met with great enthusiasm. Most notably, *Slash*'s Claude "Kickboy Face" Bessy hailed the single as "lethal" and "truly inspiring," going on to rhapsodize "this is the stuff the Dead Boys and other puppets wished they were made of. Dipshits beware, this music leaves stains on well balanced brains."[32]

With two singles and an entire unreleased album to their name, the Misfits decided late in 1978 that it was time to begin playing outside of Jersey and New York. The band, at this point considered just another hobby band by their Lodi classmates and friends, had only gigged twice outside of New York or New Jersey so far—a pair of somewhat disastrous shows in Canada the previous December wherein they were to be the openers for jump-suited New Wave icons Devo. After a grueling ten-hour drive from Lodi to Toronto's Shock Theatre, the Misfits were informed by venue management that Devo had cancelled both performances. The Misfits still played, albeit disheartened, as did a local band known as the Skulls. Recently migrated from Vancouver, the Skulls arrived in Toronto hoping to tap into a punk scene more vibrant than the one they left on Canada's west coast. The band collapsed before accomplishing anything greater than recording a demo tape; singer Joe Keithley and drummer Ken Montgomery returned to their native Vancouver, where Keithley assembled the celebrated trio D.O.A. with Montgomery's brother Chuck (who dropped his surname in favor of "Biscuits") and bassist Randy "Rampage" Archibald.

Eager to spread their art, the Misfits booked a Midwestern tour for October of 1978. Unfortunately, this jaunt had to be wiped practically as soon as it began—after just two dates in Michigan, Frank LiCata announced his sudden overwhelming desire to leave the band. LiCata, who claims the Misfits never "had words" or fought while he was in their ranks, was dutifully shuttled back to Lodi along with the Misfits' immediate dreams of conquering the North American continent (though the quartet did manage to return to Toronto later in the month to fulfill a pair of dates, with the Victims' Rick Riley filling in on guitar).

Today Frank LiCata dismisses his original explanation of travel paranoia hastening his exit from the Misfits, instead pointing to creative differences. "It wasn't that," LiCata reflects. "That's what I said, but I think I started having thoughts, like, I wasn't into what Glenn was singing about. I don't know. At that time, I thought I could do something else. I was not into the horror stuff. I was never into that whole scene. So I felt I wanted to go try another type of band, y'know?" Frank LiCata did just that, forming the jittery keyboard-based Active Ingredients before giving up music for good. Active Ingredients self-released a pair of singles in 1980, "Laundramat Loverboy" and the positively affecting ADD anthem "Hyper Exaggeration," both of which presented a rougher edge to the new wave format that Devo was purveying at the time.[33]

The Misfits barely had time to blink following their guitarist's departure before their drummer followed suit. Jim Catania didn't have any issue with the band's strange image but found himself bored by punk's limiting percussive styles. He preferred the freedom afforded to him in his other band at the time, Continental Crawler (which included former Koo-Dot member Steve Linder on vocals and guitar). Thus, Catania left the Misfits to concentrate on that project; the in-demand percussionist would also go on to play in other Lodi-specific bands such as the Adults and Aces and Eights. As with LiCata, Catania stresses there was no bad blood between himself and the Misfits, despite the fact his sudden departure left them in the lurch.[34]

"There was so much horror around back then," says White Zombie guitarist Jay Yuenger. "Everybody grew up on comic books and cheesy horror movies. Every movie theater when I was a kid would show third-run horror movies for a dollar fifty. You'd waste the afternoon watching three horror movies in a row, and it was a totally normal thing. So I'm sure *Static Age* would have connected. Plus, those tunes are huge. They cut above everything else from that time with the brilliant doo wop songwriting. The melodies are just incredible."[35]

Had Mercury Records released *Static Age* the year it was recorded, the record might have been counted as one of the last great gasps of punk rock's founding East Coast wave alongside the Ramones' *Road to Ruin*, the Talking Heads' *More Songs about Buildings and Food*, and the Dead Boys' *Young Loud and Snotty*. Anchored by Glenn Danzig's harrowing melodies and the moody, turgid swirl of the band, this earliest material represents a bold statement unlike anything else at the time. This music is not campy or tongue-in-cheek (even compared to the depraved Dead Boys, who were not above silly double entendres and quasi-ironic pop covers). It has no agenda, political or otherwise, aside from startling violence and frustration-spiked apathy in equal measure. It's mysterious and odd, amateurish certainly—capturing almost perfectly the feeling of creaking through the cobwebs and dust of a long-sealed upstairs attic in search of unknown treasure—but like all great art *Static Age* is also affecting, unique, and enrapturing. As rock writer Mike

Stax notes, "On *Static Age* they hadn't quite fallen into the formula yet. The records that came later, like *Walk Among Us*, weren't as pure."[36]

"If it would've come out then, everything would have moved up five years," theorized Jerry Only in 1993. "We would have been the forerunners of the new scene. . . . The main problem with our band [was] that we didn't focus and get somebody to sit down and look at the imagery. But, y'know, we were a band and we were having a good time, and we could give a fuck, y'know?"[37]

Static Age's suppression is occasionally mourned in the same manner by fans, though the album would eventually see the light of day in the wake of intense legal wrangling. Certain band members regret more the dissolve of the *Static Age* lineup. LiCata in particular—with "no disrespect to the players who came" later—feels his version of the Misfits was "really the best" and laments that he lacked the "insight" Glenn possessed ("I just couldn't see beyond the immediate. If I had stayed with them and realized that was the thing . . . I don't know").[38] Pictures of the Misfits from this period definitely show a sense of camaraderie not always present in later incarnations. In a series of images taken by Jerry's younger brother Ken, the quartet stroll down Lodi's snow-caked Arnot Street in a tight cluster; Glenn Danzig grins widely when he isn't offering cutesy faux sneers for the camera, his band mates mugging behind him. Free of the ghoulish dime store accoutrements that would later become the hallmarks of the Misfits' attire (only LiCata seems to be cultivating some kind of character with his blazer's numerous enormous campaign buttons and the way he shrinks his face below several popped shirt collars), here the band appears like an actual functioning unit with interpersonal relationships in some basis of reality. In short, they seem normal and relatable, not half-zombies who just emerged from some frightening netherworld to feast on warm flesh.[39]

The insight of Glenn Danzig that Frank LiCata mentions—not to mention focus, hard work, and determination—would soon see to it that the Misfits reached a nationwide audience. In fact, the band's next three singles would serve to cement their legend in the underground and contribute to a musical subgenre they would forever rule.

Chapter Three

Horror Business

I remember the Misfits jumping off the record player as super dense, bright, exciting music. —Bruce McCulloch, The Kids in the Hall [1]

Twenty-something drummer Joe Poole was one of many New Jersey natives in 1978 who spent his days working in the Garden State (in his case, at a racetrack) and his nights bumming around New York City, looking for excitement. In November of that year the baby-faced Poole, who hailed from Englewood, crossed paths with Jerry Only and Glenn Danzig at Manhattan's Libra Studios. The latter pair were of course looking for a percussionist for their band, and Poole was always open for playing with new people. A week later Poole visited the Caiafa family garage for an official audition. The Misfits were impressed with Poole's primitive pounding and invited him into the fold. Liking the material, the drummer accepted, at first changing his name to the glam rock-sounding Joey Pills before settling on the slightly more opaque Joey Image after a nudging from his new band mates.

The vacant Misfits guitar slot would be filled shortly thereafter by a figure some felt was contentious right off the bat. "I was dead against [Bobby Steele]," Joey Image told *Ugly Things* in 1993. "I didn't dig the way he played from the get-go . . . he had a 'twang' in his guitar. He just wasn't good for the band, but Glenn thought he was alright . . . it was Glenn and Jerry's band . . . I was a part of it but it seemed they made all the decisions and shit." [2] Rail-thin guitarist Robert Kaufhold went by the nickname Bobby Steele in reference to the metal leg brace he had worn as a child to help overcome his crippling spina bifida; adolescent bouts with polio and a spinal cord tumor further weakened Steele, forcing him to walk with a cane intermittently from his teenage years on. [3] A veteran of several bands including The Living End and Parrotox (which counted among its ranks Smithereens

bassist Mike Messaros and future developer of blood-soaked video game hit
Mortal Kombat Bill Pidgeon), Steele was playing with the Whorelords in
1978 when he placed an ad in New Jersey music trade paper *The Aquarian*
looking for an established act to join that already had management and a
record deal. Danzig saw the ad and, despite the Misfits meeting neither of
those requirements, responded.

At first, Steele was dubious. "All I knew about the Misfits was 'Cough/
Cool' and I was kind of like, 'I don't know if I want to fucking play in that
kind of band,'" Steele would later recall. "But [I thought], 'Okay, I'll give it
a shot' . . . it was a good gamble, because they didn't sound anything like that
record [anymore]." Steele became immediately enthused by the band's dark,
intense take on punk rock and corresponding imagery. He easily envisioned
the Misfits becoming the new, more credible version of Kiss.[4]

Despite Image's misgivings, Steele proved a great fit for the band with his
fierce determination and guitar tone awash in angry fuzz. Emboldened, a
spirit of togetherness was forged between this Misfits lineup, and the music
similarly gelled. This can be heard in a bootleg live recording of the group's
December 20 gig at Max's Kansas City in Manhattan (only their third performance together). A relaxed confidence permeates the material as the band
swings through twelve songs, barely missing a beat as they flex their prowess. The menace is there, but so is a sense of fun. To wit: Danzig giggles to
himself when the band momentarily fudges the newer "Horror Business,"
and the set ends with a thirty-second rendition of the Elvis holiday standard
"Blue Christmas" that smashes right into "We Are 138." "Blue Christmas" is
tailor-made for Danzig's vocal range, and he gives Presley's soulfulness a
serious run for its money in the one verse he sings.[5]

As impressive as their chops were, the Misfits of this era quickly gained a
reputation in the New York punk scene for their somewhat outrageous and
rowdy behavior. Mocking the People's Temple massacre at Jonestown that
had taken place just two weeks earlier, Danzig capped off a December 3 gig
at Max's Kansas City by splashing the crowd with grape-flavored Kool-Aid.
The following March, Max's banned the Misfits for life after Steele allegedly
beaned an audience member with a glass bottle during the band's performance. Slightly more embarrassing was Steele's interaction with John Len-
non at the Mudd Club five months later—soused beyond belief, the Beatle-
worshipping Steele inadvertently vomited all over his hero's feet just seconds
after introducing himself. In August, Danzig and Only were jailed for one
night after they were caught throwing bottles from a balcony at Manhattan's
bohemian hangout the Chelsea Hotel.

Creative savvy was not lost because of these melees. In fact, the Misfits
made one of the smartest decisions of their career during this period. Centered on the flyer promoting the March 28 Max's gig that resulted in their
banishment was a highly contrasted photo of obscure screen villain the Crim-

son Ghost.[6] This criminal mastermind, bedecked in red robes and identity hidden by a frighteningly accurate skull mask, starred in his own serial for Republic Pictures in the late 1940s. If *The Crimson Ghost* series was remembered for anything in the late 1970s it was for the presence of future *Lone Ranger* star Clayton Moore as one of the titular character's sneering lackeys.[7] Eerily enough, Bud Geary, the uncredited actor behind the Crimson Ghost's mask, was killed in a car accident nine months before the serial premiered and would never get to see his ghoulish performance onscreen.[8]

Danzig and Only found the picture of Geary in his costume one afternoon while searching for images to silkscreen on T-shirts.[9] They decided to adopt the creepy grinning skull as their de facto mascot, and one of rock n' roll's greatest brandings was born. The decaying, bleach-white visage of the Crimson Ghost proved beyond striking, a wordless calling card perfectly projecting the base fear and haunted house mystique of the Misfits' entire oeuvre.

The Crimson Ghost would reappear on the cover of the next Misfits single, "Horror Business." While more muddled production-wise than "Bullet," "Horror Business" is just as arresting as its predecessor. The opening chords of the title track might as well be stabs from the very knife Danzig sings about sinking into the listener. Allegedly based on the unsolved murder of Sex Pistols groupie Nancy Spungen, the Misfits never suggest who the protagonist is supposed to be but makes it clear that the victim's stabbing was no accident as they howl the chorus ("With you, I'll put a knife right in you!") over delicious waves of overdriven guitar and Joey Image's hissing cymbals. And yet, despite its gratuitous violence, "Horror Business" (the title a grim play on Chuck Berry's 1956 tale of pedestrian beleaguerment "Too Much Monkey Business") offers a bluesy feel at times, almost as if nothing more is at stake than the melody. By the time the song is hurtling through its conclusion of several consecutive refrains it almost feels like a campfire stomp between a gaggle of old, grizzled friends.

On the single's flip side, "Teenagers from Mars" presents more stuttering riffs under ominous declarations from a conquering alien race unconcerned with human suffering as they "land in barren fields" to inseminate our females ("We take your weak resistance and throw it in your face," Danzig spits in his UFO conqueror persona). A third song, "Children in Heat," roars along more on its raw adolescent rage than the gross-out visuals of bloody urination and presents another fiery performance by Steele. Released in August of 1979, "Horror Business" was greeted by the growing Misfits fan base as an instant classic, even if it didn't exactly spell everything out in layman's terms.[10]

"The first [Misfits] singles just knocked me out," says Minor Threat's Ian MacKaye. "They were so interesting and mysterious. I had no idea what to make of them. The legend was [the Misfits] played [live] only on Halloween. We also heard they were all crippled, y'know, because Bobby Steele had a cane and you didn't see any pictures of them back then. [And Glenn] was deeply talented, a genius as a kid. His lyrics puzzled me. 'Paint my mirrors black for you'—what the fuck does that mean?"[11]

"Horror Business" represented a watershed moment for both the Misfits and the subgenre of horror punk they spearheaded. Though it was always obvious that the band had a violent edge, this single made clear a platform dedicated firmly to the macabre, the supernatural, the grotesque. From the Crimson Ghost staring out at the listener beneath the blood red "HORROR" on the cover to the flip side where black-and-white portraits of the individual band members shared space with a rendering of Lon Chaney as the Phantom of the Opera to the aggressive music held within—this was the ultimate marriage of Ramones and Romero. To drive the point home even further (almost to the brink of self-parody), various copies of "Horror Business" were stuffed with an insert claiming the band had recorded the single in a haunted house and that "strange voices and noises" defying any explanation were heard when the group mixed the tracks later at a New York studio.

Of course this story was hooey. "Horror Business" was recorded at C.I., the same studio where the band completed their shelved debut album a year earlier,[12] though Joey Image would later note the session was not without incident. Tensions rose when Danzig demanded the band record as many songs as possible during the allotted studio time in an attempt to save money; Steele, meanwhile, had difficulties keeping his "twangy" guitar in tune.[13] Compounding the tension was the sudden appearance at the session of Ann Beverly, mother of Sid Vicious, who had overdosed just a few months before while out on bond for the alleged murder of his former lover (and "Horror Business" inspiration) Nancy Spungen. Jerry Only had attended the small party Vicious hosted in February at his new girlfriend Michele Robinson's Greenwich Village apartment just hours before he died on February 2. Upon learning of Sid's death the following morning, Only reached out to Beverly and subsequently brought her to the studio.[14] A potentially awkward situation to be recording a song about a perceived murderer with said murderer's mother standing just a few feet away, but maybe not: Prior to Sid Vicious's death, the rumor about town was that the Misfits were in the running to potentially back the bassist-turned-singer on his eagerly anticipated debut solo album.

Playing second fiddle to a washed-up junkie would have been a massive step back for the Misfits, whose identity in concert was quickly becoming as wickedly ghoulish as their music. Danzig had taken to dressing in a skeleton costume for live shows complete with face paint meant to emulate the Crimson Ghost logo. Bobby Steele and Jerry Only created a punk zombie look by wearing tight black clothing with matching (often smudged) eye makeup. Only also dyed his electric blue hair back to black, greasing it up and letting it grow—especially in the front, where his punky spikes were drooping down into a point just above his nose. This hairstyle, later adopted by the other band members, would be dubbed "the devilock" by a disapproving Lodi mother.

As much as his appearance was influenced by a bare-bones love of horror, Danzig also drew inspiration from Japanese manga character Captain Harlock. A bit character created by famed artist Leiji Matsumoto who was spun into his own animated television series in the late 1970s, the space pirate Harlock was a slender rogue who donned a black jumpsuit with a large skull and crossbones across the chest to fight interstellar corruption. The character's hair was a thick shock that hung in his face to obscure his identity as well as various facial injuries incurred during his battles. Captain Harlock starred in various films, comic books, and television programs over the years but never crossed over to American shores in the same manner as Astro Boy or Akira. Regardless, the Captain made an indelible impression on Danzig, who soon crafted his own skull and crossbones T-shirt that aped Matsumoto's design and made sure his devilock was always a tad wider and hairier than that of his musical counterparts. It should be noted, however, that Danzig's favorite Japanese animation character has long been the feisty red-winged superhero Devilman, the Hell-spawn alter ego of a meek young boy the singer once claimed he "could related to . . . on a personal basis."[15]

The Misfits of this era also proved their knack for showmanship by preceding their live performances with projections of classic horror movies (usually the wretchedly awful *Plan 9 from Outer Space*) on flimsy sheets of paper they would kick their way through to start the show.[16] This style of theatrics was borrowed directly from the interactive spook shows of the 1960s wherein cinemas used electric seats or costumed employees during movies like *The Monsters Crash the Pajama Party* to give the audience an extra scare or two.1[17]

Such ghoulish flair extended even to the Misfits' press releases. A typed two-page biography circulated by the band shortly after the release of "Horror Business" is strewn with all sorts of unverifiable (and often laughable) yarns concerning the band members. To wit: Danzig "almost died when he was born at Hackensack Hospital"; the black rings under Jerry Only's eyes are "the result of a rare pigment defect . . . which left his face permanently discolored in that area"; Bobby Steele is related to British actress Barbara Steele and spent his youth "skinning live cats"; Joey Image (here still referred to as "Joey Pills") has "been intimate with every young female in New York he's met." The music of the Misfits was of course powerful enough that it didn't necessitate or warrant such outlandish boasting, but the band clearly felt otherwise (Only has the best quote when he comments that his family is "bigger than a breadbox and twice as empty").[18]

On Halloween of 1979, the Misfits released the logical "Horror Business" follow-up single "Night of the Living Dead," though they weren't entirely thrilled about it. An error during the mastering process gave songs on the "Dead" discs an extraordinarily bass-heavy sound, reducing the guitar to a thin, trill background noise. Thankfully, the band's songwriting muscles remained strong. The title track swings with a sick sense of glee as Danzig outlines a zombie uprising that most assuredly "ain't no fantasy," a dreadful situation where humans are being "ripped up like shredded wheat." In place of a proper chorus, "Night of the Living Dead" features an elongated chant of "No-oh-oh," as if the band themselves are decrying this undead apocalypse before them. The B-side offers "Where Eagles Dare," a crude pounder whose blustery chorus challenges you to take it seriously ("I ain't no goddamn son of a bitch! You better think about it, baby!"). The final song, "Rat Fink," finds the Misfits being goofy for no real discernible reason, covering novelty nebbish Allan Sherman's parody of the country standard "Rag Mop." Still, they manage to give the dumb thing some bite.[19]

That evening the Misfits hawked copies of their latest single at the door of their Irving Plaza gig. The show itself was said to have been among the group's best. The Misfits had shown up early to decorate, festooning Irving Plaza with all manner of rubber bats, fake skeletons, and plastic jack-o-lanterns. A giant version of Glenn's hand-drawn Misfits logo hung above the stage as the band performed; the set ended with Joey Image smashing his black Ludwig drum kit to pieces.[20] Unbeknownst to anyone at the time, this would be the final American performance for this version of the Misfits. They were about to embark on a foreign adventure that would effectively place a stick in their fast-moving spokes.

The Misfits were not the only punks in the late 1970s toying with ghoulish imagery, though they were by far the most distilled. The Cramps, who settled in Manhattan after forming in California and spending some time in singer Lux Interior's hometown of Akron, Ohio,[21] sang celebratory tales of werewolves and zombies in a bed of Hasil Adkins–inspired "psychobilly" guitar riffing (though the group's sexual undercurrent would always be stronger than its devotion to the macabre). Los Angeles bands like T.S.O.L., 45 Grave, the Flesh Eaters, Kommunity FK, and Christian Death focused on a grim, discordant, and echoey musical offering very much in line with overseas goth proprietors such as Bauhaus and Joy Division. The artwork associated with these self-dubbed "death rock" bands also skewed European—the cover of Christian Death's 1982 debut *Only Theatre of Pain* features a sketch of an emaciated ghoul akin to any given figure from the German Expressionist movement; similarly, the front of T.S.O.L.'s 1981 virgin effort *Dance with Me* depicted the Grim Reaper in front of a severely disturbed grave, his hands clasped, a layer of fog obscuring the landscape. The Angelino death rockers had their brief flashes of humor—45 Grave's first single was a cover of Don Hinson's 1964 "Monster Mash" cash-in "Riboflavin-Flavored Non-Carbonated Poly-Unsaturated Blood"—but for the most part, there was little correlation between these depressed outfits and the rowdy punk showmanship of the Misfits.[22]

Closer to the Misfits were British punk pioneers the Damned, who by 1979 had transformed themselves from a vague Ramones clone into an undeniably distinct and acutely extrinsic keyboard-driven rock band. Smoky-vocaled singer Dave Vanian, whose backstory included an alleged stint digging graves, routinely wrapped himself black capes and white stage makeup like Bela Lugosi; other members included the Renfield-esque Rat Scabies on drums and oddball guitarist Captain Sensible, whose penchant for mohair occasionally made him look like a neon gorilla. The Damned's records routinely featured gloomy aural exercises like droning injury ode "Feel the Pain," demented carnival creeper "These Hands," and the band's most celebrated depression ode "I Just Can't Be Happy Today." Even some of their rawer material suggested a penchant for evil, such as nihilist's delight "Born to Kill" and the surprisingly catchy "Stab Your Back."[23] The Misfits saw the Damned if not as a direct influence than at least kindred cobwebbed spirits.

In June of 1979 the two bands shared a bill at Hurrah's in New York City, a hot ticket if one goes by some of the musical luminaries who attended (reformed Stooge Iggy Pop and Blondie chanteuse Debbie Harry). Afterwards, Jerry Only engaged Vanian and the Damned's management in a brief conversation about the Misfits supporting the Damned on a tour in England that fall. The Damned camp regarded the conversation as little more than after-gig pillow talk, but Only took their word as bond. Six months later, on November 21, the Misfits flew to the United Kingdom (funded by Only's father) for their orally agreed upon tour with the Damned.[24]

The month that followed was an unmitigated disaster. The Damned were not prepared to have the Misfits show up on their doorstep; they had already booked an opening act called Victim for this six-date tour of their native land. Trying to be nice, the Damned's management added the Misfits to the bill anyway, but an awkward tension hung in the air. Various members of the Damned and their entourage made no bones about disliking their forward American guests. There was also the issue of payment—the Misfits would receive none, as the exposure to British audiences was to be considered valuable enough.[25] The tensions compounded when the Misfits decided the musical equipment provided for them was substandard (Joey Image in particular would complain his drum kit was the "rinkiest dinkiest" he'd ever seen[26]). Feeling disrespected, the Misfits cancelled their remaining appearances on the Damned tour and tried to find arrangements of their own. A mysterious figure named Derek befriended the stranded punks and offered to help the band get dates opening for rising British punk heroes the Clash, but days stretched into a week or so and still nothing was confirmed.

The malaise was beginning to get to the Misfits. On December 2, Glenn and Bobby tried to alleviate their hotel-based boredom by attending a Jam concert at London's famed venue the Rainbow. Outside the concert hall, a group of skinheads began harassing the duo. Things quickly escalated. Somehow Bobby slipped away in an attempt to find some authorities; Glenn stayed behind, arming himself with a broken bottle.[27] When police eventually did arrive they arrested Glenn and Bobby for disturbing the peace. The Misfits spent two nights in Brixton jail, an experience that birthed one of the group's most solemn and memorable dirges.

"I just turned to Glenn [in the cell]," recalled Steele in 1993, "[and] said, 'We should make a song about this called "London Dungeon."'" We were like sitting in this cell, it was like ten feet perfectly square, you know, solid painted walls, it was real echoey in the room . . . and we were just like slapping the beat out on our legs and humming . . . it sounded so cool . . . [and] Glenn took it from there."[28]

Glenn and Bobby were released on December 4, and a week and a half later there were still no gigs in sight. Fed up with the stagnant situation, on December 15 Joey Image flew back to America by himself, effectively leaving the band for good.[29] Three days later the rest of the Misfits returned to New Jersey, metaphorical tail between their legs, having done little more than spend Jerry's father's money and obtain arrest records in England. At least the financially fruitless overseas jaunt had provided a jolt to the band's creativity. In addition to "London Dungeon," the Misfits came home from England with a great title for their next vinyl offering.

The EP *Beware* was released in January 1980 and took its name from a series of confusing road signs the band noticed in England marked "Beware Bollards." A bollard is a traffic control structure similar to a traffic cone; the Misfits at first thought a bollard might be some kind of strange cryptid like their own Jersey Devil.[30] Combining the "Bullet" and "Horror Business" singles, *Beware* was originally planned as something of a catch-all record the Misfits could bring with them on their failed UK tour (the cover, a fun house mirror rendering of the band, was not completed in time, however).[31] *Beware* would prove landmark anyway because of its final song, the previously unreleased punch drunk anthem "Last Caress."

The violent, nihilistic lyrics of "Last Caress" outline the bold confessions of a remorseless killer and rapist and are delivered by Danzig with such romantic melody that the crimes almost seem like triumphs. Ostensibly on death row, our protagonist moans in the chorus about his yearning for the inevitable arrival of "sweet lovely death," suggesting it may somehow release him from the pain and apathy he feels. "Last Caress" is punctuated by the most dramatic of pauses at the end that finds the instruments stalling so Glenn can offer a clear affirming snarl of "One last caress!" This moment, coupled with the song's similar roustabout opening where Glenn proclaims

"I got somethin' ta say!" over a lone guitar chord, helped put an already excellent creation over the top to become a defining punk rock salvo on the same cathartic level as "Anarchy in the U.K." or "Psycho Killer." Incredibly, "Last Caress" was nearly left off *Beware* as Danzig didn't feel the recording was good enough. At the urging of Bobby Steele, the song was tacked on at the last minute.[32]

Joey Image continued playing in punk bands following his departure from the Misfits, turning up in the likes of the Whorelords, the Undead, the Strap-Ons, Human Buffet, the Mary Tyler Whores, Jersey Trash, and the Bell Ringers (the feisty punker also later took a bride, the alluring Patty Mullen, a one-time Penthouse Pet who gained infamy in 1990 by portraying the title character in the horror farce *Frankenhooker*).[33] Rendered Image-less at the dawn of 1980, the Misfits would not find a new drummer until four months after the release of *Beware*. Joe McGuckin, a gaunt Queens native who preferred to keep his hair closely shorn in a blonde shock and had previously played in his older brother Thomas's new wave band the Accidents,[34] joined the fold when his girlfriend, a mutual friend of Bobby Steele's, brokered a successful audition.

McGuckin chose the pseudonym Arthur Googy for his stint in the Misfits—an inexplicable tag that appears partially inspired by late nineteenth-century New York gangster Googy Corcoran. Googy quickly impressed the band with his zeal and dedication. The drummer would make the roughly two-hour journey from Queens out to Lodi several nights a week for practice in the Caiafas' garage, mostly via public transportation.[35] Unfortunately, Googy's percussive fundamentals were a considerable step down from those of Jim Catania and Joey Image, giving the Misfits a more savage and unsteady beat. The drummer often fell behind in the live setting as well. Government Issue vocalist John Stabb said, "We were always playing shows with the Misfits, and our running joke was, 'Wait up for Googy! Wait up for him! He's still trying to catch up!' . . . [It was] embarrassing . . . I saw them and thought, 'People like this shit?'"[36]

Arthur Googy may not have been the world's greatest drummer, but he was enthusiastic and available and, at the time, there were no other applicants jockeying for the Misfits timekeeping position. The same could not be said for the band's guitar slot. Jerry Only claimed that Steele was showing up late and unprepared for practices; the bassist also expressed concern that the frail Steele would have difficulty keeping up with the Misfits growing stage show (namely, the bassist couldn't see the cane-wielding guitarist kicking his way out of a prop coffin).[37] Only wanted to bring in his sixteen-year-old brother, Paul Doyle Caiafa, to replace Steele. Doyle, as Paul preferred to be known, seemed like the perfect replacement: he was healthy, agreeable, and built like the high school linebacker he actually was. Steele couldn't deny his weak condition but claimed any rehearsal or studio absence was because of Only lying to him about the Misfits' schedule to make it appear he no longer saw the band as anything beyond a hobby.[38] Danzig, unsure of how to handle the situation but feeling pressured to resolve the struggle quickly, acquiesced to Only, who informed Steele he was out of the band just before Halloween.

Doyle immediately made an impression. Rosemary's Babies singer Vincent "JR" Paladino said, "When I met Paul he was a pretty big guy and he always had a serious look on his face. I kept thinking, 'Does this guy wanna fight me? Man, fuck him!' Eventually I asked [a mutual friend], 'Does he have a problem with me?' And [the friend] goes, 'No, I don't think so.' So I started talking to Paul and, yeah, we got along great."

Doyle's expression of stone and similar physicality may have been a better aesthetic fit for the Misfits (the band members were just starting to lift weights to they could appear more imposing and monster-like onstage), but Jerry's little brother was just as inexperienced on his instrument as Arthur Googy. Doyle often pounded his guitar strings so barbarically they'd go out of tune after just one song, forcing the axeman to spend long stretches of gig time desperately trying to re-tune. The younger Caiafa wasn't particularly adept at solos yet, mangling in his early outings the guitar breaks in "Horror Business" and "We Are 138." From this point forward, the Misfits live experience would often descend into haphazard mess, the saving grace of which was usually the sight of these strange ghoulish men pounding out their racket.

Initially relations between Bobby Steele and the Misfits remained friendly. Danzig financed the recording of *9 Toes Later*, the debut single from Steele's other band the Undead (Danzig even offered to release *9 Toes* on Plan 9; the Undead took a deal with England's prominent Stiff Records instead). Things soured between Steele and the Misfits a short time later, something Steele has long blamed on the music press's quick appraisal of the Undead as a better, more productive Misfits. Whatever caused the shift, suddenly Bobby Steele was persona non grata to his former band.[39] A year later the two groups performed together at the Ritz in Manhattan; the Misfits threw bottles at Steele during the Undead's set and taunted him during their own, infamously altering the chorus of "Teenagers from Mars" to "Bobby Steele's an asshole, that fuckin' cunt" (a practice they would continue in concert for a number of performances).[40]

Bobby Steele's Undead would soldier on for several decades in various forms, at one point even including fellow Misfits castaway Joey Image. In 1985 the guitarist achieved a unique milestone when he scored work as an extra in filmmaker Martin Scorsese's critically acclaimed comic thriller *After Hours*—milling about in the background during one of the movie's bar scenes, Bobby Steele became the first Misfit to appear in a horror movie.[41]

The year 1980 signaled a new era for the band. "Around 1980 or 1981 I started hearing about the Misfits," remembers Death Piggy's Dave Brockie. "I didn't know what to make of them . . . it kinda didn't make sense. These guys, these big lugs—these palookas!—dressing up like vampires? Then I heard their music and I thought it was *really* cool. They were like a 'roided out Damned. They always seemed kinda dangerous. They scared people."[42]

Indeed, many people started hearing about the Misfits as the 1980s broke open, as their proverbial heat continued intensifying. On Halloween Day 1980 the band made their television debut, appearing on Garden State cable *Pee Wee's Playhouse* precursor *The Uncle Floyd Show*. As the titular character, comedian Floyd Vivino welcomed the sneering black-clad Misfits to his colorful spoof of 1950s kiddie shows and allowed them to lip synch to a couple of their less intense offerings. That evening Doyle came out as a Misfit, as it were, when the band opened a show at Irving Plaza for none other than Screamin' Jay Hawkins; the Eisenhower era wild man had never stopped performing but was still a few years out from his underground renaissance. Fulfilling Jerry Only's vision while also paying homage to forbearer Hawkins, the Misfits started this show by bursting out of four individual coffins. In his own act of tribute to the sci-fi gods of yesteryear Doyle sported a blue Star Trek uniform shirt under his guitar during the performance which gave him the appearance of a mutated Vulcan warrior. Eclectic pioneering rocker Frank Zappa was among the revelers at Irving Plaza this night, blowing off steam from his own two-date stand at Manhattan's neighboring Palladium.[43]

The following year found the Misfits playing their first Midwestern and West Coast dates where the Lodi foursome crossed paths with brewing legends such as lewd Michigan shock troopers the Meatmen, California pop princes the Dickies, and caffeinated Texan weirdos the Big Boys.[44] Also in 1981 the band released two more singles: April's "3 Hits from Hell," noted for its secretive cover that displays nothing more than the band members' eyes, included the aforementioned "London Dungeon" (a brooding, bassleaning drag that opened up room for one of Glenn's most powerful vocal performances), a by-the-numbers spook scare called "Horror Hotel," and the expertly arranged "Ghouls Night Out" whose Orbison-inspired melody change in the second verse proves nothing short of transcendent.

In October the Misfits followed up with "Halloween," the ultimate 4/4 stomp dedicated to their favorite holiday. Reverb washes over the song as Danzig rhapsodizes about "brown leaf vertigo" and poisoned candy, ultimately concluding, "This day, anything goes!" In an interesting move, the flip side takes the same song, slows it down, and adds Latin phrases pertaining to lycanthropy. The record's black-and-white cover photo, surrounded by a frame of skulls on a field of orange, once again only gives a partial view of the Misfits as they linger menacingly in the shadows. On the far right, Doyle bares his teeth like a caveman. Closer to center, the lighting illuminates Googy's face in such a way that he eerily resembles the Crimson Ghost. Danzig, hunching over between his drummer and guitarist, barely looks human at all. Above the band is a brand new Misfits logo, written in the same font as treasured horror geek magazine *Famous Monsters of Filmland.*[45]

Both "3 Hits" and "Halloween" garnered critical praise. England's *New Musical Excess* heard these new singles and declared the Misfits superior to UK spook rock heroes the Damned. Just as shocking was *Wave Sector* placing "3 Hits" ahead of any Cramps release in terms of "ghoulish fantasy" before pegging "London Dungeon's" lyrics as "the most evocative and agonized" of the year.[46]

Many have wondered how a relatively unknown band from New Jersey could afford to pump out so much material so quickly. Were they really turning enough of a profit? The only band member with an outside job was Jerry Only. Working at his father's machine shop, Only would often pull double shifts before a tour or release to make sure expenses were covered. Another benefactor was a neighbor of the Caiafas, George Germain. A former musician himself, the portly Germain lived across the street from the Caiafas and was known around Lodi as a kind of Svengali to struggling musicians. The Misfits were apparently just one of many bands Germain, a few generations ahead of the late 1970s crop of punks, helped—not only with production expertise (passing down various secrets regarding "studio magic") but also financially, throwing cash behind several of the group's earliest recordings.

It's rumored that trouble with the IRS kept George Germain largely in the shadows at his own behest, especially as the legacy of the Misfits grew. Many who worked with Germain, though, describe the focused, dedicated craftsman as a sweet and kind soul who may have simply preferred the young musicians have all the credit. At least one New Jersey musician referred to George Germain as the Phil Spector of the East Coast, a knob-twiddler of meticulous nature who would think nothing of spending hours trying to squeeze the best possible sound out of an enclosed space and who put his work with artists far ahead of anything else in his life.[47]

Despite Germain's quiet support, the Misfits were still releasing everything themselves via their Plan 9 label, pressing singles in relatively low numbers—usually between 2,000 and 3,000 copies. That, coupled with various artwork variants created both on purpose and accidentally by the band during sleeve copying/folding sessions (artwork that was more visually arresting than the standard Xerox-heavy punk rock image paradigms of the day), has ensured the rarity and value of every Misfits single among punk collectors. A separate encyclopedia set could be written about the market that exists for original Misfits seven/twelve inches and their now equally valuable bootlegs. Luckily, the advent of the cassette tape help disseminate the music within those singles after all the vinyl had been snapped up, which perhaps only compounded the mystery of this band. Generally fans didn't replicate artwork or liner notes on the blank tapes they passed around containing fragments of "Beware" and "3 Hits." With nothing to go on but the music, this band seemed even more mythic and foreboding. [48]

Soon, the Misfits would emerge from their relative obscurity to stake a firmer claim on the punk scene. During the summer of 1981 the group booked time in several different New Jersey studios to begin work anew on a full-length album. The resulting piece of vinyl would prove one of the most stylish, affecting, and explosive records of punk rock's second wave.

Chapter Four

Astro Zombies

Those comic book lyrics, [Danzig] took it seriously. And he was a really morbid, depressed guy. One time he was walking around the supermarket going, "Don't you ever feel like the human race just disgusts you, man? Like you want it wiped out?" And it's like, "No, Glenn." The guy just takes everything way too seriously. —John Stabb, Government Issue [1]

Punk rock was roughly a half decade old by March of 1982, and the genre that put safety pins and glue in a new context was experiencing growing pains. The Ramones, America's flagship band of the genre whose string of peppy late 1970s albums the music press cherished but mass audiences ignored, faced the harsh reality that they might never break through after a 1980 collaboration with reclusive producing legend Phil Spector failed to bring Top 40 stardom (the record in question, the stuffy *End of the Century*, also sapped the Ramones of their trademark buzzing guitar sound; it wouldn't fully return until four albums later). [2] English upstarts the Clash began as Ramones imitators but quickly distinguished themselves with a rootsier, more anthemic sound; oddly, they moved away from punk rock with smashing results, shooting up the Billboard charts and garnering a five star review from *Rolling Stone* for 1980s world music fusion triple platter *Sandinista!* In May of 1982, the Clash experience their greatest commercial success with *Combat Rock*—the album's dance-infused third single "Rock the Casbah" became a Top 10 hit across the globe, securing the group's position on countless future "Hits of the '80s" compilations. [3]

The surviving members of punk rock's most infamous assembly, the Sex Pistols, all softened or significantly altered their signature soundscapes following the group's messy 1978 dissolve and the sudden 1979 death of bass player Sid Vicious. Guitarist Steve Jones and drummer Paul Cook formed a meat-and-potatoes hard rock group called the Professionals who fizzled out after two albums in 1980 and 1981. Pistols singer Johnny Rotten reverted to his Christian name, John Lydon, and put together an experimental post-punk group Public Image Ltd. Incorporating elements of dub reggae, pure noise, and Lydon's newly relaxed caterwaul, Public Image crafted affecting atonal exercises that came to help define the post-punk movement.[4] Naturally, the spirit of Lydon's former band informed his latest—an appearance by PiL on Dick Clark's *American Bandstand* in May of 1980 went down in history for the singer's counterproductive behavior (refusing to play the part of lip-synching pop idiot, Lydon summoned the audience to the stage to dance while he hid behind various set pieces).[5] Public Image also famously locked horns with NBC's Tom Snyder on the *Tomorrow* program that June, admonishing the host for his lack of preparation and generally being standoffish. At one point during the interview, seeming to acknowledge punk rock's failure as a form of revolution, the still wild-eyed Lydon addressed *Tomorrow*'s viewers by saying, "I'll find a way to your hearts yet, though, I'll tell ya!"[6]

Hardcore, punk rock's faster and angrier derivative, was rising so quickly by early 1982 it seemed in danger of burning out more quickly than its predecessor. Hardcore's two figurehead bands were Washington, D.C.'s Minor Threat and California's Black Flag. Minor Threat, authors of pounding livid rants such as 1981's "Filler" and the anti-drug "Straight Edge," splintered apart when guitarist Lyle Preslar left to attend Northwestern University; Preslar would ultimately abandon school because he missed the fury and excitement of his band. The reformed Minor Threat would only last a rough year, though, breaking up again in 1983 over creative differences.[7] Black Flag, the California collective that practically invented hardcore with 1977's rage-soaked "Nervous Breakdown" single, were by 1982 rapidly moving toward a slower heavy metal sound.[8] Also floating away from their core genre were former Misfits colleagues the Damned—touched by the rumblings of the paisley underground, the Damned dedicated their later albums to churning out progressive rock sounds more in line with the fare of any given classic rock radio station.

In short, punk rock's playing field was clear in March of 1982 for a brief, brutal, reaffirming aural statement. That's exactly what the genre received in *Walk Among Us*, the Misfits debut full-length release, with a hot pink cover on which the band plants itself inside the action of 1959's martian terror picture *The Angry Red Planet*. Thanks in part to nimble work by engineer Pat Burnette (nephew of rockabilly legend Johnny Burnette)[9] , *Walk Among Us* boasted a sleeker, cleaner sound than all previous Misfits recordings—which would spurn some purists to bemoan the loss of the band's sloggy amateur charm. *Walk*'s raised production values helped to zero in on the band's ferocity as they rollicked through a host of angry schlock anthems. Danzig's vocal menace was similarly amped as he unleashed on the material with renewed authority. The album opened with the churning "20 Eyes," a primal blast in which the protagonist is either lamenting or celebrating his ocular mutant status, before segueing into the heart-pounding (and somewhat literal) alienation anthem "I Turned into a Martian." The immediacy of "Martian" was felt in its tense verses before they give way to a chorus of cathartic "whoa-oh" chanting. Less therapeutic were the doomsday visions of evil-hewn nightmares outlined in "All Hell Breaks Loose" (the menace is accented instrumentally by a lack of cymbals and palm-muted guitar for the first two-thirds of the song). The robot/human love diatribe "Nike-a-Go-Go" was similarly foreboding, rocking ahead on a stuttering beat and football-type chants.

Curiously enough, the Misfits chose to break up their debut's slick presentation midway through with a very rough live recording of the proto-speed metal half-joke "Mommy, Can I Go Out & Kill Tonight?" (taken from a performance the previous December at Manhattan venue the Ritz). The slightly off-time performance is an interesting palate cleanser but manages to keep thematically with the rest of the album's frustrated outcast mantras, telling of an outcast school boy who knows he'll "laugh last" regardless of his peers' taunting. The turgid opening prologue stomps along before abruptly stopping so Danzig may belligerently inquire, "Mommy . . . can I go out . . . and KILL tonight?" to an eerie silence. The band then launches into a messy double time as Glenn growls angrily about keeping the toes and teeth of a girl he slaughtered at Lover's Lane.

Singling out a hit on *Walk Among Us* is tricky business, but most point to the thrashing delight "Skulls," a twisted love letter in which Danzig dreams of sharing warm blood baths and showing off his severed head collection to his betrothed. Danzig imbues so much passion into this performance (quieting down to a whisper at certain points to drive his longing home) that one tends to forget the startling reality of his words—not to mention the rudimentary smashing of the chord progression beneath him. More nuanced but just as romantic is the explosive empowerment anthem "Astro Zombies," which pairs an addictive descending guitar riff with bold bellowing about a quest for intergalactic power to impress an unknown ingénue. Much like "I Turned into a Martian," "Astro Zombies" sews a succession of elongated "whoaohs" into its refrains; this particular melodic cry in "Zombies" would become another celebrated Misfits hallmark akin to the ending of "Last Caress." *Walk Among Us* offers an unprecedented third love song, a shockingly straightforward ode to the ultimate horror hostess Vampira where Glenn concedes his power and begs the micro-waisted and "feline-faced" female ghoul to "come a little bit closer" (Maila Nurmi, the actress who portrayed Vampira, would learn of the tribute shortly after *Walk*'s release; touched, she eventually met up with the band at a record signing to express her gratitude).[10]

Of course, the lean sadomasochist ode "Devil's Whorehouse" offers *Walk*'s one pure dose of raw kink, a song about a "demon slut" dominatrix who "loves carnality." The Misfits peppered "Devil's Whorehouse" with simulated whipping noises—a rare moment where the band actually employed the type of cheesy sound effects found in the Z-grade films they took inspiration from.

Those searching for levity on *Walk Among Us* found it perhaps in the wry commentary "Violent World" offered about that era's trend of gore-based tabloid journalism; more likely, the lighthearted ate up the album's closing thirty-second chant "Brain Eaters" in which the Misfits ache about their limited dining options of "brains for dinner [and] brains for lunch." They would prefer some "guts," they heartily intone.[11] A video was later filmed for "Brain Eaters" that captured the goofy spirit of the song; the clip features the Misfits and their friends around a dinner table at Boston's storied Durgin Park restaurant, pounding and chanting as they're served all manner of squishy innards (procured earlier that afternoon by the Caiafa brothers, in full stage regalia, from a local butcher shop).[12]

In what might be construed as a bit of overkill regarding their evil image, the Misfits sandwiched a quote from Revelations on the back cover of *Walk Among Us* between the track listing and production credits; the quotation reads: "Here is wisdom. Let him hath understanding count the numbers of the beast, for it is the number of a man; and his number is six hundred threescore and six." The blue-tinted close-up shot of the band also featured on the album's back cover works just as well as a final spook—Glenn, Doyle, and Jerry peering out at the listener from behind their thick devilocks, clear glint in their eyes, ready to feast on your soul (or your innards, whichever comes first).

Among Misfits fans *Walk Among Us* was an instant triumph, the record everyone had patiently been waiting for since *Beware* and "Horror Business." Underground fanzine *The Terror Times* praised the album in a writeup the same month it was released, saying, "This unpleasant upheaval of sound will grind on your brain for as long as you can bare the pain . . . there is no compassion shown for anything here except for death, hate, and complete annihilation . . . what reason could you not have for buying this wonderful record?"[13] WNYU DJ Tim Sommer hailed *Walk Among Us* as "awesome" in a May issue of *Sounds.*[14] *Forced Exposure*'s review cut more to the point, stating bluntly, "Just [buy] this fuckin' record."[15] Writing about *Walk Among Us* decades later for AllMusic.com, Ned Raggett noted that part of the album's charm is that it "willfully violated so many [of punk's] rules . . . [it's] utterly devoid of political confrontation or social uplift . . . the Misfits just want to entertain and do their own thing."[16]

Originally the Misfits planned to release *Walk Among Us* through their own label, Plan 9. That changed when I.R.S. Records, home of punk's all-female breakout stars the Go-Gos, contacted the band about releasing the record on their label. Wary of rumors surrounding the way I.R.S. treated their talent but intrigued by the prospect of greater distribution power,[17] the Misfits sniffed around other companies and decided in the end to hand *Walk Among Us* over to Ruby Records. An imprint of Slash Records (home of cultish Cali punk band the Germs and itself an extension of West Coast punk chronicle *Slash* magazine), Ruby Records was basically a one-man operation run by Chris Desjardins of Los Angeles band the Flesh Eaters.

Desjardins, a Misfits fan who dutifully snapped up all the of the band's early singles, already had two releases under his belt on Ruby—his own band's second album and an EP by bluesy punks the Gun Club—when he first touched base with Glenn Danzig about working together (Desjardins can't recall whom initiated their first conversation, although he doesn't discount the story that Danzig called him looking to purchase ad space for Plan 9 in *Slash* magazine). A contract was eventually brokered for a one-album deal. Impressed with the demo tapes from a 1981 New Jersey recording session, Ruby flew Danzig out to Los Angeles for a final marathon twelve-hour mixing session with Burnette.[18] Despite the huge chunk of time spent meticulously tweaking and repurposing various aspects of the recordings, in the end the Misfits weren't entirely satisfied with *Walk Among Us*. Danzig in particular commented years later that he wasn't sure the record accurately reflected the specific sound for which they were known. There were also issues with the album's art work. "I remember I flipped out on [Ruby] because [the cover] was supposed to be in all these different colors," Danzig said in 2009. "Such as red, black, and orange, but the way it came out was truly awful. . . . they had not shown us any proofs beforehand. Because it was this little label, it was a really big nightmare working for them."[19]

Desjardins remembers things differently, claiming he and Glenn "got along great" during *Walk*'s mixing and production—at least when it was just the two of them. "When the whole band came back out to do some [concert] dates when the record was released, he was much more . . . I don't know, hardcore?" Desjardins opines. "The brothers who played guitar and bass, Jerry and Doyle, they were pretty hard guys. I didn't have a rocky relationship with them personally, but it just seemed everything was very adversarial in general. Glenn was like that when he was around them."

Though there was no question from fans regarding the greatness of *Walk Among Us* inside and out, exact sales figures have long been hard to nail down. Danzig began claiming as early as 1983 that *Walk Among Us* had moved upwards of 20,000 copies and even greater numbers overseas (he also bitterly charged Ruby with never paying the band royalties on these large sales and that legal action would be their only recourse). According to Desjardins, Danzig's numbers are most likely inaccurate, as general sales on the high end for most of Ruby's releases at that time fell somewhere between

2,500 to 5,000. Real-time sales figures were not always forthcoming to Ruby from Slash's accounting department, however, so there is a possibility Danzig's claims had some basis—though not enough, apparently, to warrant the aforementioned litigious pursuits.[20] "It's possibly an accurate number," muses Minor Threat's Brian Baker of Danzig's five-figure sales claims. "Our record *Out of Step* has to have sold 15,000 [copies], and my perception is the Misfits were bigger than Minor Threat. I mean, some of the shows on the *Walks Among Us* tour were huge. They were playing to over a thousand people sometimes."[21]

Whatever the reality concerning its sales figures, *Walk Among Us* would eventually rise above its arbitrary numbers to be revered as one of the most invigorating and vital releases in punk history, an entity that forever married casual gore and hard rock, providing the template for a succession of spookier, more aggressive horror rock acts. White Zombie, a lo-fi punk band formed by Parsons School of Design students Sean Yseult and Rob Cummings in 1985, mutated the basic *Walk Among Us* vibe into a heavy metal beast that grooved along on crushing riffs and undead shlock for a decade-plus (earning the seal of approval from pop-culture giants like MTV). Cummings, who later christened himself Rob Zombie, and Yseult have both admitted to openly worshipping the Misfits in their youth; guitarist Jay Yuenger, a punk rock veteran from Chicago who joined White Zombie in 1989, asserts that *Walk* is "the definitive statement" from the Misfits, a record of "a dangerous sound with sweet melodies . . . it's just so unique, and so uniquely American. It made a huge impact on everyone I knew."[22]

Further south in Virginia, the influence of the Misfits helped transform what began as a low-budget horror movie production merged with a comical band called Death Piggy to form a space-suited rock n' roll opera about aliens called Gwar. Gwar didn't sing about monsters because they presented themselves literally as the monsters, a cadre of creatures from a distant planet (adorned in homemade foam rubber costumes) who came to our planet to conquer the human race one profane concert at a time. Rather than douse their fans with faux poison Kool-Aid, this band preferred to build an enormous penis cannon to soak attendees in fake ejaculate as their ears were similarly pummeled by songs such as "Slaughterama" and "Sexecutioner." Gwar singer Dave Brockie, whose stage persona is that of rugged interplanetary leader Oderus Urungus, singles out *Walk Among Us* as a nearly perfect album, hailing the Misfits' imagery in songs like "Skulls" as "spot on" and simply "classic." "They were a huge influence," says Brockie. "They were the punk rock Kiss, but they were a million times better than Kiss! They never made any shitty music!"[23]

Walk Among Us also found devotees in the straight-laced pop world, a testament to the album's unshakable melodies. Cases in point: the beautiful acoustic cover of "Skulls" recorded by bubblegum grunge stars the Lemonheads in 1990[24] and the Nutley Brass's equally touching instrumental re-working of the same song finding its way into *Saturday Night Live* star Andy Samberg's 2007 daredevil farce *Hot Rod*.[25] Unfortunately, at the time of their debut album's release in 1982 the Misfits were still relatively unknown and in desperate need of money, so much so that they'd soon sacrifice a band member over a financial matter that amounted to less than a dollar.

"Seeing [the Misfits] live, I realized they were more of a comic book," says Ian MacKaye. "I don't mean that dismissively. They simply had a shtick. I had no idea what to make of them before. When the Cramps played, it was clear they were not in costumes. The Misfits were more like Kiss."[26]

Glenn Danzig has always vehemently denied any link between Kabuki-faced hard rock titans Kiss and his own band despite the similarities in visual execution and general bombast. Countless interviews find Danzig dismissing Gene Simmons et al. as a poor recreation of the New York Dolls, a band he truly did admire. Jerry Only, on the other hand, openly admitted his apprecia-tion for Kiss, having won the group's first album in 1974 at a carnival game during a trip to the Jersey Shore with his parents and seeing the band in concert a year later on the *Hotter Than Hell* tour.[27] Kiss's stage energy is visibly incarnate in Only when you watch videotaped performances from the halcyon days of the Misfits—like Simmons, the bassist expends a great deal of energy trying to menace the crowd, thrashing his instrument about, curling his lip into a sharp sneer and staring into the darkness ahead when he isn't screaming along with Danzig. Only also made sure to adorn the sleeveless leather jacket he wore onstage with enormous spikes protruding from various angles. Fans were often afraid to approach the bassist lest they accidentally receive a gaping flesh wound.

Shticky as the Misfits may have been—particularly during the *Walk Among Us* period, as their hairspray-soaked devilocks grew to obscene lengths and the Crimson Ghost logo spread across all their equipment and *Mad Max*–inspired garb (Danzig in particular was taken with the *Mad Max* film series, bragging to *Flipside* that he saw the trilogy's second entry *The Road Warrior* in the theater on at least five separate occasions[28]). Sometimes the violence surrounding the band was all too real, though. Consider the first West Coast date of 1982 the band played on April 10 at San Francisco's Elite Club. The support acts included Desjardin's band the Flesh Eaters, California gloom rockers the Undead (not to be confused with Bobby Steele's band of the same name), hardcore pranksters JFA, and an early incarnation of alterna-tive superstars the Meat Puppets. The concert promoters made the unwise decision to sell canned beer at the gig and not enforce any strict ID policy, leading to an impossibly rowdy atmosphere—especially when the Meat Pup-pets took to the stage with a set list comprised of medium-paced country and western–leaning material. "The kids were not hep to that," Desjardins recalls. "There was a virtual storm of beer cans thrown at the stage, but the Meat Puppets refused to stop playing, to their credit. They were batting the beer cans back into the audience with the guitar[s]. It was crazy. I'm surprised that none of them got badly hurt."[29]

The Misfits were certainly not wont to put up with this kind of abuse. Five songs into their set, Arthur Googy leapt out from behind his drum kit and, with the aid of middle Caiafa brother Ken (traveling with the Misfits as a roadie), physically attacked one particular audience member who was repeatedly attempting to peg Doyle in the head with beer cans. A concert-stopping fistfight ensued. Doyle, in a moment of teenage non-clarity, decided to try and separate the violent attendee from his band mates with the pointy end of his pointy Ibanez guitar. Miscalculating distance and speed, Doyle swung down too forcefully, smashing his aggressor square in the head and breaking his instrument in the process. The audience member crumpled to the floor. Aghast, the crowd was now beside itself with rage. A full-scale riot nearly broke out. "I remember Doyle telling me they ran up the stairs backstage really fast, but everyone followed them," says later Misfits road manager Tim Bunch. "They were standing at the top of the stairs, and all these kids were coming up one at a time to fight them. Doyle just stood there, [and claims he was] punching them out one by one."[30] "You know, we don't take that kind of shit," Danzig would tell *Flipside* that December. "If we don't want people throwing shit at us . . . what do I give two fucks if that makes us rock art or something? We don't care. Maybe [what Doyle did] was [necessary], maybe it wasn't, what would anybody else do in that situation? It's a split second thing."[31]

A longstanding and completely false rumor is that Los Angeles punk provocateurs Fear were also sandwiched on the bill between certain bands for this infamous Elite Club show. This seems reasonable considering the general time frame and Fear's reputation for being present at or even directly responsible (via their fierce crowd-baiting) for outbreaks of untamed punk rock violence. Desjardins, who personally booked the evening's acts, says Fear was absolutely not there and were never even considered for the show; a freak appearance by Fear on NBC's *Saturday Night Live* approximately six months earlier at the behest of super fan John Belushi—wherein the destructive actions of Fear and their cadre of slam dancers is said to have caused several thousand dollars' worth of damage to famed Studio 8H—had increased that group's concert draw to the degree they could no longer be considered an opening act.[32] As Fear drummer Spit Stix put it years later explaining the SNL effect, "We were industry mud for about a year, but we were kings on the street."[33]

The Misfits escaped the Elite Club with their lives intact that wild April night but a with slightly injured reputation—punk rock periodical *Maximum-*

RockNRoll would later depict the band in crude cartoon form, penises sprouting from their foreheads in place of devilocks, thrilled at the prospect of cracking concert members' heads open for money (Doyle, apparently flattered by any artistic representation, would later deem said cartoon "cool").[34] Two weeks after the Elite Club fracas, Chris Desjardins was contacted at the Slash/Ruby offices by the San Francisco police department. The victim of Doyle's attack had fallen into a coma, and now the cops were looking to get a hold of the Misfits to possibly file charges against their eighteen-year-old guitarist. Desjardins informed the SFPD that the Misfits had long since returned to New Jersey. Luckily, the audience member in question recovered and the matter wasn't pursued.[35]

On April 14, 1982, an equally legendary but more lighthearted incident occurred when the Misfits invaded the famed Whisky-a-Go-Go for their official Los Angeles debut. As the story goes, Mötley Crüe front man Vince Neil sauntered into the bar with a friend during the band's soundcheck. The band began heckling the aspiring glam rocker almost immediately, who then did a quick about-face and exited the Whisky. The Misfits would later brag that they followed a visibly frightened Neil outside the Whisky to chase him down the street ("We just went running out," remembered Glenn in 1999. "And they were just scampering up the hill or the street or whatever"[36]), but little evidence outside the band's own boasts suggests there ever was any interaction between the horror punks and Vince Neil.

Writing about that evening's Whisky show in the *Los Angeles Times*, Craig Lee noted the Misfits' "muscular necro-metal pose" masked what amounted to a "speeded-up version of the Ramones . . . in Kiss clothing." Lee went on to call Danzig's voice "gutsy," registering surprise that it "actually cut through the feedback." Apparently on the fence regarding the whole affair, Lee ended his write-up by dismissing the band as "corny and disposable" but praising the "shocking, visceral" song "Bullet" as "one of the most jolting punk songs ever written."[37] David Chute of the *Herald-Examiner* had kinder words for the band, announcing that the Misfits "growled their way through a tight and infectious set" while "mak[ing] the morbid nihilism of hard-core punk seem playful and ingratiating . . . the boyish dress-up games and gleeful grossouts [sic] suggest a refreshing larkish attitude toward the standard pose." Chute also took care to note that *Walk Among Us* "seems to signal [the Misfits'] real arrival," particularly because the "Superfreak" himself, crossover funk star Rick James, was in attendance that night.[38]

Financially, the *Walk Among Us* tour had not proven very successful. Stiffed consistently by sleazy concert promoters who knew they could get away with ripping off no-name punk bands, the Misfits had not recouped the $3,000 Jerry Only borrowed from his father to fund travel for this stretch of California dates.[39] Mid-April found the tired and frustrated band members looking forward to rounding out the final three dates so they could return home and begin work on the follow-up to *Walk*, the already titled *Earth A.D.* Unfortunately, a meal stop at a Los Angeles McDonalds would torpedo all those plans while simultaneously bringing an end to what many believe was the most classic of Misfits lineups.

About a year before *Walk Among Us*, Glenn Danzig released his first solo record, a dizzying single dedicated to the murder of his favorite actress. "Who Killed Marilyn?" spun around on a sloppy two-chord riff as Danzig recounts *Dragnet*-style the facts surrounding Marilyn Monroe's sudden 1962 expiration, surmising by the chorus that her death is "no mystery" to him. The flip side, "Spook City, U.S.A.," was a crude anthem to an unnamed American haunting that leans ever so slightly toward Christian Death in its employment of background moaning and basic atmospheric frights.[40] "Who Killed Marilyn?" was a project encouraged by Misfits booster George Germain and spurred by a break in band activity when it appeared the Caiafa brothers were more interested in partying than rehearsing. Danzig is credited with performing all instrumentation on the single, though others have claimed there were outside musicians involved who, to this day, remain unidentified.

Arthur Googy's name comes up a lot during the debate over "Marilyn's" credits; while the jury's still out on his participation, the drummer was equally frustrated in the autumn of 1981 with Doyle and Jerry's slipping dedication to the Misfits. Coming together over this issue, Googy and Danzig briefly considered dumping their band mates to form a new project.[41] By April of 1982, though, the bond between drummer and singer was broken—relations between the pair had become openly hostile. A *Touch and Go* interview from shortly before this period finds Danzig and Googy never missing an opportunity to take a swipe at one another. Googy curtly declares to the magazine his disapproval of Danzig's "Who Killed Marilyn?" solo single, the very piece of music that spurned their discussion of a new band ("I think it sucks, myself"). Meanwhile, Danzig chides Googy over his repeated requests to meet "nice girls" ("Enough about fuckin' horniness, Arthur!"). The petty squabbling continues over whether *Walk Among Us* was intended to have thirteen songs, where the "Horror Business" single was recorded, and Googy's unhip love of pot (Googy: "I lit up a joint [outside Club 57] and they started saying, 'Aw, reefer sucks!' and all this shit. . . ." Glenn: "Good, they should have killed you").[42]

Another thorn in Danzig's side was Googy's assertion in the Misfits tour van that he would happily perform fellatio on himself if he were limber enough. In a letter to Meatmen singer Tesco Vee circa this time period, Danzig highlighted and condemned this sexual desire of his band mate's as simply too bizarre to sit with ("Everybody in the van went, 'What!!!,'" Glenn wrote. "And so he repeated it and we kicked him out of the van.").[43] The singer clearly construed Googy's statement as a homosexual desire, which, as several pieces of press from the era prove, is something for which Glenn Danzig had little tolerance. Case in point: a 1982 interview with *Flipside* that finds the Misfits leader calling San Francisco "fucking Homo Land" where "everyone's pushing [homosexuality] on you." ("You go to the supermarket to use the phone and it's, 'Oh, yeecch,' [makes kissing sound]. 'Fuck you, leave me alone for five seconds!'")[44] In his letter to Vee, Danzig speculates further on Googy's sexuality, noting that the groupies his drummer consorted with were "old . . . fat and ugly."[45] Disheartening sentiments from a member of an allegedly more liberal-minded musical revolution but not terribly surprising considering the time period and geographic location in which the Misfits were bred.

At any rate, Googy's days with the band were numbered, and had been since shortly before the 1981 studio sessions that would later make up the bulk of *Walk Among Us*. A few clandestine Misfits rehearsals were held at this time with a former Lodi High School football buddy of Jerry Only's, Jim Murray, on drums. Though band members have never confirmed or denied his story, Murray claims he asked to replace Googy and would have, had his girlfriend not strongly objected to his participation in a demonic punk rock band. A confrontation between Murray, his girlfriend, the girlfriend's parents, and the Misfits is said to have broken out one afternoon on the Caiafas' front lawn, just as the band was leaving to go log some time recording their debut album. The tense argument ending with a sullen Murray slinking away from the band, leaving punk rock history in his rearview mirror and forcing the Misfits to fall back on Arthur Googy.[46]

The Danzig/Googy feud reached its climax on April 15, the band's day off between California tour dates. Dining at McDonald's (a favorite eatery of the band), the famished drummer demanded a meal of two cheeseburgers instead of the single burger he was to be allotted for the day. Danzig refused, citing the band's dire financial straits. Within moments, a fistfight had broken out between the two, frightening neighboring diners and annoying the Caiafa brothers. "Me and Doyle said, 'Hey, you two guys better just sit down,'" Jerry Only later recalled. "'This sucks enough. You guys are fightin' over cheeseburgers—I gotta go back and tell my old man I blew three grand!' . . . [in the end] pretty much Googy told [Glenn] to kiss off, and I don't blame him a bit. If Doyle wasn't in the band at that point, I probably would have packed it up too, y'know?"[47]

Showing some mettle, Arthur Googy toughed it out for the final three gigs of the *Walk Among Us* tour before flying back to New York City, making good on his McDonaldland resignation. Googy later joined New York hardcore band Antidote, whose platform was the spread of peace and unity among warring punks; still, Antidote's approach was rage-heavy, and their blistering 1983 EP *Thou Shalt Not Kill* (which clocks in at a mean seven minutes) is considered to this day to be one of hardcore punk's finest recordings. In a slightly more ironic post-Misfits career move no one other than Bobby Steele has been able to verify, Arthur Googy allegedly appeared in a nationally broadcast television commercial for Burger King circa 1984, happily consuming a Whopper that may or may not have been his second hamburger of the day. Googy's work in a Levi's ad from the same time period is stuff of similar legend. "Just to put it in the simplest terms, this guy was a wacko," Bobby Steele later said of Googy, who played with the drummer during his final months with the Misfits. "This guy was just like so hyper . . . when I was driving him home, after his audition [with us in 1980], he admitted to me that he had never played an entire song [on the drums] before, in his life, y'know, and it was like the guy was incredible. [He] always seemed to be like the kind of guy that he sets his mind to something [and] he does a great job of it."[48]

Less than a month after the release of their debut album, the Misfits had lost their third drummer in six years over a thirty-eight-cent cheeseburger.[49] Googy's departure killed the momentum they needed to break *Walk Among Us* on any kind of larger scale (the Slash/Ruby release later remembered for dominating 1982 is Fear's dark debut, simply titled *The Record*). This unexpected inactivity bred enough tension and resentment within the band to prove fatal. Not even the addition of a storied hardcore punk superstar would save the Misfits from slipping into the grave forever.

There were more pedestrian matters directly at hand, though—namely, Doyle's graduation from high school in June. By all accounts, the ceremony went far smoother than the guitarist's passage from Thomas Jefferson Middle School several years earlier. That graduation ceremony erupted into vague chaos when fourteen-year-old Doyle, hair freshly dyed pink with matching jacket and pants, was initially refused his diploma by Principal Gary Carabin for violating Thomas Jefferson's dress code. Doyle sat on the stage long after Carabin purposely neglected to call his name; the audience began shouting in the youth's defense, and Doyle made his feelings known with a one-fingered salute. After some give and take, Paul Doyle Caiafa was finally awarded his diploma once the ceremony concluded. The angry Doyle promptly crumpled his award up and discarded it—the school had accidentally put someone else's name on the paper. "I just wanted to liven things up," Doyle told a *New Jersey Herald* reporter later that day. "It was all so boring and they were such a bunch of duds."[50]

Doyle, the third and most menacing Misfits guitarist, Goleta, CA, 1983. *Kevin Salk.*

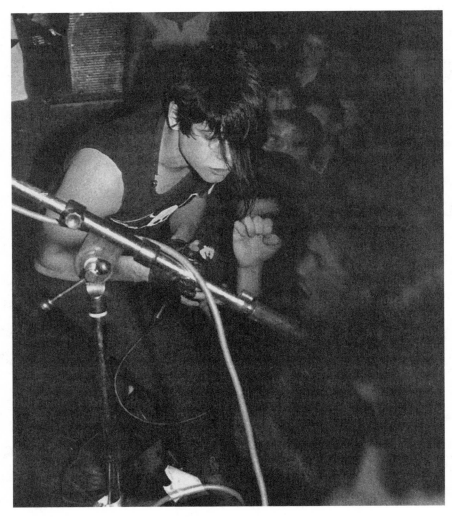

Singer Glenn Danzig, on the blurred line between stage and crowd, Goleta, CA, 1983. *Kevin Salk.*

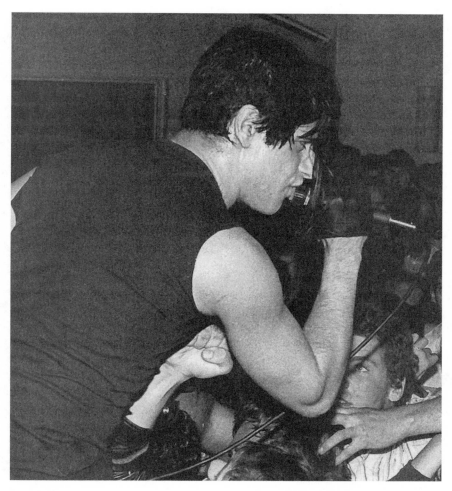

Danzig shows some of the musculature that would later define him, Goleta, CA, 1983. *Kevin Salk.*

Doyle and Glenn in classic pose; note the overwhelmed fan in the background, Goleta, CA, 1983. *Kevin Salk.*

Bassist Jerry Only in full regalia, Goleta, CA, 1983. *Kevin Salk.*

Jerry's past as a high school football star shines through, Goleta, CA, 1983.
Kevin Salk.

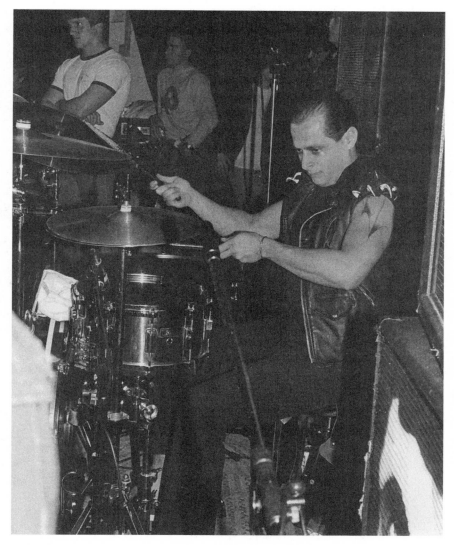

Fifth Misfits drummer Robo helped usher the band into hardcore, Goleta, CA, 1983. *Kevin Salk.*

Chapter Five

Die, Die My Darling

"Whom the gods love die young," was said of yore. —Lord Byron

The Misfits were not generally known during their so-called glory years for spending time with fellow punk rock bands. Granted, the group took a handful of younger like-minds under their wing: Manhattan sleaze rockers the Victims were the only outside band allowed to release anything (in this case, a self-titled 1979 EP) on the Misfits' Plan 9 label; fellow Lodi punks Rosemary's Babies were also chums to the degree that Babies singer JR still considers Glenn Danzig "a really supportive big brother" type and fondly recalls him helping to load the band's gear into clubs for gigs;[1] and the Necros were another somewhat macabre outfit from the Midwest who began regularly touring with the Misfits after a pleasant experience opening the latter band's first Detroit show. For the most part, however, the Misfits locked horns with their contemporaries, making enemies of some of the punk scene's bigger names over seemingly ridiculous matters.

San Francisco agitators the Dead Kennedys, for instance, were labeled "assholes" because they released a song called "Halloween" in the wake of the earlier Misfits composition.[2] The Misfits also began hating the Flesh Eaters—despite singer Chris Desjardins's role in the creation and distribution of *Walk Among Us*—as they believed the band to be "homos."[3] The Cramps and the Ramones faced Danzig's ire because neither band would allow the Misfits to share concert billings when the groups were all still in their infancy in the late 1970s (even though both these trendsetting New York bands helped paved the way for the Misfits in many regards). Such venom was typical and often returned in favor; during a 1982 gig with the Misfits in Michigan, unhinged Crucifucks shrieker Doc Dart jabbed the image-heavy headliners by asking the audience, "What's the difference between the Misfits and Ronald McDonald?" After a brief pause punctuated a few stray shouts, Dart spat, "Oh, you can't tell the difference either!"[4]

One outfit the Misfits didn't pick fights with was Black Flag, the California hardcore founders whose explosive anger at authority figures was expertly outlined on their 1981 debut album *Damaged*, right down to the cover depicting the meaty fist of singer Henry Rollins smashing into a mirror. Black Flag's lethal guitar-heavy approach resonated with the equally agitated Lodi assembly who were more or less at the same level of underground popularity. The two groups forged a mutual respect playing together a handful of times beginning in 1981; on June 11, 1983, the Misfits made clear how much they valued Black Flag by traveling across the country for a one-off performance at that group's auspicious "Everything Went Black" reunion concert.

"Everything Went Black" was a reference to the 1982 compilation album that Black Flag was forced to release without their name due to ongoing legal entanglements with MCA imprint Unicorn Records.[5] The concert found three former Flag vocalists—Keith Morris, Ron Reyes, and Dez Cadena—coming back to the fold for one blow-out night of throat-ripping memories at the Santa Monica Civic Center alongside Flag's fourth and final singer, the aforementioned Henry Rollins. Rollins was such a Misfits devotee he had two Crimson Ghost tattoos—one for each arm, and one more than Misfits singer Glenn Danzig had himself at the time (for the record, Doyle was the Misfit with the most drawings of the Crimson Ghost permanently inked on his body, brandishing four inside a fiery design near his right shoulder).[6]

Second on the bill that night at the Civic Center after SoCal skate punks the Vandals, the Misfits set their towering amps emblazoned with the Crimson Ghost atop a blood red stage carpet and plowed through their material at lightning speed. Video of this gig shows the band as the consummate showmen they were. Glenn Danzig stalked the stage like a man possessed in his full body skeleton costume while the Caiafa brothers lumbered shirtless just outside the spotlight. A Misfits logo on the bass drum glowed in a certain light; pounding away behind that drum was the newest Misfit, a Black Flag graduate of stout proportions and Colombian heritage named Julio Roberto Valverde Valencia. Friends knew him better by his nickname, Robo.[7]

Valverde was a South American national who entered the United States on a student visa in 1975. By 1978 the hobby drummer had joined Black Flag and was providing the perfect rigid backbone for guitarist Greg Ginn's overwhelming steamroller guitar work.[8] Robo's drumming was, as Ian MacKaye puts it, "square geometrically, and metered out in real blocks"[9] (hence the mechanical nickname). Yet Robo could also play with a unexpected amount of finesse, as heard on *Damaged*'s intricately arranged social commentary-cum-sing-along "T.V. Party"; copping moves from Black Sabbath's Bill

Ward, Robo made it through that piece on rolls and accents, hardly playing a straight drum beat once. Humble by nature and generally soft-spoken, Robo nonetheless lent great character to Black Flag, a powerful, handsome Hispanic with piercing eyes, a monosyllabic name, and an indeterminate background some say was steeped in misdeeds at the hands of the Colombian government. Perhaps inevitably, Robo became a legend in his own right.

In the winter of 1982, Black Flag embarked on a tour of England to support the release of *Damaged*. Unfortunately, just hours before the band were due to fly home, UK officials detained Robo at Heathrow Airport because of nagging passport issues. With dates in the US already scheduled and never ones to simply cancel a leg of tour, Black Flag bit the bullet, recruited a new percussionist, and closed the book on their time with Robo. [10] The stranded Robo was eventually allowed to reenter the United States in July of 1982. Upon his return, he quickly learned of the drum vacancy in the Misfits, one that remained open despite offers to both Rosemary's Babies drummer Eric Stellmann and Kenny Caiafa (Stellmann, already regularly working with the Misfits as their semi-official photographer, turned it down to focus on his own group; Kenny Caiafa wasn't confident enough with his skill set to officially level up). Being a long-time fan of the Misfits, Robo telephoned Danzig and, thanks to mutual admiration, was immediately brought aboard. [11]

Acquiring this storied Black Flag powerhouse was quite a "get" for the band considering their previous technically unimpressive drum roster, but it wasn't entirely clear where in Lodi the their newest member could live. Jerry and Doyle's parents balked at the idea of a homeless and prematurely balding Colombian shacking up in their house. "My mom said, 'I don't mind taking in two Midwestern bands that are passin' through town, but Robo looks older than me,'" Only remembered in a 1994 *FEH* interview. "I told Glenn my mom wasn't psyched about Robo livin' with us, so I says, 'Why don't he bunk with you?' and Glenn says okay. In the meantime, Robo came to work [with us at the machine shop]." [12]

As pedestrian as their lives in Lodi seemed, on the road the line between reality and ghoulish cartooning was increasingly blurred for the Misfits. No incident better exemplifies this than the band's arrest for criminal trespassing in a New Orleans cemetery in the middle of their Evilive Tour—undertaken to support the forthcoming raucous concert EP of the same name—on October 17, 1982. Following a lively gig at Tupelo's marked by the backstage antics of two strippers from Atlanta named Poison and Venom who repeatedly placed Robo's drum sticks in their vaginas, the Misfits journeyed with approximately thirty hangers-on—including the strippers and support band the Necros—to one of the city's historical cemeteries, as many first-time visitors to New Orleans are wont to do. The band members joked as they entered St. Louis Cemetery No. 2 some time after midnight that they were on the search for stray bones and the tomb of nineteenth-century voodoo figure-head Marie Laveau (a hairdresser of mixed ethnicity, Laveau was believed to retain incredible psychic powers and inspired an early 1970s Marvel Comics character of the same name; she is actually buried in neighboring St. Louis Cemetery No. 1).

Residents of a housing project near the graveyard were alarmed by the racket the punk rockers were making and immediately called authorities. Tagalong Mike IX Williams, just fifteen at the time, remembers the melée that ensued. "We were there for what felt like half an hour but was probably closer to ten or fifteen minutes before the cops surrounded the place," says Williams. "We saw the [patrol cruiser] lights and the searchlights . . . and people scattered everywhere, trying to get to their cars. I just happened to end up at the edge of cemetery where the cop cars were. That's when they nabbed me, and then I saw them walking the Misfits over, one by one—Glenn, then Jerry, and so on—in handcuffs." [13]

Eighteen people total were arrested (discounting the Necros, who managed to convince the earliest arriving police unit they weren't with the trespassing party [14]), but only fifteen were of age and could be legally charged. Williams recalls the arresting officers as "complete assholes" who made a spectacle out of hauling to the station this cadre of menacing-looking punks, harassing them every step of the way. ("They took stuff I had outta my pockets and just balled it up and threw it away. They were taking everyone's wallets and dumping them out.") At one point, a mohawked teenage female in the party was smashed in the face with a cop's mag light after she refused to answer the question, "Are you a girl or a boy?" While Williams and the other two underage arrestees were eventually bailed out by one of their parents, the Misfits themselves spent the night in jail.

The next morning the Misfits were released on bail, courtesy of Ken Caiafa, but they didn't stick around for their scheduled arraignment. The band soldiered to Florida for their next scheduled tour date. [15] Meanwhile, the *New Orleans Times-Picayune* reported the incident under the headline "PUNK-ROCK MUSICIANS ARRESTED IN CEMETERY." The story made sure to note that the Misfits wore "dramatic facial painting" and their "album . . . features an offer to buy a Misfits T-shirt that shows President Kennedy at the moment of his assassination." [16] A month later, Glenn, Jerry, Doyle, and Robo returned to New Orleans for their rescheduled court appearance. Scolded by the judge, the Misfits were basically told to stay out of the Big Easy and paid a fine of a few hundred dollars.

While the New Orleans incident was the kind of PR other horror rockers would kill for and bolstered the band's intense legend, there was one casualty of the whole affair: The set of free weights the Misfits brought with them on tour to help maintain their impressive musculature were missing from the tour van when the New Orleans PD returned the vehicle to them the morning of their bailout. The cops had left the bright red vehicle, doors ajar, in the cemetery after the arrests. Further drawing attention to this abandoned van was the large unmistakable painting of Spider-Man's face on the side door. Despite the selection of expensive musical equipment held within, the weights were the only item local thieves—or perhaps the cops themselves— pilfered.[17]

The *Evilive* EP the Misfits were touring in support of during their grave-yard dustup was released that December. The disc culled seven live tracks from two raucous Googy-era performances by the Misfits, one in New York and another in San Francisco. The production values on *Evilive* were only vaguely better than any given third-party recording distributed at the time; instrument levels rise and fall, a strange distortion permeates the entire EP, and a long stretch where Doyle tunes his guitar one string at a time remains curiously unedited. Yet *Evilive* captures the Misfits live show as it was— raw, frantic, unrelenting. The tension spikes during "Horror Business": taken from the New York gig, where a last-minute lineup change unexpectedly paired the Misfits with Bobby Steele's Undead, Danzig firmly intones to an audience member and Undead supporter pelting him with ice, "One more fuckin' time, you asshole, and you die!" (it should be noted the crowd was merely following the Misfits' lead—this was the Ritz gig where Danzig and Only spent the Undead's set hurling bottles at their former band mate).[18] Later, just before *Evilive* peaks with the swelling anthem "Hatebreeders," Danzig angrily answers a heckler's taunts with a vaguer threat: "You think you'll get outta the hospital in time?" Even the EP's cover photo managed to convey the Misfits' singer's ever-present rage: as Only, Googy, and Doyle mercilessly pound out a racket behind him, Danzig stands at the foot of the stage, hand outstretched as if reaching to strangle someone, ignoring the audience members cheering wildly for his band.[19]

Evilive was originally only available via the Fiend Club, the fan organiza-tion the Misfits started to reward their followers with promotional stickers, buttons, and news direct from Lodi. Listeners who wrote to the address on the back of Misfits records would receive mass quantities of such ephemera in envelopes and packages as ornately decorated as the record sleeves them-selves. The average Fiend Club envelope boasted a close-up image of the Crimson Ghost underneath the Misfits logo, the return address stamped just underneath the Ghost's eye sockets. During interviews, Danzig and his cro-nies would invite eager fans to pay the band back by mailing any bones, skulls, or dead animals they had lying around. Occasionally a dyed-in-the-wool fiend would comply, and the Misfits would open a package to discover a long-deceased rodent or bat rotting away in their hands.[20]

Seven months after the New Orleans arrest, at the aforementioned Santa Monica gig Robo slammed away with his usual aplomb, propelling the Mis-fits through a set of classics peppered with a handful of newer, darker compositions like the barren "Green Hell" and the ferocious "Hellhound." The band played quickly, but each song was decipherable and things did not deteriorate into the cacophonous blur heard on so many other Misfits live recordings from this period. The catharsis can certainly be felt at the close of "Devilock," the penultimate song that evening; the band bounces between the two final notes, rocking back and forth incessantly, as Danzig screams in pain before letting out a final exorcising exclaim of, "Oh my fucking God!" The song collapses and you can almost see the dust rising up from the devastation.[21]

As together as horror punk's biggest act seemed on stage that night in Santa Monica, the end was nigh. In the hours following the "Everything Went Black" gig—where the Misfits had played before 3,000 rowdy punks, their biggest crowd to date—Danzig confided to Henry Rollins that he was planning to leave the band.[22] He was tired of dealing with the other members, whose lack of shared creative vision Glenn believed was holding him back. The singer felt Jerry and Doyle weren't committed enough to punk rock and was fed up with the pair's open worship of Van Halen and insistence on dramatically smashing their guitars in concert a la Pete Townshend. The Caiafas, according to Glenn, also spent too much time offstage draped in attire bearing the logo of their gridiron heroes the New York Giants as opposed to the leather-and-spikes Misfits uniform.

A more serious issue was Only's growing cocaine habit, something that tested the relatively clean-living Danzig's mettle (although he sang of absolute horrors, the singer rarely touched anything harder than rum and coke). Glenn would later remark that he could "see the Misfits becoming exactly the things that [he] got in a punk band to avoid."[23] "They would give me this rap that if I didn't get the band lots of money [by writing commercial songs], they wouldn't be able to do it anymore," Danzig commented later to *Hard Times*. "But they would waste money on things like smashing guitars . . . [*This Is Spinal Tap*] kind of epitomizes what was going on . . . with the amps that go up to eleven."[24]

Jerry Only would lay much blame for the Misfits deterioration with Danzig's inability to comfortably coexist with his de facto roommate Robo. There was open resentment on both sides concerning the fact Robo spent his days working at the elder Caiafa's knife factory with Jerry and Doyle, earning money for the band, while Glenn stayed at home running the Misfits' Plan 9 record label. After a full day's shift, all Robo wanted to do was drink beer and watch television. Glenn would chide the drummer, trying to force him into folding and glueing record sleeves. This cycle went on for some time; by August of 1983, Robo reached his limit and announced his departure from the band. He moved out of Danzig's basement and back to Los Angeles.[25]

Danzig, seeing his opportunity to finally pull up his stakes, canceled three pending concert dates in Canada so he could fly to Washington, D.C., to meet with Minor Threat guitarists Lyle Preslar and Brian Baker about forming some kind of punk rock super group. Preslar later recalled: "[Glenn, Brian, and I] all decided that we would go after Chris Gates of the Big Boys for bass and Mark Stern of Youth Brigade for drums. . . . Those two guys had the good sense and foresight to back out without a note played, and Brian and I started trying to work with Glenn . . . from the earliest efforts it was obvious that we couldn't work together in a million fucking years, and Brian bolted, but I accepted Glenn's offer to play with him [later] in a new thing."[26] With the punk super group on hold, Danzig began working on material for a darker horror band he intended to call Samhain with various friends around New Jersey and New York, including Al Pike from celebrated Queens peace punks Reagan Youth, Eric Stellmann, and Stellmann's guitar-playing band mate from Rosemary's Babies, Craig Richardson.[27]

There were a pair of important bookings on the horizon, though, that would keep the Misfits together until the end of 1983: their annual tent pole Halloween gig, which that year was scheduled for October 29 in Detroit, and a brief November tour of Germany to support the overseas release of *Evilive*. Walking away from the band at this point would potentially cost them all a great deal of money—the German tour alone allegedly boasted guarantees of $2,000 for every show (foreign promoters were eager to have the Misfits for their first gigs ever in continental Europe), so the horror punks decided to tough it out until the December release of *Earth A.D.*

The only immediate problem facing the band was, once again, the absence of a drummer. In September, Jerry Only got back in touch with Arthur Googy to see if the wayward drummer be up for at least playing the Halloween show. If things went well, Only told Googy, he would be welcome to come along for the German tour. Googy, now deeply entrenched in his new hardcore band Antidote, considered the offer but told Jerry he'd only play with the Misfits again if payment was received entirely upfront. Only figured this was fair and was ready to cut a check until Danzig caught wind of his bass player's unsanctioned olive branch. Danzig curtly vetoed Googy's participation as he feared the drummer would simply play drug buddy to the elder Caiafa brother (aside from Van Halen and New York Giants football, one of Jerry Only's favorite pastimes was allegedly smoking Herculean amounts of marijuana).[28]

Danzig actually had his own drummer for the Misfits in mind, someone he had tried to audition for the band previously but the timing had just never worked out: Brian "Damage" Keats, a hard-hitting percussionist in his teens best known for his work with New Jersey sleaze punks Genocide. In the fall of 1983, Keats was living in San Francisco and playing with Verbal Abuse. A huge Misfits fan, Keats remembered in a 2005 interview being sought out by his heroes: "I got a call from my New York roommate, saying that Glenn Danzig called, asking me to join [the Misfits]. At the time, I don't think I'd ever actually met Glenn. I think he had just seen me play in bands or had heard about me through other people. Without hesitation, I dropped everything and moved back to New York. I took the bus out to Lodi and went to Glenn's house for my audition . . . I didn't know the band was about to fall apart or about the dysfunctional relationships within . . . I found out pretty quickly, though."

Speaking volumes, perhaps, about these dysfunctional relationships—or at least speaking to Danzig's claims that Jerry and Doyle were completely obsessed with mainstream heavy metal at this point—is Keats's memory of the Caiafa brothers arriving at the Misfits practice space in "a monster truck, blasting Van Halen's 'Unchained' on their way home from working out at the gym—not the exact image of [these guys] I had in my head." Keats rehearsed with the band that October afternoon, running through as much material as possible, before he was invited to play with them in Detroit. This would be the only instance prior to the Halloween gig in which the Misfits would attempt to rehearse with their brand-new teenage drummer (the Caiafas were working double shifts to ensure they'd have enough money to cover their pending German tour expenses). On the morning of October 25, Brian Keats met up with the Misfits again in Lodi to make the grueling ten-hour drive west to Detroit for the Halloween performance.[29]

The show itself was booked at Graystone Hall, a palatial showroom space that held at least 1,000 people. Drummer Todd Swalla, whose band the Necros were also on the bill that night, was excited for the show but was also curious regarding the future of the Misfits. It was no secret there were tensions within the band over creative direction: Jerry was happy turning the Misfits into a punk reflection of Kiss while Glenn desperately wanted something more akin to Australian blues-based post-punk upstarts the Birthday Party (who used gothic and horror themes in a less ham-fisted way than mainstream groups like Kiss or Iron Maiden . . . or, sometimes, even the Misfits). The family bond between the Caiafas also presented problems. "Glenn did not want Doyle on guitar," Swalla remembers. "And, of course, Jerry was not going to fire his little brother . . . Jerry and Glenn were increasingly at odds, yeah, [but] no one knew this [Detroit gig] would be their final show."[30]

Keats, a good friend of Swalla and the other Necros, began drinking with the opening act after the Misfits soundcheck that evening. When it was time to play, Keats realized he was "seriously buzzed," making an already difficult situation even worse. With no written set list and unable to discern from the deafening roar of the amps exactly what song he was supposed to be playing, Keats stumbled. After two botched songs an angry Doyle physically ejected Keats from the stage with one forceful forearm motion in favor of Swalla (who had already sat in with the band numerous times).[31]

The Misfits continued their blaring aural assault on Graystone Hall. However, for Danzig (who that evening was adorned in a sadomasochist's dog mask with a large pentagram painted on his chest), Doyle's physical removal of Keats proved to be the straw that broke the camel's back. After the fourth song in the set, "Death Comes Ripping," Glenn made a firm, faithful announcement that no one bothered to challenge: "This is our last show— *ever.*"

The Misfits then played for over an hour, one of their longest sets on record, frustration and apathy painted on their faces. Doyle and Jerry eventually sat down on their amps as they joylessly hammered everything out. The only one who seemed to be having any fun on stage was Swalla, who always thrilled to play with his favorite contemporary punk band. The crowd also seemed to be unaffected by the Misfits' onstage implosion—they surged as one giant mass, chanting along to their favorite songs and more or less luxuriating in the anarchic revelry.

The endless stream of stage divers and stage dancers, however, only served to further fray Danzig's nerves. Following "London Dungeon," the singer addressed the Graystone crowd with the following irritated rant: "If you guys come up here, then come up here and stage dive or do whatever the fuck you wanna do. But don't stand in the way of, like, so if we go crazy and you get hit and then you start cryin' to your mama or somethin' . . . like, if you're gonna jump, jump! If you're gonna go crazy, go crazy! But don't stand up here and, y'know, [makes jerking off motion] 'bluh, bluh,' pull your dick off . . . alright? 'Cause we're tryin' to play up here, and it's fucked up." Naturally, the crowd began cheering loudly as soon as the singer started feigning masturbation. Later, in lieu of water, Danzig requested that someone bring him a glass of schnapps.[32]

The unfortunate truth concerning this disastrous final performance was the Misfits could not simply go their separate ways once it was over (for the record, the absolute last song Glenn Danzig sang with the Misfits was "Night of the Living Dead," the same song they began their set with that evening). They were still a good half a day away from their home base of New Jersey. That evening, the seething band members—none of whom were speaking to one another—were invited to spend the night at the home of Detroit punk promoter Russ Gibb. Gibb stumbled into a strange kind of worldwide pop culture notoriety on October 12, 1969, when, as a radio deejay for Michigan's WKNR-FM, he took a call from a listener who put forth the creepy theory that Paul McCartney had died in a car accident in 1966 and the remaining Beatles had hired a McCartney doppelganger as a cover-up; this notion endures today as one of music's greatest conspiracy theories. In the early 1980s Gibb ran a fledgling punk rock video production company out of his house called Back Porch.

Mat Hunt recorded the Graystone Hall performance for Back Porch that night and recounted in a 2009 blog post the scene the following morning at the Gibb homestead: "I walked in . . . and handed Russ the tape of the Misfits show from the night before. I went into the kitchen and saw [the band] eating breakfast around a tiny table. From around the corner, [Russ's mother], holding a spatula and wearing an apron, said with a thick Scottish accent, 'Would you boys like some more scrambled eggs and sausage?' To me, it seemed like Anywhere, USA, but it was the fucking Misfits. The guys, hung over, exhausted, pissed, with long black sexy hair in their face[s], barely raised their head[s] and said, 'Yeaaaaaa, I'd like some more eggs please, Mrs. Gibb.' It was the 'please' that got me . . . the expectation was that they were rock stars, but here it was grandma with some regular boys."[33]

This same morning found Brian Keats apologizing profusely for his blunder to no avail ("I was so fucking sunk by the whole thing. . . . like I'd just probably caused the breakup of my favorite band"). The Misfits refused to acknowledge him, even during the ten-hour drive back to Lodi. Keats would never speak to any of the Misfits again but did manage to carve out a career as an in-demand session drummer. In the ensuing decades he racked up credits with a who's who of punk and new wave musicians, including members of the Dead Boys, Devo, the Damned, Blondie, the Bangles, the New York Dolls, and Gang of Four. The drummer would later credit his Misfits gaffe as something of a professional awakening, saying it lead him to "take the responsibilities of performing . . . way more seriously from that point on."

Sadly, Keats would be the first Misfit to die, succumbing to colon cancer in 2010 at the age of 46.[34] To their credit, the Misfits—or Jerry Only, at least—never directly blamed Keats for their Detroit meltdown. Only would eventually state that Keats was "a nice kid" who "did try" but ultimately "sucked." The bassist blamed Danzig for "pick[ing] [Keats] up . . . because of his haircut," apparently misinformed or unaware of Brian's work with Genocide and Verbal Abuse. "Glenn forgot the first rule: the music comes first and all the bullshit is for later," Jerry told *Jersey Beat* in 1990. "You don't sacrifice your music for a look. . . . [After Detroit], that was that. We said, 'Cancel the German tour.' It was then that I realized he wasn't competent enough to run things. He just wants to be on the cover of some magazine."[35]

After seven years, the Misfits had come to a crashing halt. Their saga was far from over, though.

Earth A.D./Wolfs Blood, the second and final original Misfits album, was released on December 12, 1983, on the band's Plan 9 label. Recorded the previous October in Santa Monica, California, this stark nine-song document is a complete departure into the subgenre of hardcore punk that leaves behind nearly all vestiges of the 1950s-style rock n' roll that characterize the band's prior recordings. The album's general mood of raw, heartless terror is set by the title track, which opens things up with a storm-like squall of guitars feeding back for roughly thirteen seconds; then, without warning, Robo's drums accelerate to an incredible pace while Danzig simultaneously lets out a massive carnal bellow. "You bet your life there's gonna be a fight," Danzig curtly warns moments later over the band's furious thrashing. After two minutes, "Earth A.D." collapses back into a wave of feedback that immediately crashes into the demented insect lust tribute "Queen Wasp." The pace is just slow enough to groove ever so slightly as the Misfits repeatedly shout the vague command "Go!" when Danzig isn't rhapsodizing about his hybrid lover's thorax.

The next three songs offer the most transparent blueprint for the heavy metal subgenres that would later claim *Earth A.D.* as a cornerstone. You can hear thrash metal's birth in the hard-charging "Devilock" wherein Doyle hammers a low E chord endlessly, each brief note change accented by a hard cymbal smash. There's more suspense in "Death Comes Ripping," a song that sounds carefully assembled with its slow introduction, against-the-beat verses, sparse vocals, and bookends of busy drum patterns. An obtuse arrangement, at least compared to the wild crunching abandon of "Green Hell" (a tribute to the 1940 James Whale film starring Vincent Price and Douglas Fairbanks Jr.). Although the speed of the album's material forces Danzig's voice into a hoarser territory, he still manages to maintain his prowess, that trademark howl cutting through the rest of the band's thick din.

Earth A.D.'s most interesting moment might be the moderately paced "Bloodfeast," which, either by design or its proximity to so many speedier songs, sounds almost like a pagan ritual. Here is where Danzig specifically shines, double-tracking his voice in various places to give it an even spookier cadence. At two and a half minutes, "Bloodfeast" is the album's longest song and, as such, acts as a fine palette cleanser before the explosive closer "Hellhound." The band sounds most furious on this final track—you can practically feel the cramping in Doyle's hands as he forces those powerful crunches from his instrument. The album ends as it began, with a final squeal of feedback that drifts into silence after one last cymbal crash.

The keen production work of SST Records mainstay Glen "Spot" Lockett helped *Earth A.D.* avoid sounding as muddled or uneven as other hardcore records of the time. Many years later Danzig would praise Lockett—who had already helped tame the outrageous noise of Black Flag, the Minutemen, and the Descendents on a handful of classic recordings—for helping capture what the Misfits truly sounded like in concert. Indeed, Lockett's work helped find the correct space between the murky Misfits recordings of their nascent years and the weird sheen that hung over *Walk Among Us. Earth A.D.*'s cover art, which is just as striking as its sonics, is a Marc Rude etching depicting the band members and their followers as a pile of fetid zombies writhing around some sort of abandoned mausoleum. The art more than anything signaled to fans that *Earth A.D.* was no cheesy B-movie shtick—this was the actual horror, the meat and potatoes, the visceral unrest generally reserved for Glenn's bold lyrics.[36]

Earth A.D.'s shift in tone caught punk fans off guard, many of whom felt the band was simply jumping on the hardcore bandwagon to compete with the rapid likes of Bad Brains and Minor Threat. From the latter band, singer Ian MacKaye in particular was disappointed with the Misfits' new direction. "You know, I *believed* them before that," says MacKaye. "The music was something coming out of deep expression. *Earth A.D.* . . . I felt it was just too fast."[37]

The lack of humor or camp value in this second Misfits record also bothered fans who reveled in the group's earlier classic dime-store Halloween presentation. The change in tone could be a reflection of how the horror film genre itself was being transformed at this time. 1978's *Halloween*, the first of the modern masked man murder scares, heralded the arrival of the take-no-prisoners slasher films and paved the way for a slew of shallow, gore-filled imitations such as *My Bloody Valentine, Slumber Party Massacre*, and the long-running *Friday the 13th* series. That same year the highly controversial *I Spit On Your Grave* hit screens and instantaneously offended mass audiences with its graphic depiction of rape and revenge-based violence; of course it inspired numerous copycats, including Charles Kaufman's *Mother's Day* and the infamous Italian production *Cannibal Holocaust*. Even science fiction films were feeling the effects—see the 1981 David Cronenberg classic *Scanners* about a group of telekinetics who invade a corporation and explode human heads like casaba melons. There was also *The Evil Dead*, the horror comedy best remembered before its sequels for offsetting its cartoony yuks with the horrifying concept of violent sexual assault by sentient trees.[38]

One of the biggest mainstream horror hits the year of *Earth A.D.*'s release was the film adaptation of Stephen King's frightening novel *Cujo*, a movie that does little more than trap two people in a car they cannot exit lest they be torn to fleshy ribbons by a giant rabid dog. *Cujo*, while not be as bloody or gruesome as most entries in the canon, showed just how much horror had changed in recent years. At this point it was all about pure, unrelenting terror. The relics of Hollywood's golden fright era that built their chills mostly on strange voices, ornate costumes, and romantic origin stories were now just that—relics, corny black-and-white spookfests that were more about atmosphere than actual horror, doomed to the prison of late-night television for the rest of eternity. Even Romero's 1968 lynchpin *Night of the Living Dead*, the film almost solely responsible for the genre's shift, seemed staid by this point in history. Perhaps afraid of falling into the same trap, the Misfits reinvented themselves as a more visceral (and less chuckling) beast.

Certain sects of Misfits fanatics outside the punk realm appreciated the band's newfound direction, and the development of heavy metal bands such as Metallica, Slayer, Megadeth, Nuclear Assault, and Exodus would prove the ultimate value in *Earth A.D.*'s dark hardcore tear. It is impossible to imagine the fury of Reagan-era platters like Metallica's *Ride the Lightning*, Slayer's *Reign in Blood*, or even a later work like Pantera's 1990 *Cowboys From Hell* existing without a guideline such as *Earth A.D.* Metallica would become particularly taken with the guiding hand of the Misfits as they fought to distinguish themselves from their long-haired competition, coloring their later work with several strong dabs from Danzig's pallet. By the early 1990s, historians would go so far as to dub *Earth A.D.* the speed metal bible, the work all speed metal dreamers should look to for inspiration and final rulings.

Not bad for an album that was more or less recorded in one eight-hour stretch. As the story goes, the band entered Santa Monica's Unicorn Studio at midnight after a gig in Los Angeles. The exhaustion does show in some places on *Earth A.D.*'s finished product—there are a couple of sloppy drum rolls on Robo's part, and the forty-second "Demonomania" barely has any reason to exist (apart from the hilarious opening declaration of "Look upon me, *I am the beast!*"). Danzig himself was so worn out during the session that he slept through the majority of it, rousing himself only to provide the titular cue in the middle of a newly recorded version of "Mommy, Can I Go Out and Kill Tonight?"[39] The rest of the vocals were recorded a year later, though the band kept Danzig's original low-volume grunting in "Mommy," ostensibly as some sort of weird joke.

Chapter Six

Green Hell

Fame and tranquility can never be bedfellows. —Michel de Montaigne

"Die, Die My Darling" was the aptly named Misfits single Glenn Danzig issued via Plan 9 Records in May of 1984 after the band's demise. A threatening staccato march in which the protagonist threatens an unknown victim with a future of entrapment in "an oblong box,"[1] "Die, Die" would prove a powerful final stamp for the band and would in time become one of the most revered Misfits songs (the single's flipside, a grinding werewolf ode entitled "We Bite," juxtaposes the famous beat of its A-side with pure unrelenting speed). With the Misfits officially behind him, Glenn focused his efforts on Samhain, whose lineup finally solidified in former Rosemary's Babies drummer Eric Stellmann, né Eerie Von (a name taken in part from horror periodical *Eerie*), on bass and Steve Grecco Zing on drums;[2] the guitar slot was filled by Minor Threat's Lyle Preslar, fulfilling his oral agreement to play in whatever "new thing" Danzig put together after the pair's planned supergroup with Brian Baker, Chris Gates, and Mark Stern fell apart. "[We] began recording an album in New Jersey," Preslar later told *Crawdaddy!* regarding Samhain's earliest steps. "I thought that the sessions went pretty well musically . . . I was playing a lot of different stuff on the songs and getting away from the strict power chord riffing that I did in Minor Threat."

Preslar as a guitarist was oft heralded for the explosive passion he brought to his playing; personality-wise, however, he was oceans away from Danzig and the brooding, twisted vision the singer hoped to put forth in Samhain. Promises were allegedly made to Preslar that this new outfit would not be a sequel to the Misfits; so he was dismayed upon arriving to Manhattan's Rock Hotel for the band's first gig in his regular outfit of T-shirt and jeans to see the rest of Samhain adorned in what he would later dub "ridiculous" costumes (complete with eyeliner). The guitarist was further aggravated that specific pieces of equipment he requested for the show were not present; Danzig apparently had his own ideas concerning how Preslar's guitars should sound.[3] Preslar's tenure with Samhain ended that night; shortly thereafter Mourning Noise guitarist Pete "Damien" Marshall stepped into his place.[4] Little love was lost between Preslar and Danzig's camp. "[Lyle] just didn't fit in and he didn't put out," Eerie Von recounted later that year. "He didn't want to do anything . . . his idea of getting into a song was moving the neck of the guitar around. 'You guys are going to love me because I'm playing an A minor arpeggio. Later you're going to say that I was amazing.'"[5]

Pete Marshall, who also played in the Whore Lords with former Misfit Joey Image and Humpty Keg, was more enthused to be working with Danzig, as were Samhain's other two members.[6] The Misfits, regardless of their successes and failures in the general punk rock realm, remained nothing short of awe-inspiring heroes to the handful of outsider youths who remained parked in Lodi and surrounding areas. Stellmann relished this second opportunity to collaborate musically with Danzig, as his decision to stick with Rosemary's Babies in 1982 after being offered the Misfits drum chair yielded no greater success. Zing, however, may have been the most excited of all; the nascent drummer had burned many hours in front of the Caiafa garage where the Misfits practiced, dreaming about what it might be like to be included in that fold. Decades later Zing wrote that Danzig's personal invitation to join Samhain "floored" him and that he couldn't sleep that evening because he was so worked up about the situation.[7]

The name "Samhain" refers to an autumnal festival held by the Celts in medieval Ireland circa the 900s, a festival comprised of tribal celebrations that marked the end of the year's "light" harvest period and the coming of the "dark" winter period. Over the course of several days Celts would partake in various solemn rituals involving bonfires and livestock believed to cleanse its participants. Centuries later scholars would tag this annual event as the Celtic New Year; this term has been adopted by both the Celtic League and existing Celtic nations.[8] Samhain's correct Gaelic pronunciation, depending on your dialect, is either "SAH-win," "SOW-win," or "SOO-win." At first, Danzig and his band mates attempted to have their followers use that centuries-old pronunciation, correcting friends, interviewers, and concertgoers. Alas, it quickly became clear that the phonetic way of speaking the name would prove less headache-inducing for all parties involved, so the band stuck with "Sam-HAYN."[9]

Samhain's debut record *Initium* was unleashed that September. The album took a more ethereal, obtuse approach, giving the instrumentation room to breathe with slower tempos while employing various atmospheric techniques such as heavy reverb, chimes, and simulated moments of paranormal activity (the title track opens *Initium* with a simulated maelstrom of ghostly winds that almost seem to be speaking; atop the din Danzig angrily intones that he is "the end" and "now is the pain"). The band would later comment that this style reflected a "darker, blacker understanding of the world, why it works the way it does . . . and has for endless centuries."[10] Plodding chants like "Samhain" and "The Shift" surely sounded like a pagan celebration. Samhain also proved their more dramatic devotion to darkness via their lyrics, not just in subject matter (ritualistic sacrifice, occult practices, biblical struggles) but in the delivery. "Feel thine end dark, we who live are ever dead, Cerberus, Cerberus!" Danzig snarls in the spine-tingling "Macabre." Later, "The Shift" culminates its evil reverie with an ascending spiral of vocal calls Danzig can't seem to get out of his body fast enough.

Yet Samhain retained a mighty edge to their music and could rock just as hard as any of their underground contemporaries—"Black Dream" tears into the listener with its jagged opening riff, and the jaunty "He-Who-Could-Not-Be-Named" was just speedy enough to be incredibly fun. A similar but somewhat odd moment (one that suggests Samhain were perhaps hedging their bets) comes in *Initium*'s reworked version of the Misfits' "Horror Business"; the song is repurposed as "Horror Biz" and speeds along several miles faster than the landmark original.[11] These purely punkish moments proved that goth was only a slightly fair term to apply to Samhain. If anything, this band was horror punk of a different, more serious strain. This notion is reinforced by *Initium*'s startling cover art, wherein the band's logo, replete with ornamental cow skull (swiped from an obscure Marvel comic called *Crystar Crystal Warrior*), sits atop a dimly lit photo of the group drenched in horse blood procured from an upstate slaughterhouse.[12] "Tortuously great power punk from [Danzig] and two new warlocks," *Flipside* hailed upon *Initium*'s release. "The songs all keep in the 'horror' motif like the Misfits . . . but this new band seems to be full of more honest vigor."[13]

On stage, the imagery was more or less the same as well—black leather, combat boots, etc.—plus the occasional gratuitous dousing of stage blood. Danzig himself gained a noticeable amount of muscle mass during the Samhain years, due to an increased interest in bodybuilding and nutrition. The singer also let his devilock grow into a shaggy mess that often obscured his entire face. As a result, Glenn looked more ursine and threatening during this period than ever before.

Samhain's less playful approach was a turn-off for Misfits diehards who appreciated the latter band's implied sense of glee. The common complaint was that Glenn's sense of humor died when he formed Samhain, the singer fully embracing demonic imagery and alleged occult practices as an entire lifestyle. Danzig's true dedication to the pagan arts was often called into question, though. To this day, even some of his former cohorts question whether or not he truly "lived it" (Glenn's famous complaint about the Caiafa brothers). "That's an odd statement," said Marshall in response. "Even back then I know Glenn [stayed] at his parents' house, and that allowed him to hang out and wear black clothing and write songs and stuff. He wasn't off in a cave somewhere."

As he did in the Misfits, Glenn retained complete control over Samhain's songwriting, recordings, image, and performing techniques—Marshall remembers being scolded by Danzig occasionally for not adhering exactly to the rhythms and nuances of specific guitar parts even years into playing them. Fed up with the uneven business of fielding his work out to record plants, Glenn sometimes forced Samhain to press their own vinyl in his bathroom, a laborious process that could take several hours.[14] Rumor has it the singer even pressed his own bootlegs of out-of-print Misfits singles and live shows to sell for extra money without a serious loss (something Bobby Steele did openly and flagrantly with the *Live '79* bootleg he hawked at his own Undead gigs[15]). The evidence to suggest Danzig bootlegged his own material are the unofficial releases themselves; often, the sound quality is as good or even better than the original distributed recordings.

Samhain lasted four years with, remarkably, only one lineup change: Steve Zing left the band in 1985 after not meshing well with the others on the road. Danzig later labeled the drummer an "effeminate" who took musical "short cuts"[16] (despite these insults and rumored issues with the singer withholding *Initium* royalties, Steve never lost his reverence for Glenn and the two remained on relatively friendly terms). Zing was replaced by former Reptile House member London May, who had struck up a relationship with Samhain when he booked the group for its first performance in his native Baltimore. Despite its brief lifespan Samhain managed to garner a dedicated fandom, even outside the United States. The group's aesthetic bent toward a more realistic or palpable form of shock rock resonated with Europe's brewing black metal and death metal contingents. Swiss rockers Celtic Frost, the perceived grandfathers of these genres who began operating at roughly the same time as Samhain, consider the band a vital entry in the underground canon. Frost bassist Martin Eric Ain cites Samhain's "heathen Satanic horror goth approach" as something "very dear to [him] personally."[17] Indeed, just a few years prior, it was more acceptable for there to be clear division between the musician and their stage persona; by attempting to posit themselves as the most authentic of their violence-obsessed ilk, Samhain helped give rise to the notion of "false metal"—bands who do not practice what they preach.

Musically, Samhain's impact is more uncertain. Disciples offer praise, but the dissonant and decidedly heathen arrangements present on *Initium,* its October 1984 follow-up EP *Unholy Passion*, and 1986's *November-Coming-Fire* full-length (generally considered Samhain's masterpiece) seldom penetrate the suffocating soundscapes of black or death metal, most of which lean on more traditional punk and heavy metal for influence. The goth and post-punk movements of the time more or less ignored Samhain as well, possibly because their level of abrasiveness (underscored by the relatively low production values) wasn't as digestible as material by the likes of more charismatic acts like the Birthday Party or England's Killing Joke.

By the close of 1986 Danzig's goth punk experiment would transform into a beast of an entirely different nature, practically overnight thanks to intervention of noted hip-hop mogul Rick Rubin. Rubin, the unkempt Long Island–bred founder of Def Jam Records (a label responsible for breaking LL Cool J, Run-D.M.C., Public Enemy, and the Beastie Boys), was looking for a rock act to groom for his new offshoot label Def American when he saw Samhain perform that July in New York City as part of CMJ's New Music Seminar. Rubin didn't care much for the music (a blunt comment about Marshall's playing made by Rubin backstage almost escalated to a physical confrontation), but the producer saw in Glenn a powerful and potentially marketable hard rock vocalist. A deal was verbally offered to Danzig on the spot.

By this point Glenn had been paying his dues musically for ten years with no other career options. He would have been rather foolish not to take a deal offered by the man who helped birth such cultural milestones as *License to Ill* and *It Takes a Nation of Millions to Hold Us Back*. Glenn accepted Rubin's deal on the condition his new group retain Von as a bassist. Marshall and May were replaced with classically trained guitarist John Christ and phenom percussionist Chuck Biscuits.[18] By the start of 1987, Samhain was no more. Glenn saddled this reconfigured outfit with his own last name, Danzig, and set out on his path for mainstream acclaim.

There would be a brief and curious stop along the way, though, on the journey from Samhain to Danzig. The newly formed group found itself recording a song to the soundtrack for *Less Than Zero*, the November 1987 film adaptation of Bret Easton Ellis's acclaimed 1985 novel. Danzig and Rubin composed the dramatic swell "You and Me (Less Than Zero)" originally for a female singer; however, after Glenn performed the song's scratch track with career-making aplomb, it was decided "You and Me" should be the first Danzig recording. The band was excited to introduce itself to the world with this song—unfortunately, an in-studio disagreement derailed that plan. Frustrated with a handful of specific directions Rubin was offering concerning his bass playing for "You and Me," Eerie Von turned his instrument over to engineer George Drakoulias, who played on the finished recording. To mark this delineation, the group billed itself on the finished *Less Than Zero* soundtrack as Glenn Danzig & the Power and Fury Orchestra. An odd hiccup that was perhaps offset for Glenn by the other work *Less Than Zero* yielded—the chance to collaborate with one of his musical heroes, Roy Orbison. The end result of the Danzig/Orbison authorship, a mournful prance entitled "Life Fades Away," is fondly remembered as one of Orbison's finest late period compositions. Danzig would later deem working with the famed balladeer so shortly before his death "an honor" (Orbison died just one year later, in December of 1988) and that he "was floored" to hear such a tremendous voice in person.[19]

Legacy of Brutality, the first Misfits compilation record, was released in September of 1985, and in many circles it would be considered quite contentious. The disc was curated exclusively by Glenn Danzig for Caroline Records, an independent label in New York City that months before signed a distribution deal with Danzig and Plan 9 Records. Consisting primarily of material from the unreleased *Static Age*, *Legacy of Brutality* proved akin to the Rosetta Stone for Misfits diehards who didn't even know songs like the brilliant "Spinal Remains" and "American Nightmare" existed. To those on the inside, however, something didn't sound quite right. The suspicions of other band members proved correct: Danzig took it upon himself to not only radically remix the material chosen for *Legacy* but to record his own guitar tracks over the half-decade old material.[20] Furthermore, he did not credit any Misfits but himself on the album sleeve.

By this time Jerry Only and Doyle had begun a transition away from music. The brothers relocated with their family to the mountainous resort area of Vernon, New Jersey, where they continued to help their father's company produce the popular Proedge hobby knife. Jerry in particular had reason to assemble a more steady life—he was raising a daughter, Kathy, born in 1982. According to most who knew him at the time, the former bassist considered the Misfits a failure. This notion was highlighted vaguely (both to Only and those on the sidelines) by the arrival that year of Hasbro cartoon "Jem," the story of a female rock star whose mortal enemies comprised a band called the Misfits. "Jem's" creators were oblivious to the existence of the authors behind such vital underground recordings as *Walk Among Us* and *Earth A.D.*[21] Since neither Only nor Danzig had ever formally copyrighted their band's moniker, Hasbro was allowed to keep using "The Misfits" as Jem's de facto villains. "Jem" and *Legacy of Brutality* surely upset Jerry Only, particularly the latter considering it found Danzig literally erasing his and his friends' contributions to history. At the time, however, taking anyone to court over the fading memory of a punk rock band that had already proven a dangerous money pit did not seem like a battle worth fighting.[22]

Jerry Only's outlook would soon change. In August of 1987, San Francisco thrash kings Metallica, already on track to becoming the most popular heavy metal of the contemporary era thanks to endless touring and a string of explosive no-nonsense albums, released an extended play of covers that included two Misfits songs. *The $5.98 E.P.: Garage Days Re-Revisited* was both a light-hearted exercise meant to help the band cope with the recent tragic bus crash that claimed the life of their bass player Cliff Burton and an easy way to break in Burton's replacement, Jason Newsted. The late Burton was Metallica's resident Misfits devotee who championed Danzig's talents not only to his fellow band mates but to the press (when asked by an interviewer in 1986 to name his top five favorite albums, the bassist stammered briefly before replying, "Everything by Glenn Danzig . . . all of his shit").[23] The shadow of Danzig's earliest works loom over such pivotal early Metallica recordings as *Ride the Lightning* and *Master of Puppets*, which fuse the Bay Area quartet's obsession with British "New Wave" metal bands like Iron Maiden, Saxon, and Motörhead with the cold punk bite of the Misfits. You can hear the DNA of *Earth A.D.* sewn into breakneck assaults like "Fight Fire with Fire" and "Battery," especially in the way Metallica's guitars (blistering with the same anger felt on livid Misfits songs like "Queen Wasp") barrel forward on the rapid drum beat and bounce between just one or two chords before giving way like a dam under pressure.

Metallica drew influence from several other punk bands, including profane hardcore pioneers the Anti-Nowhere League and proto-crust punks Discharge, but of that genre only the Misfits proved worthy enough to be included on *Garage Days*. The record concludes with a searing run-through of "Last Caress" and "Green Hell" as if they were one song. The track proves an exemplary tribute to both the Misfits and the fallen Burton's rabid fandom. Of the countless thrash bands who worshipped at the altar of the Crimson Ghost, none would be as blatant as Metallica, and certainly none would be as popular—the *$5.98 EP* would chart at no. 28 on the Billboard 200, one spot higher than the band's previous effort *Master of Puppets*.[24] In turn, an entirely new—and much vaster—generation of bored, restless rock fans were introduced to this mysterious Misfits group and their hyperviolent music.

Suddenly more and more devotees were squirreling out the Caiafa brothers in the rolling hills of Vernon, professing their love for the Misfits and begging for any trinkets left over from the glory days. Jerry Only knew Danzig might prove a potentially valid source for promotional Misfits merchandise to help satiate the growing number of fans, but the bassist was wary of reaching out after such a bitter dissolution. Exercising some degree of caution, Only contacted a mutual friend to ask for a box or two of T-shirts from Glenn. The response was not friendly. "Glenn said that if we want [shirts] we could go out and buy them," Only recalled in 1989. "I paid for half of the records that are ours from my pocket. I was laying out cash left and right. Now I don't see why the dude has to turn to me and say, 'Buy the stuff.'"[25]

A year prior, Caroline Records had released *Misfits*, another assembly of recordings compiled by Danzig that spanned the group's entire existence.[26] In October of 1987, the Misfits concert disc *Evilive* (previously an exclusive item via the Misfits Fiend Club fan organization) was also distributed by

Caroline.[27] From these two releases and *Legacy of Brutality*, only Glenn Danzig was receiving royalties—which were on a steady rise thanks to Metallica's unexpected endorsement (Danzig also of course benefitted financially from *Garage Days'* worldwide sales, as his was the sole songwriting credit). These factors, combined with the T-shirt insult, spurred Jerry Only and his brother to take definitive action. At first the Caiafas wanted to avoid any costly legal entanglement, contacting Danzig directly about the royalty situation. Only later claimed that Danzig offered his former band mates $13,000,[28] a paltry sum considering the perceived monies flowing into Glenn's pockets. The Caiafas allegedly countered with a $250,000 settlement sum, which Danzig quickly rejected. Unsure of their next move, Jerry and Doyle temporarily distracted themselves with a brand new musical venture.

Rechristening himself Mocavius Kryst ("Mo the Great" for short), Jerry Only spearheaded a viking-themed heavy metal act with Doyle called Kryst the Conqueror. Joined by fellow Lodian Jim Murray on drums, Kryst the Conqueror embraced a galloping power metal sound a la Helloween or Manowar. The overt Christian themes were difficult to ignore, however, not only in the band's name but on their singular release, 1990's self-pressed *Deliver Us from Evil* EP, which boasts songs such as "In God We Trust" and "Trial of the Soul."[29] There were also "Mo the Great's" various fan club writings at the time. To wit: "In the final days of the second millennium, I, Mocavius Kryst, and my men now swear this pact with God. For it is by His command that I now open the gates, unleashing the fury of His vengeance . . . behold the power of truth for it burns its light up the sword of my brother."[30] "We don't want people to come out and say, 'They were great, but they're into that devil shit,'" Only explained to *Yeszista*. "That's not it, all of our songs are about going out and chasing the son of a bitch. That's what it's all about . . . if I made Kryst with a 'C,' people are gonna say, 'He's making fun of God.' We've come in *His* name to do the job."[31]

Former cohorts would question the validity of the Caiafas' sudden conversion to ultrapiousness ("They're about as born again as Anton LaVey," Bobby Steele snorted to *MRR* in 1992).[32] Further doubts surrounded Jerry's proclamation that Kryst the Conqueror was on par with Led Zeppelin and that the band's music would sustain for a minimum of three decades. When push came to shove, "unleashing the fury" ultimately proved somewhat tricky for Kryst: The band never managed to employ a full-time singer as Jeff Scott Soto, the vocalist who sang on *Deliver Us from Evil*, was under contract to Swedish guitar sensation Yngwie Malmsteen at the time and could not commit fully to another project. In fact, Soto couldn't even legally be credited in *Deliver Us from Evil*'s liner notes—the vocalist listed on the sleeve is, in fact, Kryst the Conqueror.[33]

Kryst also never played live, partly because of the sticky singer situation but also because Jerry Only was adamant that his new band never succumb to the perils of being an opening act (read: they only wanted to headline).[34] Only also refused to entertain any record contract that didn't include "big money" for videos and merchandising. In 1990 the bassist claimed that no less than Atlantic Records, home of Led Zeppelin, initiated the kind of deal he was looking for until the company discovered he had zero control over the Misfits back catalog.[35] No comparable labels came calling for Kryst, apparently, as the full album the quartet recorded remains unreleased—though the material has been bootlegged and passed around the tape trading community for years by curious Misfits completists. Regarding Kryst's relative quality: there is certainly more acutely cringe-inducing heavy metal hailing from their time period, though none of it has the same pedigree. It is difficult to believe the same musicians who played on such authentic Misfits songs as "Hatebreeders" and "Astro Zombies" are responsible for a Jesus-themed viking band with songs bearing such names as "March of the Mega-Mites" and "Thunder Thruster." The mind also staggers when one realizes *Deliver Us from Evil* was released two years after the first Nirvana album. Grunge clearly took its time in clubbing heavy metal to death.

And so it came to pass: the first chapters of the Clinton Decade rolled by and Kryst had conquered nothing—not even the proposed comic book that was to coincide with their ultimately unreleased debut album. The project flatlined completely shortly after *Deliver Us from Evil*'s January 1990 release. In an angry all caps fan club missive announcing the end of the Doyle Fan Club (what Only renamed the Fiend Club following the Misfits 1983 breakup) that also read like a makeshift obituary for his latest musical project, Jerry Only wrote, "STRENGTH COMES FROM THE WILL TO STAND AGAINST FEAR AND EVIL AND TO STRIVE FOR THE RIGHT REGARDLESS OF THE PAIN . . . THIS PROJECT HAS LOST A LOT OF MONEY, BUT THAT DOES NOT MEAN IT IS A FAILURE." Only ended the letter promising an early 1991 release for Kryst's unnamed LP.[36]

That never happened. Kryst the Conqueror's debut album stayed in the crypt and the only public appearance from the Caiafa brothers in 1991 came when Doyle and younger brother Ken were inadvertently caught on camera during the ABC network's televised interview of the first person in line for Super Bowl XXV outside Florida's Tampa Stadium on January 27 (Doyle and Ken were second and third in line; their beloved New York Giants would clinch the trophy that night in a harrowing one point victory over the Buffalo Bills). The failure of Kryst was just as well, though. A more complicated task loomed on the horizon for the Caiafas, albeit one with a potentially massive financial reward.

Glenn Danzig began a slow and steady climb to rock stardom after signing with Def American in 1987. His group's self-titled 1988 debut was embraced by critics and fans looking for a powerful, authentic antidote to the superficial hair metal that ruled the airwaves at the time. Danzig the band would prove "real" enough to weather the storm of grunge that descended just a few years later, wiping so many other metal bands into a figurative sinkhole. Of course, by squeezing themselves into extraordinarily tight pants, festooning their videos with sultry bikini-clad woman, and sporting the requisite flowing heavy metal coifs (even Glenn was parting his hair to the side at this point so as to better accentuate his Travolta-esque facial features), Danzig managed to prove themselves far campier than the Pearl Jams, Mudhoneys, and Soundgardens to come. Regardless, positive press from no less than *Rolling Stone* and England's *Melody Maker* helped the leather-clad quartet gain an international foothold, expanding the audience for Danzig's snarling brand of rock into countless foreign markets.[37]

Sensing an opportunity, Warner Bros. Records (who had acquired the rights to the Slash/Ruby Records catalog years before) reissued the Misfits' *Walk Among Us* on vinyl and cassette that July, one month before *Danzig* had even come out (following the newer record's positive reception, Warner released *Walk* on CD in November).[38] Glenn had long held that he and the Misfits had never been fully paid for the original release of *Walk Among Us* and was furious to learn of the reissue. He briefly considered filing suit against Warners, talking up a potential lawsuit in various interviews at the time, but ultimately never followed through. He had too much to focus on as it was. A long time was spent prepping the conclusive Samhain release, 1990's *Final Descent*, a compact disc offering five previously unheard outtakes and the *Unholy Passion* EP that served as an aural tombstone for the band. Danzig the band's popularity also seemed to be growing by the minute; their 1990 sophomore effort *Danzig II: Lucifuge* and its 1992 follow-up *Danzig III: How the Gods Kill* proved even more popular than *Danzig* (*How the Gods Kill* was even given a full four stars by the finicky *Rolling Stone*[39]) while simultaneously finding the synergetic quartet growing musically into a slightly more complex animal. Case in point: *Danzig III*'s opening track "Godless" begins as a hard-charging call to arms before slowing down to the pace of a funeral procession for the majority of its six and a half minutes; through all that time, the listener's attention is rapt as Danzig preaches from his pulpit of perceived atheism and pagan birthrights. The band ebbs and flows behind Danzig, creating a tense backdrop for the singer's howls of religious pain.[40] In particular, the performance of Chuck Biscuits on "Godless" is impressive; the drummer's work here is regularly cited by percussive freaks as one of the best hard rock tracks of the 1990s.

Amid his eponymous band's rise to glory Glenn Danzig found the time to write and record of all things a classical album, *Black Aria*, a 1992 album the singer issued himself via Plan 9. The driving, gothic platter of stirring instrumental orchestrations partially inspired by Milton's *Paradise Lost* shot up to number one on the Billboard Classical Charts shortly after its release, though this may have been due to fans of Danzig's primary band mistakenly purchasing it. Clearly few heeded the written warning from Glenn himself on the cover of *Black Aria* that read in part: "This is not a rock record. It does not sound like anything I have done previously. Some people won't get it. That's o.k. I'm used to that."[41]

Also taking note of Danzig at this time—specifically, his physicality—were some of Tinseltown's biggest players. Various producers and executives had begun the lengthy process of setting up a film based on Marvel Comics' popular X-Men series; Glenn, with his short muscular stature, perpetually furrowed brow, and Idaho-sized sideburns, struck the Hollywood types as a natural selection to portray the most championed X-Man of all, the hot-tempered super soldier Wolverine. Danzig took a meeting with 20th Century Fox to discuss the role when legendary *Superman* director Richard Donner was attached to produce.[42] Comic fans in general were pleased when news leaked that the brooding rocker was being courted for Wolverine. In the end, however, Danzig couldn't commit himself to the nearly year-long shooting schedule, fearing it would derail his presence on the music scene. It didn't matter anyway as the X-Men film languished in development hell until the new millennium. Commenting years later to *L.A. Weekly* on Hugh Jackman's performance in director Bryan Singer's finished *X-Men* film, Danzig said his interpretation of Wolverine would have been "less gay" and expressed relief he wasn't involved in the movie (one of 2000's most popular) as it was "terrible."[43]

Breaking out of the underground gutter to claim these larger stakes of American pop culture did little to alter Glenn Danzig's basic personality; his gruff, loutish demeanor led to memorable altercations with journalists who tried to pry into his past (notably MTV's *Headbanger's Ball* host Rikki Rachtman), club owners who provided substandard equipment, camera-happy fans, and other musicians who got in his way. One of the more famous incidents occurred at Germany's Rock Am Ring festival on May 30, 1993, when Glenn, mingling near the festival's food tent with a bowl of soup, made a rude remark to Def Leppard guitarist Vivian Campbell's wife. It incited another member of Def Leppard to violently kick Danzig from behind, spilling his meal to and fro. A donnybrook seemed imminent, but the warring parties eventually cooled down and went their separate ways.

This heavy metal gossip took on a life of its own in the days before Internet message boards and twisted into one of two variations: Danzig beat up Def Leppard or Def Leppard beat up Danzig. Def American later issued a press release stating only that Glenn had "challenged" Def Leppard and that no one had put their foot near anyone's posterior; an employee of the record company was quoted at the time as saying, "Glenn tells us there was, you know, he did run into them, and there was kind of a little huff going back and forth, but nothing really happened out of it. No one punched anyone and that whole big thing."[44] Danzig himself would eventually echo these claims, explaining to an interviewer that the consternation arose when Def Leppard and their entourage absentmindedly crowded near the entrance to the festival's catering tent. Unable to get through the crowd, Glenn raised his voice with one or two expletives; Glenn deemed it "a bunch of bullshit [where] nothing happened" and said "nobody threw any punches."[45]

A slightly more serious incident alleged to have occurred around this time found Danzig arriving late to a radio interview in New York City, delayed by a traffic jam stemming from the presidential motorcade. Once on the air, Glenn made some remark about maiming or killing Bill Clinton for delaying him. As the tale goes the FBI caught wind of Glenn's tossed-off threat and opened an investigation on the cult heavy metal star. Documents released under the Freedom of Information Act since this rumored incident have yet to yield any concrete proof of the government's interest in Glenn Danzig. The absence of evidence is not the evidence of absence, though, and this story helps explain the photo included in Danzig's fourth album showing a Bill Clinton impersonator congratulating a sniper in front of the band's four murdered bodies. But the story of the FBI investigation could simply be a dash of myth-making to explain an otherwise odd artistic decision).[46]

Contentious altercations aside, in 1993 Danzig achieved something nearly as unexpected as his conquering of the classical music charts: Glenn's band scored themselves a bona fide pop hit that came within a chest hair of entering the Billboard's Top 40. Granted, a number one hit or even a top twenty hit would be more impressive, but considering "Mother" is, at its heart, a snarling manifesto about killing one's parents, that it rose above the two hundred mark is a wonder in itself. Add in the fact that the song in question was no less than six years old and the version that charted was a canned live rendition, and the success proves itself a true anomaly.

Danzig's 1993 concert EP *Thrall: Demonsweatlive* contained a true live version of "Mother" along with three other tracks recorded during a 1992 Halloween gig at Irvine Meadows, California. Def American, still committed to this fist-clenching anthem that was buried on the group's first record, tacked a remix of the original studio version on the end of the EP (as the hidden ninety-third track). That July, the label cobbled together a music video for what would come to be known as "Mother '93" comprised of live footage from the Irvine Meadows show. Fake crowd noise was dropped into the clip and the whole thing was sent to MTV.[47] Incredibly, the clip went into heavy rotation. The following March, "Mother '93" was released as its own single and quickly shot up the charts to 43 on the Billboard charts.[48]

"Mother" is a song that walks a precarious line: Mick Mercer drew attention to this in his original *Melody Maker* review of *Danzig* when he singled out the song as both "hair-raising" and "moronic." Mercer offered a rather airtight metaphorical defense for these contradictory notes when he rhetorically asked, "Did you never thrill to the sight of William Shatner trying to run?"[49] Indeed, one man's treasure can also be that same man's grime-streaked trash, gloriously so, without question, without guilt. However you feel, one cannot deny that "Mother" is the song on *Thrall: Demonsweatlive* (or any other Danzig release, for that matter) with the greatest pop sensibility. It's a straightforward swagger that simmers with moderate intensity, a concise prideful boast that offers Glenn's most memorable melody, and cache of quotable lyrics. To this day, it remains the only sure bet for a Danzig composition at any karaoke bar.

The original 1988 black-and-white music video for "Mother" kicked up a small controversy for its depiction of a live chicken being torn in two as part of a vague pagan sacrifice—a clear nod to one of Danzig's forefathers, Alice Cooper. Danzig was adamant the animal was in no way harmed during the filming of the clip ("We had a chicken handler there and I like animals a lot," the singer told *Concrete Foundations* at the time[50]) but that mattered little to MTV: The footage looked too real, so the networked censored it by literally placing a giant black "X" over the entire scene. The fact that "Mother's" lyrics outlined the potential murder of a mother and father by their only child apparently was of no concern to the massively successful cable network . . . just so long as the video did not depict a chicken being maimed.

The success of "Mother" inched Danzig toward more media exposure, including an AOL Internet chat (where fans asked him questions about how much he could bench) and profiles by catch-all rags like *Entertainment Weekly*. The exposure had to be slightly bittersweet if only for the fortuitous timing of Jerry Only: a year earlier, in September of 1992, Only, along with Doyle, Frank LiCata, and Julio Valverde, filed suit against Glenn Danzig, Plan 9 Records, and Caroline Records over the copyrights and publishing royalties pertaining to their former outfit.[51] Now, just as Danzig was moving forward with his greatest success, he was being dragged back to his past life by a cadre of rightfully angry ghosts. The singer had to decide how much the Misfits were worth to him, both literally and figuratively. The battle would stretch on for several agonizing years, yielding results that no Misfits fan could have ever foreseen.

Chapter Seven

Night of the Living Dead

When the Misfits reunited, I was like, "Whatever. Everyone needs money."
—Brian Baker, Bad Religion [1]

The most popular band to emerge from the late 1980s Los Angeles hair metal scene was undoubtedly Guns n' Roses, a drug-soaked quartet who dialed down their glammy look to emphasis the wild abandon of their snarling bluesy tears. The group's reckless spin on heavy metal's various tropes—and at times equally reckless behavior in public—resonated with the danger-hungry public at large and by 1992 Guns n' Roses had grossed a staggering $57.9 million for their efforts. [2] On November 23, 1993, Guns released *The Spaghetti Incident?*, a covers album that was the highly anticipated follow-up to their 1991 double album/career apex *Use Your Illusion*. *Spaghetti* gave the world, alongside material originally composed by obscure rabble-rousers like the U.K. Subs and the Dead Boys, their own take on the Misfits' "Attitude"—a song that, more than any other Danzig work, seemed to provide the blueprint for both GNR's adrenaline-heavy sound and Axl Rose's temperamental stage persona (strangely enough, Axl allowed Guns bass player Duff McKagan the lead vocal track on "Attitude"). *The Spaghetti Incident?* quickly became a top five album in over nine countries, piquing a pronounced global interest in the Misfits. [3]

Several months earlier, a landmark in Misfits-related journalism was published in underground garage rock zine *Ugly Things*. Mike Stax, the publication's founder, was a rabid Misfits fan who felt vexed that so little information regarding the band's history was available for public consumption. Thus, Stax set out to interview Jerry Only; he hesitated contacting Danzig as he had heard too many stories concerning the singer's nasty disposition. Stax phoned a New Jersey record store called Box Shop where it was rumored

Only sometimes hung out, and although he missed the bass player by a matter of minutes the first time he called, Box Shop's owner was already familiar with *Ugly Things* and promised to put the two in touch. Shortly thereafter, Only and Stax connected, and the former granted the latter an unprecedented twenty-some-page interview that served for its time as the ultimate history of the Misfits. Granted, it was only one member's side of the story, but it touched upon nearly every aspect of the band's existence from the "Cough/Cool" single to the Detroit collapse with Brian Keats. Only, flattered that *Ugly Things* sought him out, even Fed-Exed the magazine several rare and never-before-seen photos of the Misfits. It was a shock for those only familiar with Glenn Danzig via his Rick Rubin albums to see the singer with a Dee Dee Ramone coif and a rather slender physique. Fans were also happy to finally be able to put faces to such storied names as Arthur Googy, Bobby Steele, and Franché Coma. "Jerry was really generous with memorabilia," Stax says. "And we actually got to be pretty good friends. At [one] point he flew me out to Jersey . . . I helped him out at the Chiller Horror Convention, and he drove me around the old neighborhood where the Misfits used to rehearse. It was pretty cool."[4]

"All Hell Breaks Loose: The Jerry Only Interview" ends with Only talking up Kryst the Conqueror, commenting that "[Glenn's] problem is he's living off his Misfits fame—he's in his own shadow and he don't even know it."[5] This is a massively ironic statement given the fact at this very juncture Only was suing Glenn Danzig partially to gain his ownership of the Misfits copyrights, ostensibly so he could have the authority to reform the Misfits without their original singer if that was his wont. Most involved in this erupting legal donnybrook were more concerned with the song publishing/royalty aspect of the fight, though. Negotiations between the Caiafa and Anzalone parties dragged as the specific value of the Misfits was something neither side could agree on—nor could they agree who deserved what royalties. Up until this point every Misfits song was credited entirely to Glenn Danzig. Was that true? Was Glenn responsible for every single note and nuance of the music? If so, did the players deserve compensation for their specific performances even if they had no hand in the actual song craft? Insiders did not anticipate a swift, tidy conclusion to this litigious disagreement. A lengthy, messy trial seemed imminent.

Finally, in late 1994, Caroline Records made a decision that spared both parties any elongated court time: the label purchased the complete rights to all Misfits recordings for $1.5 million, allocating Glenn Danzig the money needed to reach settlement.[6] This action allowed the warring Misfits to breathe easier and specifically helped Danzig avoid a costly trial that more than likely would have forced him to acquiesce a significant percentage of songwriting credits/publishing rights. Historically, courts view musical acts as collaborative efforts and tend to rule as such. Two years earlier a U.S.

Federal Court ruled in favor of two former members of Frankie Lymon's group the Teenagers who claimed they had co-written Lymon's 1956 doo-wop hit "Why Do Fools Fall In Love?" (the fact the two men in question, Herman Santiago and Jimmy Merchant, waited three decades to file their lawsuit cast doubt on their legitimacy and eventually lead to the original decision being reversed).[7] A more famed legal action from 1994 awarded contentious Beach Boy member Mike Love co-credit and royalties for numerous songs originally believed to be written solely by Brian Wilson, including the 1964 hit "I Get Around," despite testimony claiming Love's contributions to these works were minimal.[8]

The purchase of the Misfits catalog was a rather dicey gamble for Caroline Records. The company, despite cultivating such globally popular artists as Smashing Pumpkins and White Zombie, was no huge conglomerate with piles of disposable income. Investing so much capital in the recordings of a band that hadn't existed in a decade seemed potentially disastrous on paper. Would anyone actually buy this music if they released it? A great deal of Caroline's profits for the following year were resting on this Misfits material and the company's ability to hawk it to an ostensibly punk-hungry public. Insiders quickly began considering their options.

Meanwhile, on December 31, 1994, plaintiffs Gerald Caiafa, Paul Caiafa, Frank LiCata, Julio Valverde, and defendant Glenn Danzig entered into a legal agreement regarding the music and rights of their former band, the Misfits. The terms of this settlement stipulated that all members relinquish ownership of master recordings to Caroline Records and that all future music royalties—via Caroline Records or anyone else—should be divided 60/40 in favor of the plaintiffs (save the first $90,000 of post-settlement royalties, which would go directly to the plaintiffs; all royalties earned prior were to be split 50/50). This document also stipulated that the plaintiffs and the defendant would co-own the Misfits name, trademark, and corresponding logos as they appeared on any and all product (including *Walk Among Us*); that neither party would have to account to the other for any revenues and also agreed not to use the names, likenesses, or visual representations of other party members without full written consent; that all Misfits song publishing rights were to be owned exclusively by Danzig; and that one party would be responsible for notifying the other should Caroline fail to do so concerning future artwork or sound mixes. Perhaps most importantly, though, this settlement decreed that the plaintiffs would own the exclusive right to perform publicly and record as the Misfits and that Danzig could not and would not receive payments from future performances or recordings (the plaintiffs also agreed to alert all concert promoters that Danzig was no longer a member of the band).[9]

On month later, on January 26, 1995, the Caiafas, LiCata, and Valverde entered their own agreement that divvied up the settlement monies—with a

small portion going to Ken Caiafa, the brother between Jerry and Doyle who
was nominated to manage whatever new incarnation of the Misfits came to
be. Some of the settlement money was also set aside in a reserve clause for
Joey Image and Bobby Steele should they decide to claim it; after two years,
said monies would revert to Doyle (the only Misfits featured on the disputed
recordings who received nothing from this case were drummers Manny Martinez and Arthur Googy, and it has been rumored over the years that both
these men sought out Danzig individually for smaller compensation and were
accommodated, which would have legally barred them from participating in
the Caiafas' case). This 1995 agreement also decreed all future royalties
derived from Caroline Records Misfits product would be pro-rated by instrument and track depending on the performer. Thus, Jerry Only would receive
a full third of *Collection I* royalties, but the third set aside for the guitar
tracks would be split up between Frank LiCata, Doyle, and Bobby Steele (as
would the third for the drum tracks between Mr. Jim, Joey Image, Googy,
and Robo).[10]

With this matter finally squared away, Jerry Only and Doyle focused on
what the New York District Court now legally allowed them to do: reuniting
the Misfits.

One of the documents used for reference in the *Caiafa v. Anzalone* lawsuit
was a sprawling discography assembled by a Misfits fan named Mark Kennedy. A high schooler in the late 1980s who became enchanted with the band
and infuriated by the lack of useful information pertaining to their recorded
output, Kennedy took it upon himself in 1989 to piece together the ultimate
Misfits release timeline, an end-all history that would separate the legitimate
albums from the myriad bootleg releases that were starting to cloud the
market. Using the *Trouser Press Record Guide* as his starting point, Mark
spent the better part of five years sussing out the Misfits discography. "By
1993, I had amassed thirty to forty pages of information," Kennedy says.
"Every record, every bootleg, just everything. At the same time, my brother
had written a letter to Jerry Only about the Doyle Fan Club, and in response
Jerry just called him. He would do that—he would just call you. Like, oh my
God, he really *is* Mo the Great!"

Kennedy's brother talked up his sibling's discography, self-published that
year as *The Misfits Book*, and Only expressed great interest due to the legal
proceedings at hand. The bassist and Kennedy began corresponding regularly, which lead to the latter unearthing even more fascinating information
about his favorite band. In May of 1994, Mark Kennedy used his close
connections to launch the Misfits Bible Internet mailing list, where other fans
could keep abreast of Misfits goings-on. Six months later, Kennedy built and
took live a Misfits website, known as Misfits Central. Not only was Misfits

Central cyberspace's first page dedicated to Lodi's most famous musical export, it was the best—Mark Kennedy's close resource pool and slavish attention to detail made sure of that.

The Misfits Bible and Misfits Central would both mushroom from tiny online enclaves to bustling centers of activity for fiends from across the globe, who were finally getting Misfits news more or less directly from the horse's mouth—or at least one half of the horse's mouth. Mark Kennedy would not have a chance to interact with the other half, Glenn Danzig, until long after his online Misfits hubs were established, though the singer was alerted to the existence of Misfits Central shortly after its creation. Naturally, Danzig dismissed the website as "probably all bullshit"; when Kennedy managed to wrangle a private audience with Danzig following a November 1999 gig in Washington, D.C., the sneering singer was convinced Misfits Central was, in fact, "all bullshit" and let its creator know in no uncertain terms. "They bring me backstage after some gig to meet Glenn, and as soon as I'm introduced he explodes," Kennedy recalls. "'YOUR WEBSITE IS FULL OF FUCKIN' LIES! I SHOULD FUCKIN' KILL YOU RIGHT NOW!' So I said, 'All right, I'm sorry, you tell me what's incorrect and I'll fix it.'" Danzig relaxed and said he'd get back to him with specifics. As of this book's printing, Mark Kennedy still has yet to receive Glenn Danzig's list of inaccuracies on Misfits Central (though a link that once appeared on Danzig's official website to Mark Kennedy's site has long since been removed).[11]

Originally Jerry Only and Doyle (the latter of whom was now fully expanding his nickname to Doyle Wolfgang von Frankenstein) wanted as close to an authentic Misfits reunion lineup as he could get. Since Jim Catania was no longer interested in performing and Joey "Image" Poole was M.I.A., the brothers turned their focus to Arthur Googy. Only, who had kept in touch on and off over the years with Googy, floated the notion to the *Walk Among Us* percussionist. Googy considered accepting but ultimately turned him down; having not played his instrument in years, the drummer was concerned he was not up for the task.

After a series of rehearsals, the Misfits settled on their Congruent Machine co-worker and high school buddy David Calabrese, rechristened Dr. Chud in honor of the 1984 Daniel Stern thriller.[12] Chud was a student of various musical genres including jazz, blues, and fusion, but his true love was in the progressive rock of groups like Rush, Yes, King Crimson, and Genesis (the very groups the Misfits by nature opposed when they first sprung up in the halcyon days of punk). The drummer considered joining the premiere horror rock band as just another step in his evolution as a player.

"Learning all I can about all facets of music [is] important to me," Chud remarked in 2007. "[I draw] on things subconsciously when needed."[13]

Pressure and interest mounted over who would fill the vacant Misfits singing slot. Vocalist auditions had begun as early as October 1994, three months before the settlement with Danzig, but Jerry wanted Damned crooner Dave Vanian to front their band. Vanian expressed enough interest to visit Jerry during an unrelated trip to the States; in the end, the British singer couldn't be convinced (a rumor persists in certain circles that Vanian backed out at the last minute when he learned Only had bedded his wife during the Misfits' disastrous 1979 visit to England). Another name the Misfits considered was guttural goth vocalist Peter Steele of Type O Negative. Type O, a dreary rock band from Brooklyn who performed such pointedly droll material as "I Know You're Fucking Someone Else" and "Kill All the White People," clearly counted the Misfits among their musical heroes. Unfortunately, the group were experiencing their greatest wave of success at this time, affording little time for outside projects. That left Jerry and Doyle the myriad of anonymous singers who were regularly visiting their machine shop compound via an ad the band placed in *The Village Voice*. Incredibly, the band recorded every one of these sessions and presented all who tried out a cassette copy of the moment with the Misfits. In the end, it was one of these unknowns who would win the coveted singing position.[14]

Twenty-year-old Michael Emanuel hailed from Teaneck, New Jersey, the son of a police officer and a stay-at-home mom. A self-described "little skate punk" with blue hair, Emanuel always knew he wanted to "be something exceptional" but had difficulty figuring out what direction his life should take. In his late teens he turned to music, hooking up with a band called the Mopes who needed an energetic front person. In the spring of 1995, while the Mopes were recording a demo, engineer Bobby Alleca, impressed with Emanuel's voice, pulled the singer aside to encourage his trying out for the Misfits. Emanuel was unfamiliar with the band and therefore wary, even after a pleasant phone conversation with Jerry Only. "The first thing that came to my mind [when I heard their name] was death metal," he says. "I thought,'Wow, I wonder if I can sing that shit?' I bought *Collection 1* and I was surprised that I had heard a lot of the songs before. They were all familiar. I quickly fell in love with the music. Those songs . . . [they] turn something on inside of you."[15]

Emanuel began a series of auditions for the Misfits, and although there was no question he was spirited and had a memorably haunting voice, the Caiafas were still holding out hope they could land a singer with marquee pull. In an act of some major audacity, Jerry and Doyle even tried to invite Danzig back. Following a show by the Danzig band in Red Bank, New Jersey, on April 26, 1995, the Caiafas, decked out in their Misfits stage gear, arrived at Glenn's hotel for a proper hatchet burial. Doyle, learning Danzig's room number from a mutual friend, took the elevator up to greet his old friend; Jerry elected to remain in the lobby. Fifteen to twenty minutes later, the elevator doors pinged back open on the first floor. Jerry turned to see his brother, slightly smirking, flanked by two burly security guards. Danzig never bothered to answer his hotel room door. "We took that as a 'no,'" Only commented to *Metal Maniacs* a year later.[16]

The search for name talent went on until October 1995, when the Misfits realized no one else was interested or available. Roadie Jonathan Grimm offered Emanuel the new moniker Michale Graves,[17] and the resurrected Misfits made their live debut just after midnight on October 31 at Manhattan's Coney Island High (the band performed a handful of songs the day before as an encore at a Type O Negative concert).[18] Taking the stage in matching sleeveless Misfits shirts, the quartet blasted through thirteen dusty classics to the delight of a disbelieving sweat-soaked audience.

The next immediate order of business for the reconstituted Misfits was, oddly enough, a movie appearance. In November of 1995 the group filmed a cameo appearance for the Matthew Lillard thriller *Animal Room* (a move that also boasts the first screen appearance of developing sexpot Amanda Peet and the presence of "Doogie Howser" himself, Neil Patrick Harris). As they had not officially recorded any material yet, the Misfits were forced to pantomime to an old Kryst the Conqueror track featuring the long-suppressed vocals of Jeff Scott Soto. An indignity of sorts for Michale Graves, but not such a loss, considering the low quality of the film.[19]

Jerry Only was looking for ways for the new Misfits to get some exposure in the industry. The bassist hired a production crew and filmed a television pilot for a revived version of the classic horror presentation program *Chiller Theater*. Only hosted, of course, with brother Doyle by his side, lounging about a medieval castle set complete with thrones, flickering candles, and stray animal skulls. The Caiafas traded jokes and trivia in simmering growls about 1959's *The Hideous Sun Demon*, the film they planned to air on this inaugural outing.[20] Sadly, no station was interested the project, possibly because the far wittier and more camera-friendly Joe Bob Briggs was holding down basic cable's late night frights on the TNT network's popular cult film vehicle *MonsterVision*. The Misfits television pilot wasn't a complete waste, though—the castle set would eventually be used for a series of great promotional photos.

The Misfits reunion arrived at a near perfect time in popular culture, when the general mood of the country seemed to revolve around the spooky or macabre. One of the biggest hits on television at the time was the paranormal drama *The X-Files,* which chronicled the adventures of two FBI agents investigating various unexplained crimes and phenomena across the country—

including but not limited to the kinds of hokey monsters (killer sea creatures, sentient trash trolls, etc.) that dotted the 1950s horror landscape that the Misfits originally drew inspiration from.[21] A year prior director Wes Craven released the alleged final installment of his campy *Nightmare on Elm Street* film series, the refreshing *New Nightmare,* an early example of the self-aware Generation X horror film that scored with audiences and paved the way for Craven's massive 1996 hit *Scream,* which used irony as sharply as knives.[22]

The inescapable news story of the time was the macabre O. J. Simpson murder trial. The majority of Americans were kept on the edge of their seats by this tense legal circus. The "Trial of the Century" was packed with enough elements of the tragic, the gruesome, and the strangely humorous (mostly from wise-cracking defense attorney Johnnie Cochran) to warrant fair comparisons to Shakespeare. Simpson's acquittal in October was stunning but did not herald its true conclusion; if Simpson didn't brutally murder his wife and her lover Ron Goldman, that means someone else did, someone who was still ostensibly on the loose in otherwise bucolic suburban California.[23]

Even with an apt cultural climate and an initial positive reaction from the crowds who saw them, without Danzig the Misfits were fighting an uphill battle against the indignation of old school fans who saw their reformation sans Glenn as offensive, sacrilegious, and just plain greedy. Much of this anger was concentrated on Michale Graves, whose relative baby-face (soon to be masked by elaborate skull makeup) and corresponding boyish stature did him no particular favors. "It was like being lit on fire," says Graves of his early shows with the Misfits. "I definitely did not find my footing immediately. Learning how complex and popular the band was, it started to frighten me because it was so much of a bigger world than I was used to. [And] the violence [of the audiences] surprised me, to be honest with you. It usually felt like me against all of them, and I took that mindset." During a gig in Stuttgart, Germany, for example, Graves fell offstage and was immediately stomped in the face by an angry concertgoer; his jaw was dislocated. On the same tour, Jerry Only fell ill with a collapsed lung. Only, worn to a nub, confided to Graves one night that he was considering calling the entire reunion off.

Such misgivings were quickly brushed aside. The Misfits toughened up and began shopping around a demo in May of 1996. The prestigious and often taste-making Geffen Records heard the demo, liked it, and saw enough potential in the reunited Misfits to sign them to a multiple album contract in December. The band soon began working on material for a new album tentatively titled *American Psycho*, but it would not prove to be an easy chore. As Graves puts it, the Misfits were suddenly playing with "big boy money" and having to deal with lawyers, accountants, and all the other business incidentals that come with being on a major label. This was an atmosphere in which the band were novices. The artistic differences between band members also crystallized during *American Psycho*'s creation. Jerry Only, convinced the band had to stick to the horror shtick at all costs, routinely chose movie titles at random to author songs around. This bucked with the less specific leanings of Michale Graves. Unfortunately for Graves, he quickly came to realize the Misfits were Only's band; the singer would later lament that the bassist took the lead on everything and rarely ceded, creating a frustrating environment that did not foster much sense of collaboration.[24]

American Psycho was released March 28, 1997, offering a highly detailed yet oddly cartoonish painting of the Crimson Ghost on its cover that suggests a clear line of demarcation between the Misfits of hazy punk rock legend and the Misfits of Geffen Records. The album kicks off with an instrumental reworking of an ominous, dread-inspiring Kryst the Conqueror track called "The Abominable Dr. Phibes." Doyle's guitar is distorted to heavy metal proportions—its bottom and roar achieved by playing the instrument through an amplifier built to highlight the low end of a bass guitar (Jerry Only followed suit by plugging his bass into a guitar amplifier, giving his instrument a natural distortion; the Caiafas both played bat-shaped guitars they constructed themselves for specific durability and thickness). After a final dramatic crescendo, "Phibes" gives way to the chipper chanting of the title track. Although "American Psycho" spends a great deal of its time jutting along at double time as Michale Graves assumes the psychotic persona of Patrick Bateman, the basic refrain is a classic pastiche of Misfits "whoaohing" that seems like a subconscious attempt to let listeners know Danzig's ghost is still present—even if the song leaned in a more modern, upbeat direction. Aside from the ultracrisp, clean production, one can almost feel the cold steel of the hook the band tries to sink into whatever was left of Green Day's popularity by this time on overly melodic entries such as "Resurrection" and "Here Come The Dead."

Michale Graves does an admirable job alternating between frothing madman and mournful ghoul on *American Psycho* as he belts out the vocals on tongue-in-cheek entries like "Speak of the Devil" and "Walk Among Us," but the vocalist doesn't really come into his own until the tail end of the album. There he tears with reckless abandon into the album's three most affecting tracks: the *Bride of Frankenstein*-inspired slammer "Hate The Living, Love The Dead," an emotional recap of the 1982 Steven Spielberg/Tobe Hooper collaboration *Poltergeist* that is strangely titled "Shining," and an incredibly catchy Ramones ape called "Don't Open 'til Doomsday" wherein Graves croons his way into the listener's heart. Naturally, *American Psycho* had its gaffes—namely, too many songs based around horror movie titles. In addition to the entries already mentioned, there's "This Island Earth," "Day of the Dead," "The Haunting," a hidden track called "Hell Night," and "Mars Attacks," the latter of which Jerry Only unsuccessfully petitioned Tim Burton to include in his film of the same name a year prior (Burton sent the Misfits back a kind note, however, pledging his long-time fandom).

Reviews of *American Psycho* were mixed: *Rolling Stone* trashed it with a harsh one-and-a-half stars ("This album feels less like the Misfits and more like Elvira . . . all this longtime fan can say is, 'Quick, Van Helsing, a stake.'");[25] *The Onion's A.V. Club* declared *American Psycho* "pretty damn good" in light of its "opportunistic" and "calculated" existence;[26] and *Entertainment Weekly* gave the album a solid B.[27] Indeed, *American Psycho* boasted enough speed, spook, and spunk to justify its existence, although being saddled with the Misfits name was a double-edged sword. From a stylistic standpoint, it's too upbeat and pop-leaning to exist in the same time zone as anything from the Danzig years; however, the merit this material does boast would have been lost to time had it been released under any other moniker. The one song on *American Psycho* that seemed to appease Misfits fans of all colors with no guilt or consternation was the moody, anthemic, and legitimately haunting "Dig Up Her Bones."[28] Michale Graves wrote "Bones" when he was just sixteen years old and had been sitting on it until the right moment presented itself. The band felt confident enough about the song to release it as *American Psycho's* one and only single.[29]

Live, the *American Psycho*–era Misfits would distract anyone who felt the music was lacking in Alice Cooper–style theatrics. Performances often began with a roadie dressed as the Crimson Ghost (as he appeared in his original 1946 form) who would haul an oversized television set to the center of the stage. Said television would play a series of gruesome clips from all manner of horror movies. Soon, Dr. Chud would crawl onstage, swathed in bloody medical scrubs, gnashing his teeth at the front row like an angry bear or wrestler of years gone by. Wrapped in a straightjacket, Michale Graves was delivered to the stage like the giant TV set—on a giant leash, writhing about the whole way in faux pain. The Caiafas entered last, pounding on their wireless instruments as the crowd cheered and the band came together to launch into their set. All this was just a smidge hokier than the gimmicks of the Danzig days that included busting out of coffins, but it played well in the larger venues the Misfits were booked into as artists on the same label as Aerosmith, Don Henley, Beck, and Cher.

With the release of *American Psycho* naysayers could not write this exercise off as a dream: the Misfits had returned, without their most celebrated figure, who for his part remained relatively silent on his former band's reappearance. Fans on both sides awaited any kind of showdown between Jerry Only's Misfits and Danzig, and one of sorts occurred Halloween night that year when the two groups performed at venues within four miles of each other. The former played Hollywood's decidedly vanilla Palace venue (capacity limit: 2,000) while the latter performed at West Hollywood's storied rock shanty the Whisky a Go Go club (capacity limit: 1,000). While it might not seem like a great disparity existed between these two concerts, the Misfits felt like victors playing the larger club. "Danzig was on such a decline," remembers Misfits bus driver Tim Bunch. "We were playing this big sold-out show on Halloween and [Glenn] was playing this little shithole down the street. So me and some of the guys [decided] we're gonna go see Danzig. We walked down there earlier in the day, but Glenn told [the Whisky] specifically, 'Do not let any Misfits crew members into the building.' So we couldn't get in." Amused, Bunch and the other crew members traipsed back to the Palace, laughing about their odd badge of honor. [30]

On July 15, 1997, Caroline Records released *Static Age*, the debut album the Misfits had recorded for Mercury Records in 1977 and subsequently shelved. Many consider this to be the greatest triumph of all the legal squabbling between the band members. Caroline executives (along with most of the world) were unaware this album even existed, even after they bought the rights to the entire Misfits catalog in 1994. It wasn't until the Caiafa brothers showed up at the label's Manhattan offices in early 1995 with a twenty-year-old cassette tape of the entire record in sequence that Caroline realized what they had. The lost first Misfits album would be extremely marketable, not just because of the story but because of the infectious music within. Obtaining the master recordings from Danzig proved difficult, though—the singer denied he had the tapes, claiming they no longer existed and that *Static Age* was simply lost to history. This was of course untrue; Caroline eventually wrangled the deteriorating masters from Glenn, which were then carefully restored for release. *Static Age* was first unleashed on the public in 1996 as a part of Caroline's Misfits box set, a four-disc labor of love presented in a small coffin that sold enough copies to more than pay off the label's gamble on this dusty horror punk band. [31]

Initially Caroline had scheduled a *Static Age* release for 1995 along with several other Misfits projects, but the results of the lawsuit left them in the unenviable position of dealing with two separate band factions that had decidedly different visions for the group's future releases and (more or less) equal power. Various other professional obligations prevented Glenn Danzig from finishing the Misfits compilation he intended to assemble as a sequel to 1986's *Misfits*; he finally found the time at the same moment when Jerry and Doyle presented Caroline with *Static Age*. Livid that the record company was fast-tracking the Caiafa brothers' project over his own *Collection II* that had been gestating for years, Danzig demanded Caroline reconsider their priorities unless they wanted to become embroiled in another sticky legal action. The tactic worked; Caroline halted work on *Static Age* to placate Glenn. Also scrapped by the record company was a limited edition "Teenagers from Mars" seven inch and *Xmas at Max's*, a recording of the Misfits' Christmas

1978 performance at Max's Kansas City featuring newly overdubbed instrumental tracks from Jerry and Doyle.[32]

When *Collection II* finally hit record store shelves on November 14, 1995, it was embraced by thirsty Misfits fans despite the fact that it contained five recordings of songs from *Walk Among Us* that Danzig re-recorded with Eerie Von in August of 1986. A sixth song from that decidedly post-Misfits session, "Mephisto Waltz," appears nowhere else in the Misfits or Samhain catalog and appears to have been composed specifically for that 1986 recording. Continuity issues aside, *Collection II* sold enough to land a number 33 position on Billboard's Heatseekers chart.[33] This meant nothing to Danzig, of course, who is rumored to have taken his aggravations with the Misfits legal situation out on Caroline in various tiny ways. Insiders say they went to great lengths to make sure Glenn was pleased with *Collection II*'s artwork only to watch the singer turn around in interviews and condemn the sepia-toned cover image of Bud Geary in costume as the Crimson Ghost. Another tale, similar to the subterfuge Danzig ran regarding the very existence of *Static Age,* concerns Caroline's difficulty obtaining the master tapes of *Earth A.D.* for the 1996 Misfits box set—Glenn claimed *Earth A.D.*'s masters had washed away in a flood at his parents' house in Lodi in the mid-1980s and forced the label to work from a slightly inferior cassette tape containing the music.

The *Earth A.D.* master tapes weren't the only storied items to (allegedly) disappear from the Anzalone house back in New Jersey. Glenn's parents Richard and Maretta remained on friendly terms with the Caiafas and always welcomed Jerry and Doyle when they dropped by the house on MacArthur Avenue to say hello (which admittedly was not too often since the 1983 breakup of the Misfits). During one such visit in April of 1995, Richard mentioned to the Caiafas the bevy of skateboard parts Glenn had left underneath his back porch. The Anzalone patriarch offered his son's former band mates as many as they could carry. The parts in question were rare skateboard decks emblazoned with Samhain logos and album imagery that Danzig had commissioned years before. When the singer moved west in the late 1980s he assumed the decks would be safe in Lodi, quietly increasing in monetary value as he focused his efforts bringing Danzig the band to fruition. Upon learning that, of all people, Jerry and Doyle had walked off with this valuable stash of Samhain relics, Danzig hit the roof. He angrily demanded his father retrieve the skateboard decks, though it is unclear if Richard Anzalone was ever able to wrangle the items back from the brothers Caiafa.[34]

Geffen's *American Psycho* sold respectably well alongside the Caroline Misfits releases, though singer and ostensible face of the new Misfits Michale Graves couldn't reconcile his increased feelings of marginalization within the band. Jerry Only and his manager brother Ken Caiafa continued to make the lion's share of decisions; Doyle and Chud, both reserved personalities who preferred to avoid confrontation, went along mostly without complaint. In May of 1998, the Misfits booked a South American tour leg for July before consulting Graves. The dates in question directly conflicted with a vacation in Colorado the singer had booked far in advance. Understandably upset, Graves placed an angry phone call to Only that ended with the former declaring his intention to follow through with his vacation plans. The next day, the Misfits rehearsed with a new singer—Jersey-bred goth rocker Myke Hideous, a friend of the band who had been one of the many to audition for the singing slot in 1995.

Word of this rehearsal leaked back to Michale Graves, leading to a furious round of communication. Graves is adamant that during this brouhaha he never said he quit the band. Regardless, the band traveled to South America with Hideous, and on May 27 Jerry Only issued a press release announcing that Graves was out of the band (Michale would learn of his dismissal via a letter from the Misfits' legal counsel).[35] Only's press release took shots at Graves for choosing "the alternative to all the work necessary to be a member of the Misfits" while dubiously praising himself for fighting "with all I had to keep the Misfits alive" following Glenn Danzig's departure. In an even stranger twist, Only concluded the written missive by revealing the band had reached out to Danzig once again to see if he wished to replace Graves (Danzig apparently declined) and that Hideous was not, in fact, a "permanent" Misfit yet: "Our tour in Europe and South America will serve a long audition for [Myke] . . . at the end of this trial period [we] will come to a decision and make our announcement."[36] Clearly the band (or at least Only) was still hedging bets on landing a Dave Vanian or Peter Steele.

Hideous—a slightly grizzled figure boasting stringy jet black hair, numerous piercings, and a hyper-intense gaze—knew he was at first just warming the Misfits microphone and was okay with that; feeling lost following the breakup of his own act Empire Hideous, Myke thought a brief jaunt with one of his favorite bands might prove a fun way to help clear his mind. However, the singer claims once Graves was officially out, the other Misfits informed him he was in for sure, despite the press release to contrary. Hideous was surprised and insulted but continued on the South American tour anyway. There he quickly recognized the Misfits were unequivocally "Jerry's band" and that his own opinion rarely counted toward anything. The singer also became annoyed with his lack of contract and erratic payment schedule. Hideous foresaw his tenure with this band not extending far, and indeed it didn't: upon their return from South America, Myke was sacked from the Misfits by Only, who claimed Doyle had campaigned hard against the singer's lackluster performance.

Hideous, who had abandoned his job and home in New Jersey to join the band under the pretense of something permanent, was shocked, as Only had allegedly told him a just short time before that he had proved himself on tour and could count on singing for the next Misfits album.[37] Still, Hideous was vaguely aware things might turn out this way, as he doubted the Misfits' devotion to their own lifestyle. "You know, you look at the Misfits and you say, 'These guys are creepy,'" Hideous remembered later of the experience. "'They're really ghoulish' . . . nah. They're a bunch of jocks. I was the truest thing they could have ever had to a real life ghoul . . . you come to my studio where I live and you'll see my collection of gargoyles, tombstones, skulls, bones, rosary beads, candles, and shellacked cats . . . you go to Jerry's house and you see posters of the [New York] Giants. You see football and wrestling on TV. You get to hang out with him while he's wearing his sweat pants and sneakers . . . [eventually] I said [to Jerry], 'Look man, no disrespect, but I know you guys. I know who you are . . . you're certainly no ghoul when you sit around in your white jumpsuit and watch football . . . your audience thinks you're a bunch of skull-crushing ghouls. You're not.'"[38]

Michale Graves was still open to being a Misfit despite his firing, and soon he was back in touch with the band. Graves was asked to "come jam"; wounds were healed, and it was as if he'd never left. Well, sort of. "They said I owed them $5,000 [for breach of contract]," Graves sighs. "I didn't care. I just wanted to play music."[39]

Chapter Eight

Hate Breeders

He who has the bigger stick has the better chance of imposing his definitions of reality. —Peter Berger [1]

On October 5, 1999, the Misfits released their second post-Danzig album, *Famous Monsters*, via heavy metal boutique label Roadrunner Records. Geffen's lackluster promotional push for *American Psycho* soured the band on the experience of being a minor fish in a major label pond. [2] Roadrunner, a smaller operation dedicated to such cult bands as Life of Agony, Machine Head, and Type O Negative, seemed a better fit. The record begins, as *American Psycho* does, with an instrumental meant to inspire dread; "Kong at the Gates" mimics as best it can the reveal of cinema's most storied giant with thumping drums, a seesawing guitar riff, and corresponding sound effects (read: monkey snorts). After a requisite pause for suspense, the album immediately offers a second song rooted in Hollywood simians—the driving "Forbidden Zone," which outlines the contentious area at the center of Charlton Heston's journey in 1968's *Planet of the Apes*. ("Back on Earth, it's all you read about," Michale Graves complains. "All the evidence destroyed!")

Though shameless in its quest to present songs based on famous horror movies, *Famous Monsters* boasts a thicker, more satisfying roar than its predecessor, a meaty snarl of more originality than the soundscape of *American Psycho. Famous Monsters* is also less concerned with its identity as a punk album, allowing its compositions to exist in a fun heavy metal framework more readily than any other Misfits release. Pinched harmonics accent the crushing riff in "Lost in Space" (which doesn't lose its menace even when sampling the robot's famous cry of "Danger, Will Robinson!"). Furious palm muting drives the verses of "Pumpkin Head," eventually giving way to one of the album's more engaging melodic refrains. "Helena," the

Misfits' ode to the 1993 surgical farce *Boxing Helena*, kicks off with a bouncy pop punk verse before a slab of fierce power metal stomps it out (proving that Kryst the Conqueror was never entirely dead).

The vestiges of the band's Reagan-era glory years pop up occasionally— see "The Crawling Eye" or "Witch Hunt," two songs that slam forward on little more than a few menacing barre chords, Dr. Chud's throbbing drums, and Michale Graves's melodic delirium. The Misfits play it a little straighter in the heart-pounding quasi-ballad "Saturday Night," which sounds ported from the same Elvisy dimension as *Static Age*.[3] One could also imagine the classic era of this band performing the giant ant creeper "Them," which strikes the best balance on the album between goofy chills, driving melodies, and memorable lyrics.[4]

Coinciding with the release of their second reunion album was the music video for its first single, "Scream," an auspicious union between the Misfits and pioneering horror movie director George A. Romero. The bespectacled *Night of the Living Dead* helmsman was gearing up to direct his first feature in six years, the odd thriller *Bruiser*, and happily accepted work on the "Scream" video on the condition the Misfits appear in his latest cinematic exercise (the band naturally agreed). The four-minute, mostly black-and-white video centralizes its visuals around a small hospital overrun by wounded Misfits fans and undead versions of band members themselves (the zombie makeup effects are enormously impressive for what appears to be an otherwise limited production budget-wise).[5] Doyle, Graves, Chud, and Jerry crash through medical equipment, soak themselves in the blood of unwitting doctors, and chase a few pretty nurses around the dimly lit halls of this treatment ward. Overall, the "Scream" video is a fun and appropriate tribute to the original 1968 zombie attack that made Romero a household name in those homes obsessed with all things cult. In addition to filming their cameo for *Bruiser*, which was released the following year, the Misfits penned the film's heart-aching title track with one of the best lyrical couplets Graves ever wound together ("If looks could kill, then death would be my name," the singer laments in its tender refrain).[6]

Famous Monsters' very existence coupled with the fact that it appeared to be forging a new sonic place helped the reunited Misfits overcome the stigma of being another post–Green Day cash-in nostalgia machine. Criticism did not escape the band, though. Accusations of the Misfits being the Kiss of punk dogged the band even back in the Danzig days, but the relentless merchandising that accompanied the reunion made comparisons between Lodi's horror punks and the cottage industry classic rockers more apropos than ever. The Crimson Ghost logo was being plastered on everything, from T-shirts to wallets to shoelaces and lunch boxes. Toy shelves soon found themselves invaded by fully articulated twelve inch Misfits action figures packaged in cardboard coffins with tiny guitar accessories. Jerry Only discussed the marketing with MTV in 1999, saying the Misfits "want to be able to sell our toys to kids and for [kids] to be able to buy our record"; the bassist then pointed out that the word "raped" in *Famous Monsters'* "Helena" was altered to "draped" to help the album avoid a parental advisory sticker. [7]

The most dubious of all Misfits cross-promotions didn't arrive until November of 1999, though, when the group began a working relationship with Ted Turner's World Championship Wrestling organization. They partnered with Halloween-themed wrestler Vampiro, and the punk band once steeped in so much mystery and confusion was now taking elbows for a basic cable audience of millions a couple of nights a week. Not all band members were enthused by this partnership. Michale Graves in particular, who admits he appreciated the resources the WCW was willing to lay at the band's feet, knew he wasn't a wrestler and was not keen on "getting punched in the face by Buff Bagwell." Jerry Only, on the other hand, embraced the venture, so enamored with this new development that he had a wrestling ring installed in his father's machine shop in Vernon so he could practice during his off time.

The Misfits partnered with WCW in the middle of the much-ballyhooed "Monday Night Wars," when the organization's *Monday Nitro* television program would go head-to-head against rival wrestling company WWF's *Monday Night Raw* in a fierce battle for several hours' worth of basic cable Nielsen ratings. "Macho Man" Randy Savage, the gravel-voiced WWF Superstar who reigned in the 1980s as a wildly gesticulating cowboy perpetually bedecked in neon fringe, defected to the WCW in the mid-1990s, [8] reinventing himself as a black-clad heel complete with buxom five-foot blonde wrapped in skin-tight leather. The woman in question was Gorgeous George, a.k.a. Stephanie Bellars, Savage's real-life girlfriend. The pair met in 1997 at a strip club where Bellars was a performer. [9] They began dating, and Savage eventually used his clout to bring Stephanie into the WCW fold as his valet. The bloom was off the rose by late 1999, though; Bellars had grown increasingly fed up with Savage's bizarre demands (the final straw allegedly came when he suggested a ménage a trois with her seventeen-year-old sister) and began looking for a new paramour. She quickly found one in Doyle once the Misfits began regularly appearing aside Vampiro. Quiet, even-keeled, and classically handsome out of his corpse makeup, Doyle was almost the mirror opposite of Randy Savage—save the similar brick shit-house physique. The guitarist was equally enamored of the flashy Bellars and their love blossomed despite the fact that Doyle already had a wife.

Randy Savage, a man known outside the ring for carrying a temper as hair-trigger as that of his beloved beef jerky-chomping character, was equal parts heartbroken and enraged when it became apparent Stephanie was shunning him for Doyle. The breaking point arrived one evening that December when Bellars stood her former lover up after the wrestling legend secured box seats at an NFL game in an attempt to woo her back. In an angry tailspin,

the Macho Man made some calls, discovered where the Misfits were performing in that night—the House of Blues in New Orleans—and immediately chartered a jet so he could finally confront and/or mortally wound Doyle.
Being one of the most famous faces of American pop culture, Savage easily
breezed past security upon his arrival and planted himself firmly backstage.
The Misfits, in the middle of their headlining performance, were flabber-
gasted when they noticed the angry Macho Man waiting in the wings, clearly
visible as he shotgunned beer after beer. Mere seconds after pounding out the
final guitar chord of the night, a very aware Doyle leapt into the crowd and
exited through the venue's front door. Moments later Michale Graves and
Gwar's Matt Maguire found themselves cornered by a frothing Randy Savage. "WHERE'S DOOLIE?" he seethed in that famous voice, violently man-
handling a trembling Graves in the process. Graves and Maguire were adamant that they nothing of Doyle's whereabouts. The pair pleaded with Savage not to brutalize anyone; after a few minutes of tense back and forth,
Savage slithered off into the night. [10]

Interestingly enough, Jerry Only steered clear of this brouhaha, which
was odd considering the amount of time he allegedly spent egging wrestlers
on before and after WCW events. The boisterous Only would openly challenge younger and more experienced industry professionals like Bill Gold-
berg to unsanctioned matches backstage, embarrassing his band mates. Jerry's dreams of conquering the squared circle became so overwhelming that
for a brief moment the other Misfits considered letting their founding bass
player go after his sports entertainment dreams. A series of talks were held
weighing the pros and cons of forming a brand new group with Vampiro on
bass. That wouldn't happen, though: Only effectively dashed his wrestling
dreams by talking up a union among the WCW stable of talent. The Misfits
were released from their wrestling contracts shortly thereafter. This brief,
contentious episode as grapplers was but a microcosm of the interpersonal
problems that continued to plague the band. Many on the inside could see the
end was coming. [11]

In 2000 the Misfits expanded their cinematic résumé and tested their comedic chops in the crime farce *Big Money Hustlas*. *Hustlas* was a vehicle for
controversial harlequin hip-hop stars the Insane Clown Posse whose murder-
ous rhymes centered around an evil entity known as "The Dark Carnival."
Big Money Hustlas leaned hardest on laughs, casting its madcap (and painfully low budget) caper with a wide range of comedic personalities including
Half Baked funnyman Harland Williams, *What's Happening!!* star Fred "Rerun" Berry, wrestler Mick Foley, porn star Kayla Kleevage, and blaxploita-
tion legend Rudy Ray Moore (reprising his most famous role of feisty pimp
Dolemite). [12]

At the helm of *Big Money Hustlas* was new director John Cafiero, an artist short on professional experience (his only prior credit was camera work on a 1995 episode of A&E's *Biography*) who had nevertheless landed the *Hustlas* job partially because of his work with the Misfits. In 1997 an animated short Cafiero put together with several other artists entitled "Misfits Re-Animated" caught the eye of Jerry Only who deemed the cartoon worthy for use in the *American Psycho* promotional campaign. The Misfits hired Cafiero shortly thereafter as a creative director for the band; by 2000, John Cafiero was managing the Misfits in place of Ken Caiafa [13] (who, after an unspecified disagreement with brother Jerry, exited rock n' roll to enter the less stressful field of swimming pool installation [14]) while simultaneously producing and directing their music videos on the strength of "Misfits Re-Animated." The same animation secured Cafiero the director's chair for *Big Money Hustlas*, [15] and Insane Clown Posse's label Island Records gave him a budget of $250,000 to complete the direct-to-video feature based around their rapping clown duo. Those monies evaporated a month into shooting, and, even worse, Cafiero's crew, irritated by the cast and film's subject matter, went on strike several times. Violent J, the more heavyset of the two Insane Clowns, had to step in at the eleventh hour with $100,000 from his own pocket to make sure *Big Money Hustlas* was completed. [16]

Hustlas wrapped without further incident, though Cafiero's issues with the self-proclaimed "Wicked Clowns" ensured he wouldn't be asked back for the inevitable sequel (2010's western-themed *Big Money Rustlas*). During their scene, the Misfits are seen attempting to enjoy a leisurely snack at a late night eatery while Harland Williams's clueless cop character (the cleverly named Officer Harry Cox) disturbs the peace by playing with his food, pretending to be a "donut cyclops." Annoyed, Doyle wings a pastry down the counter that hits Williams square in the temple. Williams is shamed as the Misfits crack up, but only momentarily—once the outfit's laughter dies down the cop puts his foodstuff back up to his left eye like a monocle and carries on as "a donut gentleman from London." [17]

It should come as no shock that *Big Money Hustlas* was not nominated for any Academy Awards the year of its release. Insane Clown Posse's virgin motion picture outing did debut at number one on the Billboard Home Video chart, [18] though, proving that two rapping carnival obsessives can succeed in this country on the strength of a 1970s action adventure farce featuring Rudy Ray Moore, the Misfits, Rerun from *What's Happening!!*, and one or two porn stars.

The curtain began to lower on the resurrected Misfits in late September of 2000 when the group was preparing for a tour through Canada. As their cramped Winnebago reached the border it was discovered that Michale

Graves lacked the proper permits to gain entry to the Great White North (a misdemeanor assault conviction stemming from a 1996 concert fracas in which Graves attacked a venue's sound man complicated his international travel issues). Graves thought the band's management had taken care of his permit problems and vice versa. Tensions rose, and a vote was held right then and there on whether to replace Graves for the duration of the Canada tour with Misfits pal and Ignite singer Zoli Téglás. The decision was unanimous: hire Zoli.[19] After eight gigs with Jerry Only handling vocal duties, Téglás joined the band in Thunder Bay, Ontario, to sing on the seven remaining dates.

Graves returned to the fold on October 21 when the band came back to the States for an East Coast tour leg.[20] The anger was still there, though—not only over the passports but the general band dynamic. Michale Graves reached his breaking point. "I was so mentally beat down by everything," remembers Graves. "There was such a bad vibe. I was writing the majority of the music, giving much more material and vision to the project, as were Doyle and Chud . . . [and] I was never respected [for it]. Toward the end, Jerry wanted to play the old songs more than the new ones. I couldn't understand that direction. He'd also say I sang 'too bluesy.' What the hell? I was ready to hang myself. It was like a never-ending episode of *Real Housewives*."

Exhausted, Michale told the band that he needed some time off. Halloween would be his last performance with the Misfits for the foreseeable future. If they wished to move on without him, he understood. Graves would in fact only make it to October 25; that night, the Misfits played at the House of Blues in the bucolic Disney-laden suburb of Lake Buena Vista, Florida. At some point during the show, an increasingly exasperated Graves announced this would be his last show with the band. What happened next is still debated fiercely by all who were in attendance. Doyle stormed offstage immediately following Graves's words, either because he was experiencing technical difficulties with his guitar or because he was upset with the singer. Graves and Chud quickly followed the hulking axe man into the stage wings, leaving a befuddled Jerry Only onstage alone to perform "We Are 138" alone. Backstage, Graves says he began pleading with an apparently unresponsive Doyle regarding the future of the Misfits, begging the former Paul Caiafa to stand up to his domineering brother. Graves felt Doyle had sway not only because of blood relation but because the guitarist owned a larger legal stake of the band than he did. Still, Doyle could not be moved.[21]

Eventually Only came off-stage to confront Graves. The aggravated and sweat-drenched bassist blew up at his younger counterpart and informed him the Misfits had recently been communicating with Glenn Danzig about a "real" reunion because "this new stuff isn't selling." As the situation grew uglier and various band technicians and roadies became involved (many of whom had grown weary of Jerry Only's tight pocketbook strings), House of Blues security escorted Michale Graves out of the venue. In a show of solidarity, Dr. Chud quit the band effective immediately and joined Graves in the parking lot. Before long the two youngest Misfits found themselves stranded at their hotel with no money or jobs as the Caiafa brothers forged ahead to the next show in Fort Lauderdale, with a Misfits that was only fifty percent intact. Refusing to swallow his pride, Jerry Only anointed himself the new Misfits vocalist, unequivocally letting the world know he was in charge (though Zoli Téglás would be invited back for one or two of the remaining 2000 tour legs).

As for the drums, Eric "Goat" Arce from tour mates Murphy's Law would fill in for the time being; in a weird stroke of luck, though, former Misfit Joey Image showed up out of curiosity to the Fort Lauderdale gig that followed the disastrous Orlando performance. After clearing the air with Only, Image happily took the stage to jam out on the material from his era. [22] It was an unprecedented but fleeting reunion; the future of the Misfits, who were just establishing themselves as a worthy Danzig-free entity, was still very much in doubt. Blame was already being placed at Only's feet; Dave Brockie, whose band Gwar toured with the reunited Misfits several times over, certainly felt the bassist erred in his treatment of Michale Graves: "Michale Graves was basically beaten out [of the band]. Jerry wouldn't let Mike be the star. Jerry wanted to be the star and he couldn't stand it. He felt Mike was just some young, dumb kid. I mean, Mike could be a prima donna, but he was *supposed* to be! He's the fuckin' singer!"[23]

Michale Graves and Dr. Chud channeled their frustrations over the crumbling of the Misfits into a new band called Graves. Joined by Empire Hideous guitarist Tom Logan and Fast Times bassist Left Hand Graham, the formerly famous monsters recorded their own excellent platter of mournful pop punk in 2002's *Web of Dharma*. Driving, gnawing songs like "Tell Me" and "Casket" were the final proof that they were no slouches creatively. [24] The band splintered apart during work on their sophomore release due to disagreements between singer and drummer; Graves would go on to form a similar outfit in Gotham Road while Chud focused his efforts on the more cartoony project known as X-Ward (best known for the wacky track "Mommy Made Luv 2 an Alien"). It should be noted that the Phoenix-based horror rock act Calabrese, which launched in 2003, had no apparent affiliation with Dr. Chud aside from sharing the Italian surname.

Fences between Michale Graves and Jerry Only were eventually mended enough that the ostracized singer would appear at a series of Misfits 25th anniversary shows that Only set up in 2001 in various parts of the country. Things stopped short of a full reconciliation, though,[25] which was just as well—Graves managed to make headlines all his own a short time later. On June 23, 2004, Comedy Central juggernaut *The Daily Show* aired one of its patented tongue-in-cheek interviews with Graves explaining the singer's very real trials and travails in the punk rock community as a hard-line, George Bush–supporting Republican. In full Misfits regalia (including painted-on skull face), Graves sat across from correspondent Ed Helms, detailing how the majority of his left-leaning peers harshly judge him. "Punks cry," Graves admitted, spurring a faux-sympathetic Helms to end the piece by taking Michale to play tennis at a haughty country club so he could be among more like-minded individuals. [26]

Various solo outings would come from Michale Graves in the wake of his *Daily Show* spotlight. Fans swiped these releases up but eagerly awaited news of an *American Psycho/Famous Monsters* Misfits regrouping; in 2008, Graves revealed to Live-Metal.net that his fractured lineup of the band attempted to reunite several years earlier—shortly after the 2002 reunion with Danzig fell through—but various personal issues prevented it from coming to fruition. "The sticking point on why that fell apart was that Doyle [now remarried to Bellars] wanted to bring his wife out on tour and wouldn't bend from it," Graves told the website. "Because Gorgeous George . . . had to be a part of the Misfits. Jerry [also] didn't even want Chud [back] in the band. Chud is a waste of human life, but he certainly deserved to be a part of the situation."

Graves was vague on his exact problems with Dr. Chud, saying only that he had "changed a lot" from the early days of the 1990s Misfits. [27] The pair eventually sorted out their problems, though, and in December of 2009 Michale joined his former drummer pal onstage with Doyle at New Jersey's Starland Ballroom to perform a brief set of songs from the two records the trio made together. Doyle was there as a special guest of Starland's headlining act that evening—Glenn Danzig.

Glenn Danzig's popularity started to wear off following the release of his fifth album, 1996's *Blackacidevil*. Parting ways with powerhouse players John Christ and Chuck Biscuits, Danzig took his band in a new direction by embracing the industrial sound so prevalent in rock at the time. [28] 1994's *4* LP had toyed with synthetic noises on intense tracks like "Cantspeak" and "Sadistikal," [29] but on *Blackacidevil* Glenn took it full bore. Electronic drums dominate the album to such a degree that Glenn is at times nearly inaudible. When he is, often it's clear Danzig has layered numerous effects upon his vocals. [30] Fans were perplexed as to why Danzig would want to ape Nine Inch Nails while simultaneously masking or hindering his powerful snarl, and sales reflected that. *Blackacidevil* was Danzig's first and only release on Hollywood Records; the band decided to leave American Recordings after a royalty dispute ended with Rick Rubin inviting Glenn to sue him as casually as one might offer someone over for tea. "He said it matter-of-factly," Glenn remembered years later. "Like it's no big thing . . . he said, 'I have no control over that kind of stuff. It shouldn't interfere with our working relationship. You'll just have to take me to court.'" The band declined to take Rubin up on his offer.

Hollywood, a subsidiary of the Walt Disney Company trying to build rock n' roll cred with obscure alternative artists like the Dead Milkmen and Seaweed, lured Danzig to their label with promises of creative freedom and boatloads of capital. Unfortunately for both parties, *Blackacidevil* didn't generate enough revenue to salve the complaints that poured in over Mickey Mouse's affiliation with these alleged devil-worshippers. Hollywood dropped the band just three weeks after *Blackacidevil*'s release.[31]

That same year Glenn would be sent up by Canadian comedy giants the Kids in the Hall in their first feature film *Brain Candy*. KITH member Bruce McCulloch based his brooding rock star character of Grivo in the film on Danzig, right down to the hairy chest and shoulder-length locks (it didn't hurt that the actor was both as diminutive and lantern-jawed as his model). "[My fellow troupe member] Scott Thompson was obsessed with the idea of Grivo being this Trent Reznor-like character," McCulloch remembers. "'Do him like a punk purist!'—and I was like, 'Well, no'. . . and then I thought of little Glenn, who has a quiet evil. [The character] is not a parody, though. It's a loving tribute. I'm really trying to do him. I think he's remarkable."[32]

Loving tribute or not, within the context of *Brain Candy* McCulloch's faux Danzig is hilarious in his titanic grumpiness, holding an open contempt for everything in his orbit. If the public at large held an opinion on Glenn Danzig, this was it—eternally sour rock star incapable of humor. This attitude changes for Grivo once he gets hooked on *Brain Candy*'s fictional antidepressant Gleemonex. Suddenly the character is inspired to abandon dissonant heavy metal for dippy, disposable pop music. Grivo's first post-Gleemonex single, the saccharine "Happiness Pie," propels him to new heights of fame and fortune while disgusting his original fan base.[33] If Glenn Danzig himself was moved, humored, or even offended by *Brain Candy* he never let on, focusing instead on his new industrial-tinged sound. In 1999 his band released *6:66 Satan's Child*, which further explored the territory staked out on *Blackacidevil*. While the songwriting remained relatively strong during this period the rock community at large was still turned off by the lack of organic sound. The returns were diminishing.[34]

Four years later Glenn Danzig took another loud knock from an über-cool trend-setting pop culture vessel: droll genre-blending folk singer Beck Hansen, whose funky acousti-rap shuffle "Loser" had by that time become the defining anthem of Generation X and whose deadpan, unaffected attitude became cooler than Morrison-like swagger or pentagrams. In a cover story for the December 1999 issue of *Spin* magazine, Hansen took their reporter around his Los Angeles neighborhood, pointedly commenting, "Everything's going upscale around here . . . except Glenn Danzig's house." Referring to a bit of clutter in Danzig's front yard, the detached wunderkind added, "He's had that stack of bricks there for about eight years now. I think it's a statement."[35]

Not one to engage in protracted wars of words (even for the sake of publicity), Danzig curtly responded to Beck's public teasing that same month, telling an interviewer, "Yeah, [the bricks are] a statement that I ain't Beck. And I ain't 'going upscale.' How's that?"[36] The lingering effect of what some lightheartedly refer to as "Brickgate" was Danzig's humble Los Feliz residence suddenly becoming a tourist attraction. Beck fans, Danzig fans, and those simply aroused by rock n' roll lore began routinely seeking the singer's abode out in the wake of the *Spin* article, snapping their photos near the famed pile of bricks and Danzig's black Jaguar (or as close as they could get, anyway—a wrought iron fence provided firm division between the yard of Danzig and curious interlopers).

That same year—perhaps prompted by his mainstream stumbles—Danzig appeared to be looking back, or perhaps coming to terms with his own legacy. That November, to promote a forthcoming box set of all their material, Glenn reconstituted Samhain for a stretch of his titular band's *Satan's Child* tour. Fan excitement was staved off by the absence of both Pete Marshall and Eerie Von. According to Marshall, Danzig decided to put Samhain's name on the tour dates before vetting any other member's availability. By that time Marshall had graduated to playing in Iggy Pop's backing band the Trolls and had prior commitments booked with that act. He was more than surprised to hear from Glenn mere weeks before the alleged reunion. "He called me at my day job," Marshall remembers. "And he says, 'Hey, we're doin' a Samhain tour, it's these dates.' I was like, 'What? When were you gonna tell me?' 'Uh, right now.' 'Well, I can't do it, I'm sorry, I'm playing with Iggy.' And of course he got all huffy, like, 'Ah, whaddya mean ya can't do it?'"

Unable to wrestle Marshall away from Iggy Pop, Danzig plugged the guitarist from his own band, Todd Youth, into his place. Von decided he would decline to participate—after all, it wouldn't be a true Samhain reunion if one member was missing. Yet Danzig didn't bother inviting Von to this reformation as the bassist had apparently already crossed the point of no return with the finicky singer (Steve Zing and London May ended up sharing bass duties during the reunion shows; Zing would play the instrument while May drummed through a set of songs from his era in Samhain, and vice versa).There has been much speculation over the years concerning what drove Danzig apart from his most frequent collaborator (they appear together on nine releases and toured side by side for a solid decade); Glenn claims that Von's affinity for southern rock like the Allman Brothers interfered with the dark, semi-industrial sounds he was interested in, and he took umbrage at a handful of unflattering remarks the bass player made about the singer once his tenure in the band was over. For his part, Eerie Von has never fully explained what fractured his relationship with Glenn Danzig.[37]

Glenn's throwback mood continued with *I Luciferi*, the Danzig band's seventh full-length released that May, a satisfying if not full return to the organic heavy metal sounds that garnered the outfit so much acclaim at the dawn of the 1990s.[38] Several months later Glenn took acute aim at his own humorless image by lending his voice to the Cartoon Network's bizarre superhero farce *Aqua Teen Hunger Force*. Rendered with a perpetual scowl and limited movement by the program's animators, Danzig plays himself in the episode "Cybernetic Ghost of Christmas Past from the Future" in which he purchases a home haunted by a menacing robot from the future. After one night together, the robot visits his neighbors (the titular crime-solving team comprised of sentient fast food menu items) to complain he "cannot live with that [Danzig] guy, he is so annoying, he is so frightening, and he doesn't wear a shirt."[39]

In the wake of the Samhain reunion and *I Luciferi*'s harkening to Danzig's original sound, many wondered if some sort of Danzig-sanctioned Misfits reunion could be around the corner. For years Glenn had steadfastly denied a reunion would ever take place, with enough furor in his statements to make it clear interviewers shouldn't bother bringing it up. Privately, however, the singer began to reconsider the Misfits—not simply for nostalgia's sake, but for profit. Financially, Danzig the band had plateaued, earning a profit only because Glenn purposely budgeted himself accordingly. Jerry Only's version of the Misfits had proven it could be a viable touring act, and the receipts were only growing as the new millennium rolled on. Jerry Only, in a stroke of genius, ensured the continued interest and monies of Misfits zealots by drafting a series of punk rock all-stars—including Black Flag guitarist Dez Cadena, drummer Marc "Marky Ramone" Bell, and his own former skinsman Robo—to help reconstitute the band in the post-Graves era. The results creating a name-studded gigging machine even the naysayers ended up clamoring to see.

Another more personal event might have played into Danzig's softening on a Misfits reunion. In May of 2002 Glenn's father Richard, who had grown enormously proud of his rock star son and happily showed off ephemera to fans who occasionally stopped by his home, passed away at the age of 76. When the singer flew from his home in Los Angeles to Lodi for the funeral he was surprised by the attendance of both Jerry Only and Doyle. Even more surprising, the trio engaged in an armistice that day, despite the litigious and press-based attacks they had inflicted upon one another. Commiserating over the loss of a parental figure, pretenses were dropped. If for just one afternoon, Danzig became Glenn Anzalone again, the Caiafas Gerald Jr. and Paul.

Security escorted no one out of the funeral home. Perhaps they didn't despise each other as much as they thought.

The bottom line for Danzig was money, and the Misfits bass player seemed to be raking it in. Impressed, Glenn seriously considered for the first time how financially beneficial a full-fledged Misfits reunion could be, a reunion that would bring both of their fan bases together in one massive profit share. Surely he and Jerry could put aside their differences for a few weeks in favor of living more comfortably. With that in mind, Danzig bought the Caiafa brothers plane tickets to Los Angeles for a meeting.

Intrigued, Jerry and Doyle flew across the country for their first meeting with Glenn Danzig in years that wouldn't involve lawyers. The tale that follows is another one of legend among Misfits fans: From the airport they were ferried directly to Danzig's residence. Upon entering, they found Glenn lying sideways on a couch, facing a flickering television. The Caiafas took their seats. Glenn spoke first, saying he was ready to let bygones be bygones for a tour and an album on the condition that Jerry not perform with his new Misfits for at least one year prior. A reasonable request—the absence of the band would create a public demand. Jerry, however, balked at this notion, complaining that he'd lose $250,000 if he called off all his planned Misfits activities for the coming year. An awkward silence commenced. Doyle's head sunk into his hands. Glenn, unwilling to argue with someone who couldn't see the potentially larger fortune at stake, simply rolled over to face away from the Caiafas, as if to take a nap, and said, "Fine, no deal."[40]

And thus, the first shot the world had at an honest Misfits reunion was dashed. Doyle would confirm this long-standing rumor in 2008 during a rare interview granted to the *Cleveland Free Times*. The tight-lipped guitarist outed his brother as the one who "put a fuckin' monkey wrench" in the negotiations with Glenn, but the younger Caiafa refused to elaborate or give specific details. "So let all the Misfits fans put that in their pipe and smoke it," Doyle was quoted as saying, aware that he was dropping a potential bombshell.[41] Danzig denied any and all stories about a reunion with Jerry, which is not surprising when you consider the following quote from a 2004 interview: "Until the contract is signed, nothing is real."[42]

Issues with Glenn aside, the real hurdle of the 2002 reunion could have been mending fences between the estranged Caiafa brothers. A year earlier Jerry and Doyle experienced a major falling out stemming from Jerry's maneuvers regarding Doyle's legal rights to the Misfits name. The bitter divorce from his first wife that freed him to marry Stephanie Bellars had left Doyle in a financial hole, and the guitarist was desperate to purchase a home in New Jersey within reasonable distance of his young children. Doyle adored his kids far more than his life as a corpse-painted Misfit and by all accounts would have done anything to remain a part of their lives. The youngest Caiafa turned to his brother Jerry, who agreed to foot the bill for the home in exchange for Doyle's legal share of the Misfits brand. Doyle signed off, perhaps figuring he'd still at least get to perform if not contribute silently to larger decisions regarding the group. His optimism proved misguided; Jerry dumped Doyle from the band in favor of Cadena shortly after acquiring his Misfits ownership percentage in May of 2001. Doyle allegedly learned of his firing via a handwritten note Jerry stuck under the windshield of his truck one afternoon while the guitarist was at work. [43]

When asked about his brother's departure from the band, Jerry Only would cite the emotional toll of Doyle's divorce and a nagging elbow injury. [44]

Despite retaining two of punk's most charismatic and talented players in Dez Cadena and Marky Ramone, the Misfits appeared somewhat directionless in the early part of the 2000s. The trio toured the globe extensively, churning out a set of not just their own songs but Black Flag and Ramones classics at both small gigs and festivals, [45] but they were slow to release any new recordings. This struck many observers as a waste of resources. When the Misfits finally did get around to recording something in 2002, it was a cover of Balzac's sing-songy "The Day the Earth Caught Fire" for a split single with said Japanese horror punk band. [46] In July of 2003 the Misfits followed this obscure piece of vinyl with an entire record of covers.

Project 1950 offers ten updated renditions of early rock n' roll/doo wop classics that allegedly inspired the Misfits. The title is a bit of a misnomer: only five of the songs presented were originally released in the 1950s. At least one, the Conway Twitty/Loretta Lynn ballad "Only Make Believe," was made in 1971. Of course, this is the same band that wrote a song about *Poltergeist* and called it "Shining," so perhaps such chronological hiccups are to be expected. At any rate, Jerry Only as vocalist tackles *Project 1950* with goofy bombast; though the band performs these songs well (guest players no less than the Ronnette's Ronnie Spector and Blondie's Jimmy Destri add to the aural construct), Only's hoary singing tends to torpedo any hope of grit or honest passion. Dez Cadena, the guitarist partially responsible for Black Flag's menacing attack, could have picked up the slack but plays with far less intensity than he is generally remembered for by punk historians.

Naturally, one of the songs the Misfits chose to cover on *Project 1950* is Bobby "Boris" Pickett's "Monster Mash." Inexplicably, they add a new syrupy line of melody to the chorus, sung by the band's then-manager, John Cafiero. Rather than do a Boris Karloff impression throughout the song, Only performs as himself, slipping into an accent only during the famed mention of "The Transylvania Twist."

As a love letter to a bygone era, *Project 1950* has its merits. As a Misfits record, it is largely embarrassing (especially in its cheap cartoon cover featuring an Igor-like creature in a Crimson Ghost hoodie).[47] Regardless, the Misfits remained an immensely popular concert attraction at this juncture. The band's continued revenue stream may have influenced Jerry Only's 2005 decision to sell the Proedge brand he had been simultaneously managing since his father's retirement from Congruent Machine in the mid-1990s to an interested party (the Vernon manufacturing shop remained open with Only remaining an operations head).[48] Details concerning the Proedge sales figures are unknown, though Congruent had valuable contracts with massive retailers such as Sears and Stanley Tool for the blade's creation.[49] When asked in 2008 what kind of financial cushion the sale provided his family, Doyle curtly replied, "I didn't get anything."[50]

Meanwhile, a larger, more public embarrassment loomed for Glenn Danzig, one that proved his era was, for all intents and purposes, bygone.

Chapter Nine

Violent World

The image is one thing and the human being is another . . . it's very hard to live up to an image. —Elvis Presley [1]

The Misfits' influence on rock music was undeniable by the earliest twenty-first century. Scores of modern rockers paid lip service to the band and covered their songs, from rootsy critical cult darlings like Ryan Adams,[2] My Morning Jacket,[3] and Will Oldham[4] to more commercial punk-based acts like AFI[5] and My Chemical Romance.[6] Green Day, the multiplatinum trio who in the previous decade had done much to make "punk rock" a household term again, paid their own odd tribute to the Misfits in 2003 by recording a robotic version of "Teenagers from Mars" for the debut album of their secretive new wave side project the Network[7] (years later, Green Day would be more assured in their Misfits fandom, covering "Hybrid Moments" at random tour intervals).

More devoted to the Misfits pulpit was Slipknot, an assembly of Midwestern musicians who helped carry on the theatrics and ferocity that began in Lodi. Totaling eight members, Slipknot wore prison jumpsuits, their faces obscured by a grotesque series of mismatched Halloween masks, and churned out a deafening assault of discordant horror metal just as blunt as it was unrelenting (Slipknot's "hit," as it were, was 2001's "People = Shit" from the dour *Iowa*). Despite a thoroughly frightening persona and thinly veiled contempt for the world around them, Slipknot managed to amass enormous popularity beyond their core fan base of colorfully termed "maggots." The group hooked up with former Danzig alley Rick Rubin for their third album, 2004's *Vol. 3 (The Subliminal Verses)*; the results went platinum in several countries and earned a Best Metal Performance Grammy for the album's tenth song, "Before I Forget."[8]

The chalky white Crimson Ghost logo had also become something of a trendy fashion accessory. Rowdy millionaire rappers wore parody T-shirts with the famous skull sporting gold teeth or sunglasses; featherweight pop stars sported the Crimson Ghost to look tough. The ghostly face popped up in television and movies by Will Smith, Adam Sandler, Chevy Chase, Ben Affleck, and Keira Knightley. Bemusing as it could be to spot someone like Boy George or Justin Bieber wandering around in Misfits apparel, at least the Crimson Ghost never aged. The Misfits themselves, on the other hand, could not stave off their mortality.

In 2004 Glenn Danzig was 49 and still grinding out a living as a touring heavy metal musician with his eponymous band. Diplomacy was still not his strong suit, and an incident that July would forever topple his carefully crafted image of satanically powered tough guy. A video camera caught a backstage confrontation in Tuba City, Arizona, between Glenn and musician Danny Marianino. Marianino chided Glenn for refusing to let his band the North Side Kings perform on the bill as scheduled. The Kings had driven six hours to Tuba City after being promised an opening slot on the show; upon arrival, they learned delays would force them to go on after the headlining Danzig. Once Glenn finished his set, however, the house lights went up and Danzig's crew began breaking down the stage. Incensed, Marianino located Glenn and began to complain. The singer, who was signing autographs at the time, listened for a moment before angrily shoving his larger, taller aggressor with a shout of, "Fuck you, motherfucker!" Marianino responded with a clumsy swing that sent Danzig to the floor. Witnesses claim they saw Danzig's eyes roll back as he fell away.

The heavy metal equivalent of the Rodney King tape surfaced two days later on the Internet and was pored over by rock fans across the globe.[9] They debated if Marianino's punch had even connected with Danzig (the angle does make it appear the former's fist only grazed the latter), if Marianino had some kind of knife in his hand as Danzig would later claim, and who was saying what in the blurry melee that followed. Danzig himself remained silent on the issue until August 20. When asked by a Sioux Falls newspaper about the dust up, the singer gruffly replied that the whole thing was "a setup for me to punch him and them to sue me for a bunch of money. If I wanted to kill that guy, he'd be dead in two seconds."[10] Jaded fans scoffed and went on to celebrate the comeuppance of a figure rumored for so long to be extraordinarily difficult, unreasonable, and posturing (not surprisingly, Jerry Only was spotted shortly after the Arizona dust-up wearing a North Side Kings shirt that added a stream of blood from the nasal socket of Danzig's famous cow skull logo).

The Tuba City fracas overshadowed a rather monumental announcement that came the same week: Doyle would be performing a special "Misfits set" with Danzig and his band later in the year on the Blackest of the Black package tour, a festival that also featured controversial Norwegian metallers Mayhem and California thrash masters Death Angel. The guitarist and singer were put in touch again by mutual friends and apparently commiserated over their individual issues with Jerry Only. Although the Blackest of the Black tour was abruptly canceled under mysterious circumstances never fully explained,[11] Doyle and Danzig would reunite onstage that December in Las Vegas[12] and continue making appearances together through 2005 and 2006. Crowds packed in to witness these Misfits sets even though they often consisted of less than eight songs. Fans were curious regarding Doyle's seemingly sudden defection to the side opposing his brother Jerry. Asked by a reporter if "things were weird" between the Caiafas now that the guitarist was spending time with Danzig, Doyle retorted, "Things have been weird with Jerry since we started playing music," wryly adding, "His name is exactly what he is . . . Jerry ONLY. Only Jerry."[13]

Doyle attempted to strike out with his own act Gorgeous Frankenstein in the late Aughts, a stomping metal punk hybrid led by the guitarist and his wife Stephanie Bellars. In concert Bellars performed a strip tease on stage as the band tore through material like "Speed Witch" and "Hell Angel." Lineup changes plagued Gorgeous Frankenstein, but the band managed to squeeze out one self-titled album in 2007.[14] Following several years of inactivity, Gorgeous Frankenstein relaunched in 2012 under the eponym Doyle and began trumpeting the 2013 release of their sophomore effort *Abominator*.[15] Bellars was absent from the new lineup and press photos, but she was never sold on being in Gorgeous Frankenstein in the first place. "We have four kids, and the only reason I wanted to come out [with the band] was to take care of [them]," Bellars told *Yahoo!* in 2009. "Gorgeous Frankenstein more or less has to do with our children."[16] Paul Caiafa also expanded the Misfits empire into foodstuffs in the latter half of the decade when he launched his own brand of hot sauce. The cayenne pepper-based "Made in Hell," which bears Doyle's green glowing visage on its label, is marketed as being hotter than Tabasco but not "so hot as to totally destroy the flavor of your food."[17]

The pervasiveness of the Crimson Ghost was of course partially due to its own striking image, but also because the Misfits worked so damn hard to make it an icon. The band printed it on nearly any kind of accessory big enough to convey its fright for an interval of nearly twenty to twenty-five years (ownership of the original Republic Pictures *Crimson Ghost* serial and its related properties changed several times over the years; at no point did any of its copyright holders come after the Misfits for their unauthorized appropriation of the character). Jerry Only was still marketing the logo aggressively into the first decade of the twenty-first century, although a 2010 legal complaint would claim the bassist was doing so without the consent and permission of the other Misfits—a violation of the 1994 settlement. In August of 2009 Arthur Googy noticed a billboard in Manhattan advertising a special brand of Misfits sneakers featuring the Crimson Ghost. Googy got in touch with Bobby Steele, the former Misfit he was closest to, and the pair filed suit against Jerry Only to the tune of $75,000 for failing to properly declare co-ownership of the Misfits name and trademarks among all former members and for falsely attempting to trademark Misfits logos in his own name in 2000. (Danzig himself commenced proceedings against Only's 2000 trademark registrations; those actions were still pending as of 2010.)

The story *Kaufhold et al v. Caiafa et al* lays out an interesting spin on the accepted Misfits story, alleging that Steele had an "already established reputation" when he joined the band in 1978 that helped the group achieve its renown. Steele and Arthur Googy "controlled the Misfits marks" during this period, allegedly, painting a picture of the two as a codependent branding machine despite the fact the pair were only in the band at the same time for a matter months. The document also states that Steele was the only former band member using Misfits imagery between the years of 1983 and 1995,[18] which is simply untrue (see the various Crimson Ghost-bedecked compilations Danzig released via Caroline during those years). This is not surprising given some of the strange theories Bobby Steele has floated out to the public in recent years. The guitarist has long claimed the 2001 cancellation of *12 Hits from Hell*, an album assembled by Caroline of a 1980 Misfits recording session that combined his own guitar work with Doyle's, was struck down at the eleventh hour because Jerry Only has been on a decades-long mission to erase Steele's existence from the history books.[19]

The official explanation for the cancellation of *12 Hits*—that Glenn Danzig and Jerry Only were unhappy with the album's layout and mixing and had in fact been largely left out of the creative process[20] —seems suspect given the fact that the album had already shipped to retailers by that time; but record companies routinely assemble product without their client's direct involvement in hopes of making a quick buck (and hoping the musicians in question will be too busy to even notice). *12 Hits* appears to be just another example akin to an umpteenth Aerosmith or Madonna greatest hits collection, a "new" Misfits release the label hoped to pop out in time for Halloween by purposely not consulting the notoriously fickle band members. Besides, had there truly been a conspiracy against Bobby Steele, the Misfits would have likely suppressed the majority of Caroline's 1996 box set.

Some have speculated that part of the complication with *12 Hits from Hell* had to do with its relative inability to exist comfortably within the legal parameters set by the band's 1995 settlement agreement. Blending various distorted guitar tracks together made correct pro-rating a headache, a few insiders say. Credence was lent to this theory in 2004 when Danzig alleged to *Circus* that Bobby Steele had snuck into a studio to add new guitar tracks to the *12 Hits* mix without the rest of the band's consent or knowledge.[21] An ironic volley considering the sonic tinkering Danzig himself did on *Legacy of Brutality* and *Collection II*. At any rate, *12 Hits from Hell* would remain buried until the rise of online file-sharing; in a curious move, Bobby Steele recorded and released his own version of the album with his band the Undead in 2007.[22]

Cursed as he may appear by the hands of fate or his previous musical collaborators, Steele had sunnier moments in life. In April 2011 the still dangerously thin guitarist wed model Jill Kethel, who appeared in the original 1988 black-and-white video for Danzig's "Mother." Steele and his bride married at Parsippany, New Jersey's Chiller Theater Expo; following the ceremony, the brand new Mr. Kethel, adorned in a white tuxedo complete with top hat, performed David Bowie's "Ziggy Stardust" with Chiller Expo staples the Dead Elvi.[23] Though love petered out quickly for the couple (by the summer of 2012 Kethel claimed irreconcilable differences over Steele's involvements with drugs, pornography, and falsified claims for government assistance[24]), it is certainly better to have loved the lithe dancer from the "Mother" video and lost than to have only seen her from the other side of the television screen.

"I appreciate Jerry working so hard," says Ian MacKaye of the relentless touring Only's Misfits trio undertook in the 2000s. "I went to see them a few years ago and that guy really *works*. He's taking care of all these things backstage while still making time for fans and friends . . . I was really impressed."[25]

Indeed, Jerry Only kept the Misfits out on the road and touring constantly in the first ten years of the 2000s, remaining his affable and personable self no matter what the circumstance, always extending himself on behalf of thrilled concert attendees. Yet this latest incarnation of the band again took their time working on recorded product to follow *Project 1950* (despite having launched their own label, Misfits Records, in 2002). Eventually the group buckled down to produce 2009's single "Land of the Dead," a tribute to George Romero's 2005 zombie film entry of the same name. A fully realized version of the Crimson Ghost skull (replete with rotting flesh and stringy bits of hair) was created by *Heavy Metal* artist Arthur Suydam for the cover.[26] Unfortunately, the song itself was too meandering and lifeless to inspire much excitement, a shame considering it boasted the triumphant studio return of Robo. Robo, who spent several years alternating live percussive duties with Marky Ramone, became the permanent Misfits drummer again in 2005 after Ramone departed over rumored pay disputes (the scuttlebutt at the time suggested Marky's several thousand dollar guarantee for each performance was too draining for Only's pockets; Marky himself later officially cited his displeasure with the sloppy versions of Ramones songs that Only and Cadena were forcing him to play).[27] Only's vocals on "Land of the Dead," while perfectly melodic, lack commitment and end up sounding rather inauthentic. Yet the band still had their supporters. "I thought they were pretty good with Dez and Robo," says Eyehategod singer Mike IX Williams. "I mean, the whole thing was pretty trippy seeing Dez up there with long hair and that face paint on, but musically they were pretty good."[28]

Finally, in October of 2011, the Misfits released *The Devil's Rain*, their seventh studio album. Helmed by noted Ramones producer Ed Stasium and including another drum shift—Robo's recurring visa issues forced his ouster in favor of Eric "Chupacabra" Arce[29] —the album has perhaps the fullest, most spacious sound of any record in the band's catalog. Still, a hokey nature abounds, from the on-the-nose opening sound effects of a coming rain storm to Jerry Only's continued lounge crooning to the spate of songs that once again appear to have been written after perusing IMDb (or perhaps it's a coincidence that the band wrote a song about "Dark Shadows" roughly the same time director Tim Burton began working on his feature film).

Bits of rich melody exist on *The Devil's Rain*, particularly in the breezy sway of "Black Hole" and the ascending UFO croon "Unexplained," but camp overrides any other quality here. See the dramatic tribute to W. W. Jacobs' "The Monkey's Paw" for all the evidence you need. Only is in full Vegas swing here—you can practically see him loosening his bow tie on stage at the Sands as he playfully strains that "tonight, [he] casts this spell." Just as corny is "The Curse of the Mummy's Hand," another phantom appendage-based track in which Only bellows about Ra so often it's surprising the solar deity doesn't materialize from your stereo speakers. It's not fair, however, to unload all the blame here for misfire on Jerry Only—a large part of the problem with *Devil's Rain* is the flat production. The oomph that made *Famous Monsters* such a rush despite its moments of dubiousness has all but evaporated here, leaving hollow guitars and softened drums.

The most interesting entry on *The Devil's Rain* is "Ghost of Frankenstein," the lyrics of which could be interpreted as a rant concerning Jerry's estranged brother Doyle. "Now these tragedies surround me," Only laments, adding he's "forever locked" with the titular spirits as they "bear the same name." Dez Cadena relieves Only on the concluding charger "Death Ray"; sadly, Cadena's voice has mellowed so much since his days of screaming for Black Flag that it's barely distinguishable from that of Only; it's hard to believe this is the same throat that once exploded over Black Flag's incendiary "Police Story" and "Jealous Again."[30] The general two-to-three star review *The Devil's Rain* garnered accurately reflect its mediocrity; summing it up succinctly in the *Delaware County Daily Times*, Michael Christopher wrote "[Jerry Only] retains the [Misfits] name in rights only, because there is no true legitimacy left within the group."[31] "The question is not whether the

Misfits are really 'The Misfits' without Glenn Danzig," added noted Internet rock critic Mark Prindle in his *Devil's Rain* review. "The question is whether any of the remaining or replacement members have had any songwriting talent at all. And the answer is Hell Fucking No. Glenn Danzig may be an irrelevant prima donna asshole in 2011, but his songwriting was untouchable between 1977 and 1994. Jerry Only, on the other hand, is just some guy. Anybody could write the garbage he writes. . . . "Remember that old Dead Kennedys song, where Jello Biafra sings 'imagine Sid Vicious at thirty-five?' Think of how much more pathetic and depressing that verse would've been with the lyric 'imagine Jerry Only at fifty-two.' Then buy *The Devil's Rain* and hear that image come to humiliating, devilocked life."[32]

Undaunted by the indifference or disappointment that greeted *The Devil's Rain*, the Misfits continued to tour through 2012,[33] playing all manner of gigs to those still holding out hope that a real reunion with Glenn Danzig might one day be forged. In fact, the title of the album could be viewed as a subtle invitation for Glenn's return; "devil's rain" is one of the more memorable phrases in the Danzig-penned "Skulls" from 1982's *Walk Among Us*. Perhaps this titular nod was meant to be little more than a reminder of the glory days; perhaps it was simply inspired by the legendarily awful 1975 William Shatner vehicle about a satanic cabal of the same name. Yet true Misfits devotees must have wondered, if ever briefly, that *The Devil's Rain* was in some way supposed to be a signal to Danzig preceding a true mending of fences—that this was maybe the first step in the reunion fans had waited so long to see. When faced with the inevitable reunion question by *Rolling Stone*, Jerry Only reaffirmed his status as a Christian family man[34] only moonlighting as a satanist when he replied, "If Glenn went and got baptized again, maybe we could talk [reunion]."

Danzig has never acknowledged the current activities of his former band and has kept his head down and forged ahead in the latter half of the Aughts. His public image may have been tarnished by the knock-out video but his bank account was not; in 2005 the singer purchased a three-bedroom home in Los Angeles for $1.5 million. The Cheviot Hills property, complete with swimming pool and decorative front-yard waterwheel, was previously owned by legendary comedienne Lucille Ball[35] and proved a considerable upgrade from Danzig's previous abode. For years Glenn had lived in a modest but cozy home in Los Feliz that, thanks to his residence, became a tourist attraction for all manner of admirers.

Perhaps expediting Danzig's move to a new home was an incident on Halloween of 2005 at the Los Feliz home wherein a deranged fan began smashing the front gate before vaulting onto the property. Danzig's bodyguard gave chase, but the intruder slipped away, leaving behind a backpack allegedly full of pornographic magazines featuring Danzig's head pasted on the various bodies of the performers. Also in the backpack: a notebook with

"Kill Danzig, October 31st" written obsessively over and over again. The entire incident was kept hush hush for years, perhaps in a calculated attempt not to undermine Danzig's ferocity in the post-knock-out video world.[36]

This could also explain the lack of activity from Glenn in the latter half of the decade. There was a six-year gap between *Circle of Snakes* and 2010's *Deth Red Sabbaoth*. Much was made of *Deth Red*'s "back to basics" approach via analog recording; the results were hailed as Glenn's greatest offering since the late 1980s (especially in Glenn's vocals, which many fans and critics feared were slipping as the years rolled on). 2010 also yielded an unexpected creative union between the usual lone wolf Danzig and Hole/ Smashing Pumpkins bassist Melissa Auf der Maur on the alternative rock stateswoman's sophomore solo effort, *Out of Our Minds*. Auf der Maur had long been a fan of Glenn's work and wrote a somber croon in his style, "My Father's Grave," that she hoped he would agree to duet on—despite the fact Danzig had never shared the microphone with anyone up to this point in his career.

Circumventing the usual channels Auf der Maur wrote a letter to Danzig care of his comic book company, Veritok; apparently touched by her earnest appeal and impressed by the song, Glenn agreed to the duet, and the two quickly cut it in a Los Angeles studio. Like *Deth Red Sabbaoth*, "My Father's Grave" throbs with the pain of classic Danzig as it lays out the heartfelt conversation between the hurt tenor of a daughter in mourning and the baritone workman who buried the man who raised her.[37] *Out of Our Minds* received waves of positive press and many reviewers made sure to emphasize the wounded beauty of "My Father's Grave" (Maria Schurr of PopMatters.com praised Danzig's performance on the song as "his sinister best").

Yet any artistic achievement was overshadowed by another Internet embarrassment, albeit one far less devastating than the North Side Kings confrontation. In October of 2010, mere months after *Deth Red*'s release, paparazzi photos began circulating online of an exhausted-looking Glenn returning from a brief shopping excursion. Clearly visible in one of his translucent plastic bags was a bright blue box of Fresh Step kitty litter, its smiling feline mascot sharply contrasting the tight black ensemble (topped off with one his band's own T-shirts) Glenn chose for the day.

Rock fans the world over were enormously amused seeing the self-proclaimed "Bringer of Death" lugging around pet supplies, and before long Internet parody artists began splicing errant cat noises into YouTube videos of "Mother." Danzig himself, apparently unaware of the inherent humor in an allegedly satanic rock star caring after house pets, was mostly annoyed by the attention. In an interview with *Buzzgrinder* shortly after the paparazzi photos found their way online the singer accused anyone interested in his cat situation of "wasting their lives." "Hey, you know what? Why do people even care?" Danzig wondered aloud. "I just play music, you know what I mean? That's what I want to spend my time talking about."[38]

The pattern of Danzig doing something great only to have it quickly overshadowed by strange or ridiculous hijinks continued in 2011. That August the singer announced he would indulge fans by performing a series of legacy concerts in the fall that would include material from all stages of his musical evolution. Audiences in Chicago, New York, Los Angeles, and Austin would be treated to a special Danzig concert in three acts—one dedicated to his eponymous group, one for Samhain, one for the Misfits. As with previous assemblies of this nature spearheaded by Glenn, the only spirit from his past invited to visit was Doyle, though Steve Zing was playing bass in Danzig the band at this time and indeed participated in the Samhain sets.[39]

The first legacy gigs went off without a hitch; Danzig appeared to revel in his trips down memory lane, even engaging in new bits of myth-making (the singer was now prefacing performances of "Bullet" with claims that the city of Dallas responded to the first gory Misfits single in 1978 by threatening to arrest the band on site). The fourth show in Austin on November 4, part of the city's annual Fun Fun Fun Fest, was marred by what event organizers later characterized as Glenn's fussbudget behavior. Audience members disappointed that the set that night only lasted an hour were later informed via Fun Fun Fun Fest's Facebook page that Danzig purposely took the stage forty-five minutes late as many of his backstage demands had not been met.[40] The festival's booking agent accused Danzig of threatening cancellation from the moment he arrived in Austin that morning, citing a severe cold—or, as he called it, a "death bug." Piping hot french onion soup, a handful of vitamins, and a Wendy's chicken sandwich were all allegedly demanded by and procured for the singer to ensure his comfort. A doctor was also summoned to the concert site, but Danzig, a long-time critic of Western medicine, refused his non-holistic treatments.

The Austin promoters went out of their way to accommodate Danzig, but to no avail. Half an hour before his time slot Danzig holed up in his trailer and refused to go on (upset over the stage size and some improperly hung banners). Eventually he was cajoled onstage, still fearful that the crisp fifty degree temperatures would weaken his health further. As ordered by the city, festival organizers pulled the plug at 10 p.m., only sixty minutes into Danzig's performance. "I guess they've never heard of a thing called a riot before," Danzig groused as his set abruptly screeched to a halt.[41] The crowd was irritated but not livid; a riot would not be forthcoming. In less than a day, however, there was a new way to mock Danzig on the Internet: images of the singer surrounded by Wendy's takeout bags and bowls of french onion soup shot around the e-world just as quickly as the previous undoctored image of Danzig hauling his cat's Fresh Step.

The fifth legacy gig on June 9, 2012, at the Bonnaroo Festival in Manchester, Tennessee, contained another segment of haughty rock star behavior from Glenn. Photographer Michael Bunch was taking photos of people in the crowd during Danzig's set when the singer suddenly singled him out mid-song, leaping off the stage in an attempt to confront Bunch for violating his "no photo, no video" rule. Startled, Bunch later told his employer NashvilleScene.com that he was sure he was about to be beaten down by the still-imposing fifty-something singer. Thankfully, security held Danzig back, who returned to the stage to grumble into the microphone about certain people spoiling a good time.[42] No explanation was forthcoming from Danzig himself regarding this or the Austin incident, but these particular episodes probably did little to engender respect from younger fans.

At least Glenn Danzig could still retreat to the studio. For his band's tenth full-length release Danzig decided the time had come for his own *Project 1950* of sorts—he began assembling an album of cover songs to pay tribute to the artists and music that touched him most profoundly. In an early interview concerning the album Danzig stated that "of course" he'd be including an Elvis song, an odd statement considering the lengths the singer went to early in his career to paint himself as not much of a Presley devotee (usually in the wake of covering the King's material). Perhaps Glenn simply caved to the perceived public groupthink that an Elvis song should be on his covers record. Danzig later confirmed the covers album would include a rendition of an unknown Black Sabbath song and a duet with Runaways singer Cherie Curie. In May of 2012, Danzig leaked the first single from the project to a handful of radio stations, a cover of the obscure biker theme "Devil's Angels" by Davie Allen & the Arrows (taken from the film of the same name).[43]

A ballsy, cocksure anthem sewn up with simmering guitars, minimal production tricks, and a rich astounding vocal laid atop by Glenn, "Devil's Angels" evokes the same passion and danger as any given vintage Misfits recording. That barely contained fury, that sense of blood-pumping danger, that carefree laughter in the face of evil as Glenn ends the bridge with a joyous cry of, "Motherfucker!"—if this song were the last Glenn Anzalone ever recorded, it would be a succulent and fitting note to end on. Thankfully, there is talk of an album soon to come.

The Misfits are not a Ramones or a Nirvana or a Radiohead; they did not single-handedly sway the course of rock music a certain way, nor did they inspire legions of imitators across several continents. They created something incredibly unique, though, mixing brutality with melody in such a fashion. It touched enough people to prove monumentally important, a firm stepping stone for purveyors of the extreme and unflinching. Their touch can be heard in various critical sonic pockets since their inception. And no other band—not Metallica nor Guns n' Roses nor White Zombie nor Gwar nor Cradle of Filth—has been able to convey the same startling passion or fury as the Misfits. No other band has had the same kind of raw voice. Like the long-running horror franchises they invoke, the Misfits are oft imitated but never truly duplicated, even when they slip into self-parody or irrelevancy.

"Once I was with my friend, at his house, talking about punk names," remembers Ian MacKaye. "I said, 'You know, Danzig's not really his last name. That's a town in Poland. His real last name is [something] Italian. But who cares?' The phone rang a few minutes later and it just happened to be Glenn. My friend said to him, "Oh, we were just talking, and Ian says Danzig isn't your real name.' Glenn goes, 'Put him on phone.' 'Hello?' 'Fuck you, that *is* my last name! Don't be talking shit about me!' I was like, 'No, Danzig isn't your last name.' 'Fuck you, yes it is!'"[44]

The story is humorous but speaks to a larger fact: he may have been born Glenn Anzalone, but for all intents and purposes he is now Glenn Danzig, not just because he legally changed his name to the latter but because Glenn has transformed into that particular character he crafted oh so many years ago. In turn, Gerald and Paul Caiafa, Jim Catania, Frank LiCata, Robert Kauhfold, Joe Poole, Michael Emanuel, and the rest are the Misfits. What are they to do if they don't like it, or if others don't like it? These men cannot escape their past. Most of them rely on it to survive. It can be strange to see the human side of figures once lurched menacingly at listeners from the cover of "Beware." They have children to feed, mortgages to pay, lawsuits to settle. But nothing can diminish the accomplishment or meaning of the band's earliest pioneering efforts. That power is still present the first time anyone lays eyes on that unblinking skull staring out from a ratty old T-shirt or experiences the powerful pause that finishes off the mournful death rattle "Last Caress." "The Who never scared me," asserts Bruce McCulloch. "The Misfits scared me."[45]

Though they are currently more popular than ever, the Misfits have never really broken into the mainstream. They are not heard regularly in prime time television commercials or movie trailers. As appealing as Danzig's voice is, he's still singing about bloated corpses and blind violence most of the time. The Misfits will probably never have their music licensed for a Target advertising campaign or appear in a Pixar movie. It's just as well; such expansion would be anathema to Glenn Danzig's original concept and attitude.

"There was one time we were hanging outside CBGBs," Rosemary's Babies singer JR recalls. "There was a guy there, a skinhead, older than me, whom I really respected. He saw me talking to Glenn and asked, 'You know that guy?' 'Yeah,' I said. 'I know him, I like a few songs by his band.' Then he says, 'I really don't like them at all.' Just at that moment Glenn came over. The guy thought Glenn had heard him and started to apologize—'I'm sorry, I don't like you guys.' Glenn said, 'Ah, I don't give a fuck.' Just like that. It wasn't a sneering affectation. It was just apathetic. He really didn't care about anyone else's opinions. That, to me, was always very cool."[46]

Such is the Misfits. They aren't concerned with winning your heart or breaking it. They just want to exist. This is a band that belongs closer to the underground, a perverse delight like *Playboy* in the 1950s or a 1970s Peter Cushing vampire movie, lying in wait to be discovered by those who covet their beauty damaged and slightly unclean. In that sense, the Misfits transcend punk rock to be a true piece of Americana, a musical roadside attraction worth more than a few stops on the dark highway of life.

Annotated Misfits Discography, 1977–2012

What follows is an updated and abridged version of the exhaustive discography Mark Kennedy published in 1993 and later posted on his website, Misfits Central.com. Eternal thanks to Mark for doing the lion's share of the research in the Dark Ages of information gathering.

SINGLES

"Cough/Cool" "Cough/Cool" / "She"
Recorded June 1977 at Rainbow Studios (New York, NY)
Mastered at the Spectrum (Brooklyn, NY)
Released August 1977 via Blank Records
500 black vinyl copies (first and only pressing)
Notes: The first and rarest Misfits release is also one of the most bootlegged; as early as 1982 third parties were pressing their own versions of this disc in attempts to rip off thirsty collectors. An original "Cough/Cool" is recognized by its thin paper sleeve and large center hole in record. The sleeve itself is also of the semi-gloss variety.

"Bullet"
"Bullet" / "We Are 138" / "Attitude" / "Hollywood Babylon"
Recorded January–February 1978 at C.I. Studios (New York, NY)
Produced by Dave Achelis
Released June 1978 via Plan 9 Records
1,000 black vinyl copies (first pressing)

2,000 red vinyl copies (second pressing)

Notes: First Misfits single to include the band's first "handwritten" logo (which was, in fact, literally handwritten by Danzig). The second pressing included the slogan "better dead on red" printed on the back sleeve to trumpet the vinyl color. "Bullet" is also one of the more commonly bootlegged Misfits records. An original can be recognized by its silkscreened cover of John Kennedy's exploding cranium that boasts a matte finish; on the record itself, there should be four to five introduction grooves before the song "Bullet" begins. Furthermore, the word "dirt" on the lyrics insert is not obscured as "dint" as on various bootlegs.

"Horror Business"

"Horror Business" / "Teenagers from Mars" / "Children in Heat"

Recorded January 26–February 5, 1979, at C.I. Studios (New York, NY)

Produced by Dave Achelis

Released June 26, 1979 via Plan 9 Records

25 sleeveless black vinyl copies (first pressing)

2,000 yellow vinyl copies (second pressing)

Notes: This single marks the first appearance on Misfits record artwork of the Crimson Ghost. Approximately 20 copies of the second pressing feature the A-side label on both sides of the record. A typographical error in the original liner notes ("note esp.Teenagers from Mars") helps to distinguish between legitimate and bogus copies.

"Night of the Living Dead"

"Night of the Living Dead" / "Where Eagles Dare" / "Rat Fink"

Recorded June 1979 at the Song Shop (New York, NY)

Produced by Danny Zelonky

Released October 31, 1979, via Plan 9 Records

2,000 copies (first and only pressing)

Notes: This single's cover image is an overexposed still from a *Night of the Living Dead* trailer (the disembodied head in question does not actually appear in the final film, however). A mastering error on this record inadvertently increased the low end to overwhelming levels; "Night of the Living Dead" and "Where Eagles Dare" were both re-mixed to their proper sound for inclusion on *The Misfits* box set; "Rat Fink," however, went into the box set uncorrected.

"Halloween"
"Halloween" / "Halloween II"
Recorded 1981 at Mix-O-Lydian Studio (Boonton, NJ)
Produced by Mike Taylor/The Misfits
Released October 30, 1981, via Plan 9 Records
5,000 copies (first and only pressing)
Notes: This single marks the first appearance of the *Famous Monsters of Filmland*–style Misfits logo that the band would continue using for the rest of their career. Ten copies of "Halloween" exist that feature a black-and-white sleeve.

"Die, Die My Darling"
"Die, Die My Darling" / "We Bite" / "Mommy, Can I Go Out & Kill Tonight?"
Recorded July 1983 at Fox Studio (Rutherford, NJ)
Produced by Spot/The Misfits
Released May 1984 via Plan 9 Records
5,000 black vinyl, 500 purple vinyl copies (first pressing)
500 white vinyl copies (second pressing) [May 1986]
Unknown amount (third pressing) [1986]
Notes: The Misfits swiped the cover image for "Die, Die" from a 1950s issue of the pulp comic *Chamber of Chills*. Fourth and fifth pressings of this record in unknown quantities were done in 1991 and 1994, respectively, courtesy of Caroline Records.

"Dig Up Her Bones"
"Dig Up Her Bones" / "Hate the Living, Love the Dead"
Recorded December 1996 at Dreamland Recording Studio (Woodstock, NY) [instruments]; January 1997 at Spa Recording Studio (New York, NY) [vocals], and Baby Monster Studios (New York, NY) [sound effects]
Produced by Daniel Rey
Released July 1997 via Geffen Records
5,000 blue vinyl copies, 1 black vinyl copy, unknown amount of CD copies
Notes: The cover image for this single is a blue-tinted profile photo of *Bride of Frankenstein* star Elsa Lanchester.

"I Wanna Be a NY Ranger"
"I Wanna Be a NY Ranger"

Recorded June 1998 at Pro Edge (Vernon, NJ)

Produced by John Cafiero/The Misfits

Released August 1998 via Non-Homogenized Productions Ltd

50 CD copies (first and only pressing)

Notes: Misfits Creative Director John Cafiero performs vocals on this single.

"Scream!"

"Scream!"

Recorded April 1999 at Dreamland Recording Studio (Woodstock, NY)

Produced by Daniel Rey/Ed Stasium/The Misfits

Released September 1999 via Roadrunner Records

Unknown amount of CD copies (first and only pressing)

Notes: The cover image for this single is a yellow Misfits logo on a field of purple.

"Monster Mash"

"Monster Mash" / "Monster Mash"

Recorded October 18, 1997, at Power Play Studios (Newark, NJ)

Released October 31, 1999, via Misfits Records

100 red vinyl, 100 gold vinyl, 800 green vinyl copies, and 1,000 CD copies

Notes: On December 29, 1999, Misfits Records issued 1,000 glow-in-thedark vinyl copies

"Day the Earth Caught Fire"

"Day the Earth Caught Fire" / "The Haunting/Don't Open 'til Doomsday" (performed by Balzac)

Recorded: unknown

Produced by John Cafiero/Jerry Only/Balzac

Released 2002 via Misfits Records (CD)

Notes: This CD single is a split with Japanese punk band Balzac, who perform two songs from *American Psycho*.

EPs

Beware

"We Are 138" / "Bullet" / "Hollywood Babylon" / "Attitude" / "Horror Business" / "Teenagers from Mars" / "Last Caress"

Recorded January–February 1979 at C.I. Studios (New York, NY)

Track 7 remixed September 1979 at C.I. Studios (New York, NY)

Released January 1980 via Plan 9 Records/Armageddon/Spartan/Cherry Red

3,120 black vinyl copies (first and only pressing)

Notes: For years *Beware* was just as widely bootlegged as "Cough/Cool" due to its relative rarity in the United States. Originals are recognized by the matrix etching on the actual record that says "max" and gray shading amid the black-and-white "fun house" image of the band on the front cover. Many European bootlegs are also pressed on colored vinyl; the one and only true pressing was black vinyl.

3 Hits from Hell

"London Dungeon" / "Horror Hotel" / "Ghoul's Night Out"

Recorded August 1980 at Master Sound Productions (Franklin Square, NY)

Released April 1981 via Plan 9 Records

10,000 black vinyl copies (first pressing)

400 white vinyl copies, 400 black vinyl copies (second pressing)

Notes: 7,000 copies of the first pressing feature a light gray label on record while the remaining 3,000 feature a red/orange label; most original copies also have "R-10261" etched into A-side matrix and "R-10262" in B-side matrix.

Evilive

"20 Eyes" / "Night of the Living Dead" / "Astro Zombies" / "Horror Business" / "London Dungeon" / "All Hell Breaks Loose" / "We Are 138"

Tracks 1–5 recorded live December 17, 1981, at the Ritz (New York, NY)

Tracks 6–7 recorded live November 20, 1981, at the On Broadway Club (San Francisco, CA)

Produced by the Misfits

Released December 1982 via Plan 9 Records

2,099 copies (first pressing)

Notes: 99 copies of the original *Evilive* were sold in 33 bundled editions that included three copies of the EP with alternate cover images of Danzig, Jerry, and Doyle. In 1983 the EP was licensed by Aggressive Rock Productions for release in West Germany; the company pressed at least 12,000 black vinyl copies and repressed it twice more through 1988. Caroline Records issued an expanded version of *Evilive* on cassette October 15, 1987, adding "Nike-a-Go-Go" and "Hatebreeders" from the Ritz performance and "Devil's Whorehouse," "Horror

Hotel," and "Ghoul's Night Out" from the On Broadway performance. Several versions of the expanded *Evilive* were also issued on 2,000 copies of green vinyl and an unknown quantities of black vinyl between 1987 and 1997. A CD version was also released in March of 1997.

Psycho in the Wax Museum
"Angel Baby" / "Death of the Fallen Angel"
Recorded December 1996 at Dreamland Recording Studio (Woodstock, NY)
Produced by Daniel Rey
Released 2006 via Misfits Records
Unknown amount of clear vinyl copies (first and only pressing)
Notes: This EP was available for free with three proofs of purchase from other Misfits releases.

LPs

Walk Among Us
"20 Eyes" / "I Turned into a Martian" / "All Hell Breaks Loose" / "Vampira" / "Nike-a-Go-Go" / "Hatebreeders" / "Mommy, Can I Go Out & Kill Tonight?" / "Night of the Living Dead" / "Skulls" / "Violent World" / "Devil's Whorehouse" / "Astro Zombies" / "Brain Eaters"
Track 6 recorded June 1981 at Newfound Sound (Fair Lawn, NJ)
Track 7 recorded live December 17, 1981, at The Ritz (New York, NY)
All other tracks recorded no later than August 1981 at Mix-O-Lydian Studio (Boonton, NJ)
Overdubs recorded January 1982 at Quad Teck (Los Angeles, CA)
Produced by Mike Taylor/The Misfits/Pat Burnette
Released March 1982 via Ruby/Slash
35,000–37,000 black vinyl copies with pink cover (first pressing)
Unknown amount of black vinyl copies with purple cover (second pressing) [1982]
Notes: An unknown amount of black vinyl copies with a darker pink cover were licensed for Italian label Expanded Music in 1982; after Warner Brothers acquired Ruby/Slash the former reissued *Walk Among Us* several times in unknown quantities across several formats between 1988 and 2012. For Record Store Day in 2012, Warner subsidiary Rhino Records pressed 1,500 purple vinyl, 1,250 red vinyl, 1,250 blue vinyl, and 500 clear vinyl copies of the album with a pink cover.

Earth A.D./Wolfs Blood

"Earth A.D." / "Queen Wasp" / "Devilock" / "Death Comes Ripping" / "Green Hell" / "Wolfs Blood" / "Demonomania" / "Bloodfeast" / "Hellhound"

"Earth A.D." / "Queen Wasp" / "Devilock" / "Death Comes Ripping" / "Green Hell" / "Mommy, Can I Go Out & Kill Tonight?" / "Wolfs Blood" / "Demonomania" / "Bloodfeast" / "Hellhound" / "Die, Die My Darling" / "We Bite"

Tracks 1, 2, 3, 6, and 7 recorded October 3, 1982, at Unicorn Recording Studio (Santa Monica, CA) [instruments] and June 1983 at Mix-OLy-dian (Boonton, NJ) [vocals]

Tracks 4, 5, 8, and 9 recorded July 1983, Fox Studio (Rutherford, NJ)

Produced by Spot/The Misfits

Released December 12, 1983, via Plan 9 Records

10,000 black, 100 green, 500 yellow, 200 purple, and 200 clear vinyl copies (first pressing)

Notes: Underground artist Marc Rude drew *Earth A.D.*'s busy cover image featuring the Misfits as zombies surrounded by fans; the sketch took him approximately 300 hours to complete. This album was licensed to Aggressive Rock Productions in 1983 and released in Germany as *Wolfs Blood/Earth A.D.* in 15,000 black vinyl copies. In 1984 Plan 9 issued an expanded version of *Earth A.D./Wolfs Blood* on cassette that included the "Die, Die My Darling" single in its entirety. Caroline Records pressed an unknown amount of copies across various formats between 1986 and 1992 (including 15,000 "gold" CD copies in 1992). In 1991 Modern Music released *Wolfs Blood/Earth A.D.* with *Evilive* on CD.

American Psycho

"The Abominable Dr. Phibes" / "American Psycho" / "Speak of the Devil" / "Walk Among Us" / "The Hunger" / "From Hell They Came" / "Dig Up Her Bones" / "Blacklight" / "Resurrection" / "This Island Earth" / "Crimson Ghost" / "Day of the Dead" / "The Haunting" / "Mars Attacks" / "Hate the Living, Love the Dead" / "Shining" / "Don't Open 'til Doomsday"

Recorded December 1996 at Dreamland Recording Studio (Woodstock, NY) [instruments]; January 1997 at Spa Recording Studio (New York, NY) [vocals], Baby Monster Studio (New York, NY) [sound effects], and Creepy Attic Studio (Lodi, NJ) [special effects]

Produced by Daniel Rey

Released May 13, 1997, via Geffen Records

Notes: *Famous Monsters of Filmland* cover artist Basil Gogos crafted the image of the Crimson Ghost that graces the front of this record. Geffen Records released an unknown quantity of *American Psycho* across a variety of formats in the US, Europe, and Sweden between May of 1997 and May of 1998. LP copies include the exclusive track "Dead Kings Rise" while CD copies contain the exclusive "Hell Night" as a final hidden track.

Static Age

"Static Age" / "TV Casualty" / "Some Kinda Hate" / "Last Caress" / "Return of the Fly" / "Hybrid Moments" / "We Are 138" / "Teenagers from Mars" / "Come Back" / "Angelfuck" / "Hollywood Babylon" / "Attitude" / "Bullet" / "Theme for a Jackal" / "She" / "Spinal Remains" / "In the Doorway" / "Studio Chatter"

Recorded January–February 1978, at C.I. Studios (New York, NY)

Produced by Dave Achelis/Tom Bejgrowicz

Released July 15, 1997, via Caroline Records

3,500 black, 2,000 red, 1,000 yellow/orange, 500 purple vinyl copies (first pressing)

Unknown amount of black vinyl copies released to U.K. (second pressing) [July 28, 1997]

Notes: The second pressing of this album was delayed due to customs issues.

Evilive II

"Intro (Creepy Church)" / "Abominable Dr. Phibes" / "American Psycho" / "Walk Among Us" / "The Hunger" / "From Hell They Came" / "Speak of the Devil" / "Last Caress" / "Dig Up Her Bones" / "American Nightmare" / "Day of the Dead" / "Hate the Living, Love the Dead" / "Shining" / "Don't Open 'til Doomsday" / "This Island Earth" / "Where Eagles Dare" / "Bullet" / "Vampira" / "The Haunting" / "Die, Die My Darling"

Recorded October 31, 1997–March 10, 1998, various North American concert venues

Released August 14, 1998 via the Fiend Club (CD only)

Notes: The cover boasts a drawing by renowned artists Pushead.

Famous Monsters

"Kong at the Gates" / "Forbidden Zone" / "Lost in Space" / "Dust to Dust" / "Crawling Eye" / "Witch Hunt" / "Scream!" / "Saturday

Night" / "Pumpkin Head" / "Scarecrow Man" / "Die Monster Die" / "Living Hell" / "Descending Angel" / "Them" / "Fiend Club" / "Hunting Humans" / "Helena" / "Kong Unleashed"

Recorded April 12–June 9, 1999, at Dreamland Recording Studio (Woodstock, NY)

Produced by Daniel Rey

Released October 5, 1999, via Roadrunner Records

10,000 CDs released in Japan (first pressing) [September 4, 1999] Unknown amount of CD, cassette, and vinyl copies; 5,000 picture discs (second pressing) [October 5, 1999]

1,500 yellow vinyl and 1,500 purple vinyl copies (third pressing) [January 2000]

Notes: Ramones Artistic Director Arturo Vega designed the packaging for *Famous Monsters*, though the cover painting of the band was crafted by Basil Gogos. This album reached no. 138 on the Billboard Rock Chart.

12 Hits from Hell

"Halloween" / "Vampira" / "I Turned into a Martian" / "Skulls" / "London Dungeon" / "Night of the Living Dead" / "Horror Hotel" / "Ghoul's Night Out" / "Astro Zombies" / "Where Eagles Dare" / "Violent World" / "Halloween II" / "London Dungeon" (alternate take)

Recorded August 5–September 5, 1980, at Master Sound Productions (Franklin Square, NY)

Produced by Robbie Alter

Scheduled for release October 30, 2001; cancelled October 15, 2001

3 black vinyl test copies, 2,000 promotional CDs, unknown amount of CD-Rs, 40,000 regular CDs (first and only pressing; all allegedly destroyed)

Notes: Outside the original Misfits releases, *12 Hits from Hell* is probably the most sought-after and bootlegged release. Despite the official line that all copies were destroyed many record stores and distributors had already received promotional and sales discs by the time *12 Hits* was officially cancelled. Thus, copies survive to this day, and high-quality files of the material float around the Internet.

Project 1950

"This Magic Moment" / "Dream Lover" / "Diana" / "Donna" / "Great Balls of Fire" / "Latest Flame" / "Monster Mash" / "Only Make Believe" / "Runaway" / "You Belong to Me"

Recorded: unknown

Produced by The Misfits

Released July 29, 2003 via Misfits Records/Rykodisc

Unknown amount of CD copies and 1,000 blue vinyl copies (first pressing)

Unknown amount of CD copies, 1,000 purple vinyl, 3,000 neon green vinyl copies released in Europe (second pressing)

Notes: *Project 1950* included a bonus DVD with CD copies that contains various live clips of the band, including three songs performed at the 2003 Phillips U.S. Open Snowboarding Championships. Japanese version swapped out the DVD for a Misfits/Balzac split single. This album also spread across several Billboard charts, hitting no. 133 on Billboard 200, no. 2 on the Heatseekers Albums chart, and no. 5 Independent Albums chart.

The Devil's Rain

"The Devil's Rain" / "Vivid Red" / "Land of the Dead" / "The Black Hole" / "Twilight of the Dead" / "Curse of the Mummy's Hand" / "Cold in Hell" / "Unexplained" / "Dark Shadows" / "Father" / "Jack The Ripper" / "Monkey's Paw" / "Where Do They Go?" / "Sleepwalkin'" / "Ghost of Frankenstein" / "Death Ray"

Recorded 2011 at Eagle Sound (Durango, CO)

Overdubs/mixing completed at KozyTone Ranch (Durango, CO)

Produced by Ed Stasium/John Cafiero

Released October 4, 2011, via Misfits Records

Unknown amount of CD and black vinyl copies (first pressing)

Notes: Basil Gogos once again painted the Crimson Ghost for this album's cover. *The Devil's Rain* peaked at no. 70 on the Billboard 200.

COMPILATIONS

Legacy of Brutality

"Static Age" / "TV Casualty" / "Hybrid Moments" / "Spinal Remains" / "Come Back" / "Some Kinda Hate" / "Theme for a Jackal" / "Angelfuck" / "Who Killed Marilyn?" / "Where Eagles Dare" / "She" / "Halloween" / "American Nightmare"

Tracks 1–8 and 11 recorded January–February 1978 at C.I. Recording Studio (New York, NY)

Tracks 9 and 10 recorded January 26–February 5, 1979, at C.I. Recording Studio (New York, NY)

Track 12 recorded August/September 1980 at Master Sound Productions (Franklin Square, NY)

Track 13 recorded June 1981 at Newfound Sounds Studios (Fair Lawn, NJ)

Overdubs/remixing recorded 1985 at Reel Platinum (Lodi, NJ)

Produced by Glenn Danzig

Released September 1985 via Plan 9/Caroline

10,000 black vinyl, 2,800 black cassettes (first pressing)

500 white vinyl, 500 red vinyl, 16 pink vinyl copies (second pressing) [March 1986]

Notes: Caroline Records issued a third pressing of unknown quantity on LP, cassette, and CD in October 1989.

Misfits/Collection I

"She" / "Hollywood Babylon" / "Bullet" / "Horror Business" / "Teenagers from Mars" / "Night of the Living Dead" / "Where Eagles Dare" / "Vampira" / "I Turned into a Martian" / "Skulls" / "London Dungeon" / "Ghoul's Night Out" / "Astro Zombies" / "Mommy, Can I Go Out & Kill Tonight?" / "Die, Die My Darling" / "Earth A.D." / "Devilock" / "Death Comes Ripping" / "Green Hell" / "Wolfs Blood"

Tracks 1–3 recorded January–February 1978 at C.I. Recording Studio (New York, NY)

Tracks 4, 5, and 7 recorded January 26–February 5, 1979, at C.I. Recording Studio (New York, NY)

Tracks 6, 8, and 10–13 recorded August/September 1980 at Master Sound Productions (Franklin Square, NY)

Track 9 recorded 1981 at Mix-O-Lydian Studio (Boonton, NJ)

Tracks 14–20 recorded at Fox Studio (Rutherford, NJ)

Overdubs/remixing recorded 1986 at Reel Platinum (Lodi, NJ)

Produced by Glenn Danzig

Released July 1, 1986, via Plan 9/Caroline

Notes: This compilation was originally untitled and originally CD-only until bootleggers began pressing it on vinyl. Caroline Records issued second and third pressings of unknown quantity in October of 1988 and April of 1994, respectively. The third pressing marked *Legacy of Brutality*'s CD debut.

Collection II

"We Are 138" / "Attitude" / "Cough/Cool" / "Last Caress" / "Return of the Fly" / "Children in Heat" / "Rat Fink" / "Horror Hotel" / "Halloween" / "Halloween II" / "Hatebreeders" / "Brain Eaters" / "Nike-a-

Go-Go" / "Devil's Whorehouse" / "Mephisto Waltz" / "We Bite" / "Queen Wasp" / "Demonomania" / "Hellhound" / "Bloodfeast"

Tracks 1, 2, and 5 recorded January–February 1978 at C.I. Recording Studio (New York, NY)

Tracks 3 and 11–15 recorded August 1986 at Reel Platinum (Lodi, NJ)

Track 4 recorded September 1979 at C.I. Recording Studio (New York, NY)

Track 6 recorded January 26–February 5, 1979, at C.I. Recording Studio (New York, NY)

Track 7 recorded June 1979 at the Song Shop Studio (New York, NY)

Track 8 recorded August 1980 at Master Sound Productions (Franklin Square, NY)

Tracks 9 and 10 recorded 1981 at Mix-O-Lydian (Boonton, NJ)

Tracks 16–20 recorded July 1983 at Fox Studio (Rutherford, NJ)

Produced by Glenn Danzig

Released November 14, 1995, via Caroline

100,000 CDs, 500 clear vinyl, 6,000 red vinyl, 3,500 green vinyl (first pressing)

Notes: Caroline issued a second pressing of black vinyl in an unknown quantity in April 1996. *Collection II* rose to no. 33 on the Billboard Heatseekers Chart.

Cuts from the Crypt

"Dead Kings Rise" (demo) / "Blacklight" (demo) / "The Haunting" (demo) / "The Hunger" (demo) / "Mars Attacks" (demo) / "Dr. Phibes Rises Again" / "I Got a Right" / "Monster Mash" / "I Wanna Be a NY Ranger" / "Scream!" (demo) / "1,000,000 Years B.C." / "Helena 2" / "Devil Doll" / "Fiend without a Face" / "Bruiser" / "No More Moments" / "Rise Above" (live)

Tracks 1–6 recorded August 2001 at the Snuff Factory (Helmetta, NJ)

Track 7 recorded March 1997 at Baby Monsters Studios (New York, NY)

Track 8 recorded October 1997 at Power Play Studios (Newark, NJ)

Track 9 recorded June 1998 at Pro Edge (Vernon, NJ)

Track 10 recorded 1998 in Phoenix, AZ

Tracks 11, 12, 13, and 18 recorded April 1999 at Dreamland Recording Studio (Woodstock, NY)

Tracks 14 and 15 recorded August 1999 at Castle Oaks Studios (Toronto, ON)

Track 16 recorded 2000 at Water Studios (Hoboken, NJ)

Track 17 recorded live July 29, 2001, at Bar Opiniao (Porto Alegre, Brazil)

Produced by John Cafiero/The Misfits

Released December 29, 1999, Roadrunner Records (CD)
Notes: This disc is comprised of various *American Psycho* and *Famous Monsters* era outtakes/unreleased material.

BOX SETS

The Misfits
DISC 1: "She" / "Hollywood Babylon" / "Horror Business" / "Teenagers from Mars" / "Night of the Living Dead" / "Where Eagles Dare" / "Vampira" / "I Turned into a Martian" / "Skulls" / "London Dungeon" / "Ghoul's Night Out" / "Astro Zombies" / "Mommy, Can I Go Out & Kill Tonight?" / "Die, Die My Darling" / "Cough/Cool" / "Children in Heat" / "Horror Hotel" / "Halloween" / "Halloween II" / "Hatebreeders" / "Brain Eaters" / "Nike-a-Go-Go" / "Devil's Whorehouse" / "Mephisto Waltz" / "Rat Fink" / "We Bite"
DISC 2: "Static Age" / "TV Casualty" / "Hybrid Moments" / "Spinal Remains" / "Come Back" / "Some Kinda Hate" / "Theme for a Jackal" / "Angelfuck" / "Who Killed Marilyn?" / "Where Eagles Dare" / "She" / "Halloween" / "American Nightmare" / "20 Eyes" / "Night of the Living Dead" / "Astro Zombies" / "Horror Business" / "London Dungeon" / "All Hell Breaks Loose" / "We Are 138" / "Earth A.D." / "Queen Wasp" / "Devilock" / "Death Comes Ripping" / "Green Hell" "Wolfs Blood" / "Demonomania" / "Bloodfeast" / "Hellhound"
DISC 3: "Cough/Cool" / "She" / "Who Killed Marilyn?" / "Where Eagles Dare" / "Horror Business" / "Teenagers from Mars" / "Children in Heat" / "Night of the Living Dead" / "Where Eagles Dare" / "Vampira" / "Violent World" / "Who Killed Marilyn?" / "Spook City, U.S.A." / "Horror Business" / "I Turned into a Martian" / "Skulls" / "Night of the Living Dead" / "Astro Zombies" / "Where Eagles Dare" / "Violent World" / "Halloween II" / "20 Eyes" / "I Turned into a Martian" / "Astro Zombies" / "Vampira" / "Devil's Whorehouse" / "Nike-a-Go-Go" / "Hatebreeders" / "20 Eyes" / "Violent World"
DISC 4: "Intro" / "Static Age" / "TV Casualty" / "Some Kinda Hate" / "Last Caress" / "Return of the Fly" / "Hybrid Moments" / "We Are 138" / "Teenagers from Mars" / "Come Back" / "Angelfuck" / "Hollywood Babylon" / "Attitude" / "Bullet" / "Theme for A Jackal" / "Outro"

Disc 1 compiled from *Misfits/Collection 1* and *Collection II*
Disc 2 compiled from *Legacy of Brutality*, *Evilive*, and *Earth A.D./Wolfs Blood*

Disc 3 includes "Cough/Cool" single and various studio outtakes circa 1979–1981

Disc 4 compiled from *Static Age*

Produced by Tom Bejgrowicz

Released February 27, 1996, via Caroline Records (CD)

50,000 copies (first pressing)

(second pressing) [June 1997]

Notes: All copies housed in a coffin-shaped box. The first pressing included a Fiend Club badge, a special jewel case for *Static Age*, and slim cases for other discs. Caroline issued a second pressing of unknown quantity in June 1997. *The Misfits* charted at no. 36 on Billboard's Heatseekers.

NOTABLE APPEARANCES ON COMPILATIONS FEATURING OTHER ARTISTS

Flipside Vinyl Fanzine Vol. 2

"Attitude"

Recorded live December 20, 1978, at Max's Kansas City (New York, NY)

Released 1984 via Flipside/Gasatanka (vinyl)

Reissued on *The Best of Flipside Vinyl Fanzines* CD [November 1993]

We Will Fall: A Tribute to Iggy Pop

"1969"

"I Got a Right"

Recorded March 23, 1997, at Baby Monster Studio (New York, NY)

Released September 16, 1997, via Royalty Records

Noted for: While "1969" is technically a Joey Ramone solo track, Dr. Chud and Jerry Only comprise his rhythm section while producer Daniel Rey plays guitar. "I Got a Right" is the full Graves-era lineup of the band.

Just Can't Get Enough: New Wave Halloween

"Halloween"

Recorded August 1980 at Master Sound Productions (Franklin Square, NY)

Released June 30, 1998, via Rhino Records

Short Music for Short People

"NY Ranger"

Recorded April 1999 at Fat Wreck Studio (New York, NY)

Released June 1, 1999, via Fat Wreck Chords

Noted for: This is a rerecording of the earlier single featuring Michale Graves on vocals.

VIDEOS

"Brain Eaters"

Taped March 20, 1983, Derkin Park, Boston, MA

Produced/Directed by the Misfits

Notes: Never released.

"Dig Up Her Bones"

Produced/Directed by John and Suzanne Cafiero

Released August 10, 1997

"Abominable Dr. Phibes / American Psycho"

Produced/Directed by John and Suzanne Cafiero

Released January 11, 1998

Notes: A 16mm film version of these clips were shown before an October 30, 1998, screening of *Mad Monster Party* in New York City.

"Monster Mash" (live)

Produced/Directed by John Cafiero.

Released October 28, 1998

Notes: This video consisted of Misfits live footage spliced together with scenes from *Mad Monster Party*.

"Scream!"

Directed by George Romero

Released October 5, 1999

NOTABLE MISFITS CONCERT BOOTLEGS

Max's Kansas City (New York, NY), December 20, 1978 [audio]

This show, the band's second at Max's that evening, is noted for as a great example of the early Misfits synergy and for its thirty-second cover of the Elvis Presley holiday hit "Blue Christmas."

Studio Zero (New York, NY), January 1979 [video]

Jerry and Glenn goof off with their friends (who include Howie Pyro and Trixie Sly) in this twenty-minute recording where they play New York Dolls songs, Stooges songs, and the Joey Dee and the Starlighters hit "Peppermint Twist."

The Pit (Lodi, NJ), September 1981 [audio]

A twenty-seven-minute recording of the Misfits rehearsing in the Caiafa family garage. Notable because it captures the band introducing drummer Arthur Googy to "Queen Wasp," which they spend several minutes trying to hammer out. This tape was allegedly recorded by Dave Schwartzman of neighboring hardcore band Adrenalin O.D. who says it only became public after someone swiped it from his car during a trip into Manhattan.

Hittsville (Passaic, NJ), December 25, 1981 [audio]

Maybe the most famous Misfits live bootleg in existence, if not for the band's constantly malfunctioning equipment then for Danzig's ridiculously livid stage patter. To wit: the singer insults not only those in attendance as "fuckin' jerks" but also derides those who chose to stay home as "asshole[s]"; later, during "London Dungeon," he bitterly announces, "I hate the fuckin' British!" This bootleg also captures one of the more venom-filled renditions of "Teenagers from Mars" featuring the anti-Bobby Steele lyrics ("We don't care that Bobby Steele sucks!" Danzig announces between lines of the chorus).

Group W Cable (Dearborn, Michigan), January 7, 1983 [video]

The Misfits perform in a storage room at a television station for a smattering of fans; the entire show is videotaped for a cable access program called *Why Be Something You're Not?* During the interview portion of the program, Danzig jokes that his real name is Slim Whitman.

Channel Club (Boston, MA), March 20, 1983 [video]

This relatively excellent multiple camera recording was originally commissioned for a Flipside video magazine but was shelved for legal reasons.

Graystone Hall (Detroit, MI), October 29, 1983 [audio/video]
The final Misfits show with Danzig, the longest show the band played with Danzig as well. "Night of the Living Dead" is played twice. A few songs into the set, Danzig goes on an epic rant about stage divers.

ESSENTIAL MISFITS-RELATED RELEASES

The Victims—s/t
(Plan 9, 1978)
Four song single from this New York City band contains sex-starved classics "Annette" and "I Want Head"; the only non-Danzig release on Plan 9 Records.

Active Ingredients—"Hyper Exaggeration"
(Active Records, 1980)
Franché Coma's after-Misfits project, reminiscent of Devo in its frenetic keyboard mania.

Glenn Danzig—"Who Killed Marilyn?"
(Plan 9, 1981)
Danzig's first solo release boasts "Spook City, U.S.A." on the flip side.

The Necros—"IQ32"
(Dischord/Touch & Go, 1981)
Explosive hardcore rager from Midwestern Misfits pals.

The Undead—*Nine Toes Later*
(Stiff/Post Mortem, 1982)
Debut from Bobby Steele's long-running Lower East Side contingent, financed by Danzig. The title references the forced amputation of Steele's infected digit.

Antidote—*Thou Shall Not Kill*
(Antidote Records, 1983)
Walk Among Us drummer Arthur Googy provides the backbone for this fierce hardcore slab still coveted by scenesters today.

Samhain—*Initium*
(Plan 9, 1984)
Haunting inaugural outing from Glenn Danzig's more visceral mutation of the Misfits.

Samhain—*November-Coming-Fire*
(Plan 9, 1986)
A perfect blend of punk rock and goth atmosphere; the last true Samhain record before the band was retrofitted into Danzig.

Danzig—s/t
(Def American, 1988)
The taut hard rock major label debut from Glenn Danzig that began a four-album dynasty.

Kryst the Conqueror—*Deliver Us from Evil*
(Cyclopean Music, 1989)
Jerry Only and brother Doyle go power metal with a friend from the neighborhood and an uncredited Jeff Scott Soto. A full album expanding on this cocksure material remains unreleased.

Danzig—*4p*
(Def American, 1994)
The final hard rockin' dance for the classic Danzig lineup of Glenn, Eerie, John Christ, and Chuck Biscuits.

Graves—*Web of Dharma*
(GDU Records, 2002)
Michale Graves and Dr. Chud prove themselves outside the Misfits with a collection of spook-drenched pop punk.

Rosemary's Babies—*Talking to the Dead*
(Ghastly Records, 2004)
Expanded edition of this forgotten Lodi group's early 1980s *Blood Lust* EP, including the bone-rattling ten-second rant "What I Hate" and the perverse ode to Vice Squad's singer "Becky Bondage."

Son of Sam—*Songs from the Earth*
(Nitro Records, 2001)
More solid goth punk from AFI's Davey Havok, Danzig's Todd Youth,
and Samhain members Steve Zing and London May.

SCRAPPED MISFITS RELEASES

"Teenagers from Mars" single (1978)
Six acetates of this seven inch were pressed, one with "Teenagers from
Mars" on both sides and five with "Teenagers" on one side and "Static
Age" on the other. The band decided not to print the single after all,
keeping two copies and giving the rest away (early Misfits supporter
George Germain received both the double "Teenagers" copy and a
regular copy; the remaining two were donated to the jukeboxes of
Max's Kansas City and CBGBs).

"Who Killed Marilyn?" EP (1979)
This twelve-inch record would have combined the tracks from "Horror
Business" with the titular song and "Teenagers from Mars." An ace-
tate was pressed but completing a run of twelve-inch records was
ultimately deemed too expensive.

Walk Among Us (Plan 9 version, 1981)
The Misfits had already put together the material for their debut album
before signing with Ruby/Slash. Aside from the specific takes and/or
mixing differences, this version of the album would have included
"Horror Hotel," "Ghoul's Night Out," and "American Nightmare."

Enter at Your Own Risk (1986)
A Misfits "greatest hits" release planned by Danzig that was absorbed
into *Collection II*.

Walk Among Us 2 (1986)
This proposed "sequel" to *Walk Among Us* would have featured alternate
versions of many of the original album's songs, ostensibly so Glenn
could navigate around Warner Brothers' alleged non-payment of *Walk*
royalties.

Xmas at Max's (1994)

Jerry and Doyle dubbed new instrumental tracks over a December 25, 1978, performance by the band at Max's Kansas City for a Caroline release; it was scrapped after complaint from Danzig.

NOTABLE FILMS THAT INFLUENCED THE MISFITS

The Misfits have drawn inspiration from myriad film sources over the years. Here is a rundown of key cinematic horror exercises that ingrained themselves into the band's DNA—for better or worse.

The Abominable Dr. Phibes (1971)

Widowed Roaring Twenties scientist (Vincent Price) with a penchant for pounding the organ avenges his wife's death at the hands of several doctors. *Absolutely Fabulous* star Joanna Lumley had her scenes as a comely lab assistant cut from this cult classic at the last minute. Directed by Robert Fuest.

The Astro-Zombies (1968)

Bitter space doctor (John Carradine) creates undead slave who goes crazy and kicks off a wild government chase. Wayne Rogers of "M*A*S*H" fame shares a co-writing credit on this film's screenplay. Directed by Ted V. Mikels.

The Black Hole (1979)

The *USS Palomino*, an intergalactic exploratory vessel, searches for answers regarding a fellow ship's disappearance in the year 2130 A.D. The first non-G rated film in the Disney canon. Directed by Gary Nelson.

Bloodfeast (1979)

A deranged caterer of Egyptian descent (Mal Arnold) goes on a gore spree in the suburbs of Miami. Considered a landmark in shock cinema, not just for what's onscreen but for the producers' publicity tactics—barf bags were often handed out at theaters presenting this blood orgy. Directed by Herschel Gordon Lewis.

Boxing Helena (1993)

Disembodied female head (Sherilyn Fenn) torments surgeon (Julian Sands) who was once obsessed with the entire woman. Kim Basinger's decision to pull out of the title role resulted in a messy lawsuit that succeeded in derailing her career. Directed by Jennifer Chambers Lynch, daughter of David.

The Brain Eaters (1958)

Riverdale, Illinois, is besieged by intergalactic parasites who can control the human mind. Shot in a mere six days with an estimated budget of $30,000. Directed by Bruno VeSota.

The Bride of Frankenstein (1935)

One of horror's earliest and greatest sequels focuses on finding Dr. Frankenstein's monstrous creation an equally odd mate. Directed by James Whale.

The Crawling Eye (1958)

Telepathic cloud of alien evil goes on a killing spree near Swiss resort. Inspired John Carpenter to later make *The Fog*. Directed by Quentin Lawrence.

The Crimson Ghost (1946)

Serial that follows a dastardly masked supervillain and his schemes to steal a counter-atomic device known as Cyclotrode X. Linda Stirling, who garnered acclaim as the feline lead in 1944's *Tiger Woman*, worked as a writer on this series. Directed by Fred C. Brannon and William Witney.

Daleks' Invasion Earth: 2150 A.D. (1966)

Beloved time traveler Dr. Who (Peter Cushing) thwarts the fiendish future plans of those fiendish mutants the Daleks. Financed by Sugar Puffs cereal—hence the shameless product placement. Directed by Gordon Flemyng.

Day of the Dead (1983)

The third entry in the *Night of the Living Dead* series wherein a team of human scientists trapped underground attempt to domesticate a captured zombie. Directed by George Romero.

Descending Angel (1990)

Newlywed (Eric Roberts) fears his father-in-law (George C. Scott) may be a retired Nazi mass murderer. Produced as a made-for-TV movie for HBO. Directed by Jeremy Kagan.

Devil Dog: The Hound of Hell (1978)

A precursor to *Cujo*, this film places a nuclear family dangerously close to the jaws of a rabid satanic dog. Features *First Blood* star Richard Crenna as the family patriarch. Directed by Curtis Harrington.

The Devil's Rain (1975)

One of William Shatner's most celebrated B-movie roles. Shat plays a rugged rancher whose entire existence is cursed by a rogue satanist (Ernest Borgnine). This film marks the only instance in which John Travolta would share a credit with Anton LaVey. Directed by Robert Fuest.

Die! Die! My Darling! (1965)

Religious fanatic (Tallulah Bankhead) abducts former daughter-in-law (Stefanie Powers) in a misguided attempt to cleanse her of sin. Ms. Bankhead's final film before expiring from pneumonia, the flu, and emphysema. Directed by Silvio Narizzano.

Die, Monster, Die! (1965)

A meteorite infects the lives of an American scientist (Nick Adams) and his crippled father-in-law (Boris Karloff). Written by famed Star Trek scribe Jerry Sohl. Directed by Daniel Haller.

The Fly (1958)

A scientist's (David Hedison) teleportation device yields horrific results when a common insect invades the test area. Based on a short story that originally appeared in a 1957 issue of *Playboy*. Directed by Kurt Neumann.

From Hell It Came (1957)

Furious tree stump monster terrorizes residents of a South Seas island; American doctors William Arnold (Tod Andrews) and Terry Mason (Tina Carver) set out to extinguish its rootsy evil. Directed by Dan Milner.

The Ghost of Frankenstein (1942)

Ygor (Bela Lugosi) and Dr. Frankenstein's son Ludwig (Sir Cedric Hardwicke) revive the undead monster from the previous films with the expected results. Lon Chaney Jr. would regularly drink while filming his role as the titular creature and often got lost inside the movie's intricate sets. Directed by Erie C. Kenton.

Green Hell (1940)

Tensions abound as a group of explorers traverse the South American jungle in search of forgotten treasure. Co-star Vincent Price considered this one of the worst films on his résumé. Directed by James Whale.

The Haunting (1963)

Spooky mansion frightens its doubting guests with all manner of ghostly activities. Considered one of best fright pictures of its era. Directed by Robert Wise.

Hell Night (1981)

Quartet of college freshman must spend one evening in a haunted house to prove their mettle; of course they start dying once the door slams behind them. Future *Shawshank Redemption* director Frank Darabont worked as a production assistant on this cult classic. Directed by Tom DiSimone.

The Hills Have Eyes (1977)

Deranged hillfolk menace all-American family traveling to California. The original edit was so violent it garnered an X rating from the MPAA. Directed by Wes Craven.

Horror Hotel (1960)

College student (Nan Bartow) runs afoul of the supernatural researching a paper for school. Known outside North America as *The City of the Dead.* Directed by John Llewellyn Moxey.

House of Wax (1953)

A sculptor (Vincent Price) wronged by his boss goes mad and starts incorporating too many human elements into his work. One of the earliest 3-D movies. Directed by André de Toth, who, in a bit of cruel irony, only had sight in one eye and therefore could not appreciate the 3-D effects of his finished product.

Invaders from Mars (1953)

Small child (David McLean) is the only human who has the knowledge to stop an alien intrusion. References several real—ahem, "real"—UFO incidents, including the Lubbock Lights. Directed by William Cameron Menzies.

King Kong (1933)

Greedy businessman (Robert Armstrong) brings massive gorilla to Manhattan; chaos ensues, and a damsel (Fay Wray) is definitely in distress. Directed by former wrestlers Merian C. Cooper and Ernest B. Shoedsack.

Land of the Dead (2005)

The zombie apocalypse is in full swing and only a small cadre of humans survive, protected by a walled fortress. The fourth film in the notter-ribly-specific *Night of the Living Dead* film series. Directed by George Romero.

The Misfits (1961)

Romance between an aging cowboy (Clark Gable) and a young divorcée (Marilyn Monroe) plays out in the Nevada desert. Gable's part was originally offered to tough guy actor Robert Mitchum, who turned it down because he didn't like the script. Directed by John Huston.

Monster from Green Hell (1957)

Enormous radioactive wasps endanger a group of African explorers. Star Jim Davis later found fame as Jock Ewing on "Dallas." Directed by Kenneth G. Crane.

Night of the Ghouls (1959)

Flim-flam man Dr. Acula (Kenne Duncan) inadvertently causes the dead to rise from their graves with his phony spiritualist act. A loose sequel to the crown jewel of terrible movies *Plan 9 from Outer Space*. Directed by Ed Wood.

Night of the Living Dead (1968)

Unknown plague causes the recently dead to reanimate and feast on the flesh of the living. The Beatles of zombie movies—it just gets every moment right. Directed by George Romero.

Plan 9 from Outer Space (1959)

Aliens attempt to prevent the construction of a bomb on Earth by orchestrating a zombie uprising. Regularly cited as the worst film ever made due to basement production values and a painful lack of coherence. Directed by Ed Wood.

Poltergeist (1982)

Suburban California parents (Craig T. Nelson and JoBeth Williams) plagued by angry spirits will do anything to rid the hellish menace. Directed by Tobe Hooper, but debates have raged for years concerning just how much control producer Steven Spielberg exercised over the entire affair.

Pumpkinhead (1988)

A small-town shopkeeper (Lance Henriksen) takes revenge on a group of teenagers who accidentally killed his son by soliciting a witch to summon the film's titular demon. Features the cinematic debut of future *Blossom* and *Big Bang Theory* star Mayim Bialik. Directed by special effects wizard Stan Winston.

Planet of the Apes (1968)

American astronaut (Charlton Heston) crash lands on a planet ruled by human-hating simians. Spawned one of science fiction's most heralded film franchises. Directed by Franklin J. Shaffner.

Return of the Fly (1959)

The son of the first film's scientist (Brett Halsey) attempts to revive his father's teleportation experiments, but that darn fly gets in there again. Directed by Edward Bernds.

Teenagers from Outer Space (1959)

Alien/human love story set amidst extraterrestrial invasion. At least once during production the director posed as a college student so as to film in someone else's home for free. Directed by Tom Graeff.

Them! (1954)

Enormous ants endanger a small desert town. The chilling sound the ants make is actually a recording of treefrogs. Directed by Gordon Douglas.

This Island Earth (1955)

Our planet is threatened by the devious aliens from Metaluna who seek to conquer and colonize humans. Notable for being the subject of Bmovie mockery program *Mystery Science Theater 3000*'s sole feature film outing. Directed by Joseph M. Newman.

THX 1138 (1971)

Humans struggle to overcome oppressive androids in dystopian future. Desperate for extras willing to shave their heads to play the enslaved, producers contacted a California drug rehab facility and found plenty of eager participants. Directed by George Lucas.

Twins of Evil (1971)

Orphaned twins (Madeleine and Mary Collison) in Victorian Europe become embroiled in a vampire mystery. Directed by John Hough.

The Wasp Woman (1960)

Makeup saleswoman (Susan Cabot) creates dubious youth cream from insect jelly, becomes horrible hybrid creature. Alternately titled in some countries as *Insect Woman*. Directed by Roger Corman.

Notes

1. STUCK IN LODI

1. Bryan Walsh, "The Electrifying Edison," *Time*, July 5, 2010, http://www.time.com/time/specials/packages/article/0,28804,1910417_1910419_1910460,00.html.

2. Jeanne Donohue, "Family/Boardwalk Tradition: Salt Water Taffy," *The Press of Atlantic City*, June 8, 2006, http://nl.newsbank.com/nl-search/we/Archives? p_product=AC& p_theme=ac&p_action=search&p_maxdocs=200&p_topdoc=1&p_text_direct-0=11224176B7C4EAA0&p_field_direct-0=document_id&p_perpage=10& p_sort=YMD_date:D&s_trackval= GooglePM; "History of the Campbell's Soup Company," CampbellSoup.com.au, accessed August 1, 2012, http://www.campbellsoup.com.au/aboutcampbells/our-history.aspx.

3. "Radio Listeners in Panic, Taking War Drama as Fact," *The New York Times*, October 31, 1938, http://select.nytimes.com/gst/abstract.html?res=F70A17FB3D5F1B7A93C3AA178BD95F4C8385F9.

4. Barbara Gill, "Lindbergh Kidnapping Rocked the World 50 Years Ago," *Hunterdon County Democrat*, 1981, http://www.nj.com/lindbergh/hunterdon/index.ssf?/lindbergh/stories/demcovr.html.

5. "The Hindenburg Disaster," Airships.net, http://www.airships.net/hindenburg/disaster.

6. Everett Rosenfeld, "Jersey Shore Attacks, 1916," *Time*, August 1, 2011, http://www.time.com/time/specials/packages/article/0,28804,2085822_2085823_2085948,00.html.

7. Ian Zanni, "10 More Roads That Will Scare You Stupid," ListVerse.com, February 6, 2011, http://listverse.com/2011/02/06/10-more-roads-that-will-scare-you-stupid.

8. Andrea Allison, "The Devil's Tree," Paranormalstories.blogspot.com, February 26, 2010, http://paranormalstories.blogspot.com/2010/02/devils-tree.html.

9. Kelleigh Dotson, "New Jersey's Devils Tower Is Haunted," Suite101, June 13, 2009, http://suite101.com/article/new-jerseys-devils-tower-is-haunted-a124961.

10. Dave Juliano, "The Jersey Devil," Shadowlands.net, http://theshadowlands.net/jd.htm.

11. Randy D. Ralph, "Ramapough Mountain People 'The Jackson Whites,'" Netsrider.com, January 2, 2001, http://www.netstrider.com/documents/whites.

12. Frank D. Cipriani, "Welcome to the Gatherer Institute," Gatherer.org, http://www.gatherer.org.

13. William H. Sokolic, "Underdog Gives Woman New Leash on Life," *Courier Post*, April 17, 1999, 2B.

14. State of New Jersey Commission of Investigation, "The Changing Face of Organized Crime in New Jersey: A Status Report," May 2004, 105–121.

15. Linda Stasi, "Story behind the Real 'Sopranos,'" *New York Post*, June 23, 2010, http://www.nypost.com/p/entertainment/tv/story_behind_the_real_sopranos_6WwWzB3HbtEfL63v KrxrFN.

16. Paul Brubaker, "Bada Bing Club Is Auctioning 'Sopranos' Memorabilia Online," *Herald News*, August 25, 2007, http://www.northjersey.com/page.phpqstr=eXJpcnk3ZjcxN2 Y3dnFlZUVFeXk3JmZnYmVsN2Y3dnFlZUVFeXk3MTg2MTAy.

17. "Welcome to Satin Dolls, The Original 'Bada Bing!' Club," SatinDollsNJ.com, http://www.satindollsnj.com/satindollshome.html.

18. "Frank Sinatra Obituary," *BBC News*, May 16, 1998, http://news.bbc.co.uk/2/hi/special_report/1998/05/98/sinatra/67911.stm.

19. Richie Unterberger, "The Four Seasons," VocalGroup.org, http://www.vocalgroup.org/inductees/the_four_seasons.html.

20. "History," KoolAndTheGang.com,http://www.koolandthegang.com/history.

21. Maggy Patrick, "Summit High Hosted Velvet Underground's First Show," Summit-Patch.com, January 28, 2010, http://summit.patch.com/articles/summit-high-hosted-velvetundergrounds-first-show.

22. Adam Bernstein, "Les Paul, 94, 'Wizard of Waukesha' Invented Guitars That Changed Popular Music," *Washington Post*, August 14, 2009, http://www.washingtonpost.com/wpdyn/content/article/2009/08/13/AR2009081301768.html.

23. Jocelyn Y. Stewart, "Actress, TV Horror Hostess Vampira," *Los Angeles Times*, January 16, 2008, http://articles.latimes.com/2008/jan/16/local/me-nurmi16.

24. Elena M. Watson, *Television Horror Movie Hosts: 68 Vampires, Mad Scientists and Other Denizens of the Late Night Airwaves Examined and Interviewed* (Jefferson, NC: MacFarland, 2000), 1–5, 265.

25. Randall Clark, *At a Theater or Drive-In Near You: The History, Culture and Politics of the American Exploitation Film* (New York: Routledge, 1995), xi, 77, 129.

26. Stephanie Boluk and Wylie Lenz, *Generation Zombie: Essays on the Living Dead in Modern Culture* (Jefferson, NC: McFarland, 2011), 5.

27. Tom Brinkman, "It's a Violent, Violent, Violent, Violent World," BadMags.com, http://www.badmags.com/bmviolent.html.

28. *Pennies From Heaven*, DVD, directed by Norman Z. McLeod, Columbia Pictures, 1936.

29. Robert Johnson, *The Complete Recordings*, compact disc, Columbia Records, 1990.

30. Joel Whitburn, *Top Pop Records 1940–1955* (Menomonee Falls, WI: Record Research, 1973).

31. *I Put a Spell on Me*, DVD, directed by Nicholas Triandafyllidis, 2001.

32. "'Monster Mash' Singer Bobby 'Boris' Pickett Dies at 69," Foxnews.com, April 26, 2007, http://www.foxnews.com/story/0,2933,268765,00.html; "Bobby 'Boris' Pickett R.I.P.," NewYorkNightTrain.com, May 1, 2007, http://www.newyorknighttrain.com/2007/05/01/bobby-boris-pickett-rip-mad-scientist-who-brought-the-monster-mash-to-life; *Monster Mash: The Movie*, DVD, directed by Joel Cohen, Prism Pictures, 1995.

33. "Guide Picks—Top 10 Ten Tragedy Songs (The Fifties and Sixties)," About.com, http://oldies.about.com/library/weekly/aatpteen.htm.

34. "Behind the Music: Alice Cooper," television program, VH1, originally aired May 2, 1999.

35. Greil Marcus, *Stranded: Rock and Roll for a Desert Island* (New York: Knopf, 1979), 294.

36. "Blue Cheer," AllMusic, http://www.allmusic.com/artist/blue-cheer-mn0000059537.

37. Steven Taylor, *False Prophet: Field Notes from the Punk Undergroud* (Middletown, CT: Wesleyan University Press, 2003): 49.

38. Stephen Thompson, "New York Dolls," AllMusic, http://www.allmusic.com/artist/newyork-dolls-p5019.

39. Kevin W. Wright, "The Indigenous Population of Bergen County," BergenCountyHistory.org, http://www.bergencountyhistory.org/Pages/indians.html.

40. Joseph R. Klett, "Using the Records of East and West Jersey Proprietors," NJ.gov, 2008, http://www.nj.gov/state/darm/pdf/proprietors.pdf.

41. John P. Snyder, "The Story of New Jersey's Civil Boundaries: 1606–1968," Bureau of Geology and Topography, 1969, p. 80.

42. Scott Fybush, "77 WABC, Lodi, N.J.," Fybush.com, May 27, 2005, http://www.fybush.com/sites/2005/site-050527.html.

43. "Richard N. Anzalone," Obituaries, *Bergen County Record*, May 3, 2002.

44. Tom Russel, "Glenn Danzig Interview," Clyde 1 Radio, BBC, September 3, 1992.

45. Dennis Diken, personal e-mail to the author, June 7, 2012.

46. Jeff Kitts, "The Dark Knight Returns," *Flux* 1 (September 1994): 50.

47. Steven Linder, telephone interview with the author, May 25, 2012.

48. "Bronze Age of Comic Books," Wikipedia, http://en.wikipedia.org/wiki/Bronze_Age_of_Comic_Books.

49. Linder, telephone interview.

50. Mariana Zogbi, "Danzig on Thin Ice," *Metal Mania* (Spring 1989): 25–27.

51. "Tour Date Archive," Black-Sabbath.com, http://www.black-sabbath.com/tourdates.

52. Tom Russel, "Glenn Danzig Interview," Clyde 1 Radio, BBC, September 3, 1992.

53. Linder, telephone interview.

54. Glenn Danzig, "Afterword," *The Stooges: Head On: A Journey through the Michigan Underground* (Detroit: Wayne State University Press, 2011), 147–148.

55. Linder, telephone interview.

56. *End of the Century*, DVD, directed by Jim Fields and Michael Gramaglia, Magnolia Pictures, 2003.

57. *The Filth and the Fury*, DVD, directed by Julien Temple, FilmFour, 2000.

2. TEENAGERS FROM MARS

1. JR, telephone interview with the author, June 12, 2012.

2. Peter S. Greenberg, "Saints and Stinkers," *Rolling Stone,* February 19, 1981, 25.

3. "Making *The Misfits*," *Great Performances*, PBS, 2001.

4. Graham McCann, *Rebel Males: Clift, Brando and Dean* (London: Hamish Hamilton Ltd, 1991), 68.

5. Steve Thorn, "The History of San Diego Rock 'n' Roll, Part One: A Sleeping Town Wakes Up," *Kicks*, no. 3 (November 1979).

6. Chas Kit, "Lost and Found," Garage Hangover, August 28, 2007, http://www.garagehangover.com/?q=lostandfound.

7. Steven Cashmore, "Northland Rock: Part Four—The Beat Goes On," Highland Archives, 1998, http://www.internet-promotions.co.uk/archives/northlands/north4.htm.

8. Nick Warburton, "Them," Garage Hangover, May 17, 2010, http://www.garagehangover.com/?q=taxonomy/term/1638.

9. Paul Grondahl, "Remembering Bob Gori, Punk Rocker," *The Times Union*, April 22, 2011, http://www.timesunion.com/local/article/Remembering-Bob-Gori-punk-rocker-1347843.php.

10. Daniel Russell, "Horror Business: An Interview with Jerry Only of the Misfits," MyKindaSound.wordpress.com, http://mykindasound.wordpress.com/interview/horror-business.

11. Mike Stax, "All Hell Breaks Loose: The Jerry Only Interview," *Ugly Things,* no. 12 (Summer 1993): 8–9; Steven Linder, telephone interview with the author, May 25, 2012.

12. Stephen Blush, "Glenn Danzig," *Seconds*, no. 44 (October 1997): 34–44.

13. Daniel Russell, "Horror Business: An Interview with Jerry Only of the Misfits," MyKindaSound.wordpress.com, http://mykindasound.wordpress.com/interview/horror-business.

14. "Discography of Official Misfits Releases," Misfits Central, http://misfitscentral.com/misfits/discog.php.

15. Eerie Von, "Liner Notes," *The Misfits*, Caroline Records, 1996, compact disc set.

16. Frank LiCata, telephone interview with the author, March 21, 2011.

17. Mark Prindle, "Jerry Only—2003," MarkPrindle.com, http://www.markprindle.com/only-i.htm.

18. Rich Lockney, "Jerry Only Interview," TVCasualty.com, http://tvcasualty.com/articles/a_jonly.html.
19. LiCata, telephone interview.
20. "Misfits Time Line," Misfits Central, http://misfitscentral.com/misfits/timeline.php.
21. Jim Catania, telephone interview with the author, November 5, 2010.
22. Dave Achelis, telephone interview with the author, July 2, 2012.
23. Daniel Russell, "Horror Business: An Interview with Jerry Only of the Misfits," MyKindaSound.wordpress.com, http://mykindasound.wordpress.com/interview/horror-business.
24. LiCata, telephone interview.
25. Stephen Blush, "Glenn Danzig," *Seconds*, no. 44 (October 1997): 34–44.
26. Steve Huey, "Jello Biafra: Biography," AllMusic, http://www.allmusic.com/artist/biafra-mn0000322642.
27. Dead Kennedys, *In God We Trust, Inc.*, Alternative Tentacles, 1981, seven-inch vinyl record.
28. Peter Buckley, *The Rough Guide to Rock,* 2nd ed. (New York: Rough Guides, 1999), 275.
29. Kenneth Anger, *Hollywood Babylon: The Legendary Underground Classic of Hollywood's Darkest and Best Kept Secrets* (San Francisco: Straight Arrow Books, 1981).
30. "Song and Name Information," Misfits Central, http://misfitscentral.com/misfits/songname.php.
31. LiCata, telephone interview.
32. Claude Bessy, "The Misfits," *Slash* 2, no. 2 (November 1978): 28.
33. LiCata, telephone interview.
34. Catania, telephone interview.
35. Jay Yuenger, telephone interview with the author, January 4, 2011.
36. Mike Stax, telephone interview with the author, March 29, 2011.
37. Stax, "All Hell Breaks Loose," 11.
38. LiCata, telephone interview.
39. "Vintage Photos," Misfits.com, http://www.misfits.com.

3. HORROR BUSINESS

1. Bruce McCulloch, telephone interview with the author, February 16, 2012.
2. Mike Stax, "Image of a Misfit: An Interview with Joey Image," *Ugly Things*, no. 13 (1994): 13–14.
3. *Kaufhold et al v. Caiafa et al*, Case No. 11-cv-01460-WJM-MF, originally filed June 11, 2010, 12.
4. "Bobby Steele Interview," TV Casualty, April 25, 1998, http://www.tvcasualty.com/articles/a_bobby.html.
5. The Misfits, "Max's Kansas City 12/20/78," live recording, 1978, cassette tape.
6. "Misfits Time Line," Misfits Central, http://misfitscentral.com/misfits/timeline.php.
7. *The Crimson Ghost*, directed by Fred C. Brannon and William Witney (1946; Republic Pictures), film; IMDb, http://www.imdb.com/title/tt0038435.
8. "Bud Geary," The Files of Jerry Blake, http://filesofjerryblake.netfirms.com/html/bud_geary.html.
9. A. J. Ryan and Pamela Hazelton, "I Am Misfit," *Lucanae*, no. 7 (April 1996).
10. The Misfits, "Horror Business," Plan 9 Records, 1979, seven-inch vinyl record (single).
11. Ian MacKaye, telephone interview with the author, January 28, 2011.
12. Mike Stax, "All Hell Breaks Loose: The Jerry Only Interview," *Ugly Things*, no. 12 (Summer 1993): 14.
13. Stax, "Image of a Misfit," 10.
14. "Misfits Time Line," Misfits Central.
15. Elena Romanello, "Captain Harlock," Anime Mundi, November 30, 2008, http://www.terrediconfine.eu/captain-harlock.html, Pushead, "Danzig," *Thrasher* (June 1986): 65–66.

16. Stax, "Image of a Misfit," 13.

17. John Waters, *Crackpot: The Obsessions of John Waters* (New York: MacMillan, 1983), 16–19.

18. "The Misfits: We Want, We Need, We Take," Misfits press release, 1979.

19. "Discography of Official Misfits Releases," Misfits Central, http://misfitscentral.com/misfits/timeline.php. The Misfits, "Night of the Living Dead," Plan 9 Records, 1979, seven-inch vinyl record (single).

20. Stax, "Image of a Misfit," 11.

21. Rachel Leibrock, "Cramps Singer Lux Interior Dies at 60," *The Sacramento Bee*, February 4, 2009, http://www.sacbee.com/static/weblogs/ticket/archives/019288.html.

22. Christian Death, *Only Theatre of Pain*, Frontier Records, 1982, vinyl record; T.S.O.L., *Dance with Me*, Frontier Records, 1981, vinyl record; Various Artists, *Darker Skratcher*, Los Angeles Free Music Society, 1980, vinyl record.

23. Ned Raggett, "The Damned," AllMusic, http://www.allmusic.com/artist/the-damnedmn0000138520.

24. "Misfits Time Line," Misfits Central.

25. Stax, "All Hell Breaks Loose," 15.

26. Stax, "Image of a Misfit," 11.

27. Stax, "All Hell Breaks Loose," 15.

28. "Bobby Steele Interview," *Punk Floyd* (October 1993).

29. "Misfits Time Line," Misfits Central; Stax, "Image of a Misfit," 11–12.

30. "Song and Name Information," Misfits Central, http://misfitscentral.com/misfits/timeline.php.

31. "Discography of Official Misfits Release," Misfits Central.

32. The Misfits, *Beware*, Plan 9 Records, 1980, twelve-inch vinyl record (EP).

33. Stax, "Image of a Misfit," 12.

34. John Carlucci, e-mail interview with the author, February 2010.

35. Steven Blush, *American Hardcore: A Tribal History* (Port Townsend, WA: Feral House, 2010), 230.

36. Mark Prindle, "John Stabb—2008," MarkPrindle.com, 2008, http://markprindle.com/stabb-i.htm.

37. Stax, "All Hell Breaks Loose," 17.

38. Geoffrey Tilander, "Bobby Steele Interview," *MaximumRockNRoll* (1992).

39. Blush, *American Hardcore*, 228–230.

40. "Misfits Time Line," Misfits Central; The Misfits, "Hitsville 12/25/81," live recording, 1981, cassette tape.

41. Mark Kennedy, telephone interview with the author, October 20, 2011.

42. Dave Brockie, telephone interview with the author, March 14, 2011.

43. Charles Ulridh, "Frank Zappa Gig List: 1980," http://members.shaw.ca/fz-pomd/giglist/1980.html.

44. "Tour Dates," Misfits Central, http://misfitscentral.com/misfits/timeline.php.

45. The Misfits, *3 Hits From Hell*, Plan 9 Records, 1981, seven-inch vinyl record (EP); the Misfits, "Halloween," Plan 9 Records, 1981, seven-inch vinyl record (single).

46. "The Misfits—3 Hits From Hell"; "The Misfits—Halloween," *Wave Sector*, 1981.

47. Tommy Koprowski, telephone interview with the author, April 15, 2012.

48. Kennedy, telephone interview.

4. ASTRO ZOMBIES

1. Mark Prindle, "John Stabb—2008," Mark's Record Reviews, http://markprindle.com/stabb-i.htm.

2. *End of the Century*, directed by Jim Fields and Michael Gramaglia (2003; Los Angeles: Magnolia Pictures, 2005), DVD.

3. *The Clash: Westway to the World*, directed by Don Letts (2000; London, 3DD Entertainment, 2002), DVD.

4. Thom Jurek, "Professionals: Review," Allmusic, http://www.allmusic.com/album/professionals-mw0000454833.

5. "Public Image Ltd.—Poptones & Careering (American Bandstand 1980)," YouTube.com, uploaded by BonzoGoesToMexico, November 26, 2009, http://www.youtube.com/watch?v=hZLhqTzjpUM.

6. "Tomorrow Show with Tom Snyder (NBC) 27th June, 1980" interview transcript, John-Lydon.com, http://www.johnlydon.com/tom80.html.

7. Stephen Thomas Erlewine, "Minor Threat: Biography," AllMusic, http://www.allmusic.com/artist/minor-threat-mn0000422947.

8. Michael Azerrad, *Our Band Could Be Your Life: Scenes from the American Indie Underground: 1981–1991* (New York: Back Bay, 2002), 40, 141.

9. Chris Desjardins, e-mail interview with the author, April 2011.

10. The Misfits, *Walk Among Us*, Slash/Ruby Records, 1982, vinyl record; Eerie Von, "Liner Notes," *The Misfits*, Caroline Records, 1996, compact disc set.

11. The Misfits, *Walk Among Us*.

12. Jaime Sciarappa, telephone interview with the author, November 7, 2010.

13. "Misfits—'Walk Among Us,'" *Terror Times* (March 1982).

14. Tim Sommer, "New York Noos," *Sounds* (May 1, 1982): 14.

15. "Misfits—'Walk Among Us,'" *Forced Exposure*, no. 2 (March 1982).

16. Ned Raggett, "Walk Among Us," AllMusic, http://www.allmusic.com/album/walkamong-us-mw0000197473.

17. Joe Matera, "The Classic Albums: The Misfits' 'Walk Among Us,'" Ultimate-Guitar.com, June 24, 2009, http://www.ultimate-guitar.com/interviews/interviews/the_classic_albums_the_misfitss_walk_among_us.html.

18. Desjardins, e-mail interview.

19. Matera, "The Classic Albums: The Misfits' 'Walk Among Us.'"

20. Desjardins, e-mail interview.

21. Brian Baker, telephone interview with the author, January 3, 2011.

22. Jay Yuenger, telephone interview with the author, January 4, 2011.

23. Dave Brockie, telephone interview with the author, March 14, 2011.

24. The Lemonheads, *Favorite Spanish Dishes*, Atlantic Records, 1990, compact disc.

25. *Hot Rod*, directed by Akiva Schaffer (2007; Paramount Pictures, 2007), DVD.

26. Ian MacKaye, telephone interview with the author, January 28, 2011.

27. Mark Prindle, "Jerry Only—2003," Mark's Record Reviews, http://www.markprindle.com/only-i.htm.

28. Glenn Danzig, "Movies," *Flipside*, no. 36 (December 1982): 51.

29. Desjardins, e-mail interview.

30. Tim Bunch, telephone interview with the author, April 5, 2011.

31. "Misfits Interview," *Flipside*, no. 36 (December 1982): 21.

32. Desjardins, e-mail interview.

33. Spit Stix, "FEAR, SNL, Halloween 1981," A Punk Chronicle, http://www.sol-i.tv/Spit/docs/5a.html.

34. "Misfits Interview," *Flipside*, no. 36 (December 1982): 21.

35. Desjardins, e-mail interview.

36. Nardwuar, "Nardwuar the Human Serviette versus Glenn Danzig," Nardwuar.com, December 1999, http://nardwuar.com/vs/glenn_danzig/index.html.

37. Craig Lee, "Horror-Movie Rock from The Misfits," *Los Angeles Times*, April 15, 1982.

38. David Chute, "Misfits Make a Joke of Hard-Core Punk," *Los Angeles Herald-Examiner*, April 15, 1982.

39. Mike Stax, "All Hell Breaks Loose: The Jerry Only Interview," *Ugly Things*, no. 12 (Summer 1993): 22.

40. Glenn Danzig, "Who Killed Marilyn?" Plan 9 Records, 1981, seven-inch vinyl record.

41. Pushead, "Danzig," *Thrasher* (June 1986): 65.

42. "Misfits Interview," *Touch & Go*, no. 18 (Fall 1981).

43. Glenn Danzig, personal letter to Tesco Vee, Lansing, date unknown.

44. "Misfits Interview," *Flipside*, no. 31 (1981).

45. Glenn Danzig, personal letter to Tesco Vee, Lansing, date unknown.

46. Sal Bee, e-mail to the author, August 2012.

47. Stax, "All Hell Breaks Loose," 22.

48. "Bobby Steele Interview," *Punk Floyd* (1993).

49. Lynne Olver, "McDonald's Hamburger Prices," FoodTimeline.org, http://www.foodtimeline.org/foodfaq5.html.

50. Stax, "All Hell Breaks Loose," 16.

5. DIE, DIE MY DARLING

1. JR, telephone interview with the author, June 12, 2012.

2. "Misfits Interview," *Forced Exposure*, no. 5 (January 1983).

3. "Misfits Interview," *Flipside*, no. 31 (1982).

4. "Crucifucks live [2/2] in Kalamazoo MI 1982," posted by souldonut666, March 10, 2007, http://www.youtube.com/watch?v=aZw4xQpnB2k.

5. Alex Ogg, "Everything Went Black," AllMusic, http://www.allmusic.com/album/everything-went-black-mw0000192996.

6. Henry Rollins, *Get in the Van: On the Road with Black Flag*, 2nd ed. (Los Angeles: 2.12.61, 2004), 94.

7. "Misfits—Santa Monica Civic 1983," posted by drinkyeflaggons, December 3, 2011, http://www.youtube.com/watch?v=EdUcVbiAiU4.

8. Steven Blush, *American Hardcore: A Tribal History* (Port Townsend, WA: Feral House, 2010), 58.

9. Ian MacKaye, telephone interview with the author, January 28, 2011.

10. Rollins, *Get in the Van.*

11. "Misfits Time Line," Misfits Central, http://misfitscentral.com/misfits/timeline.php.

12. Geri Nible, "Jerry Only Interview," *Feh,* no. 12 (September/October 1994): 24–27.

13. Mike IX Williams, telephone interview with the author, October 2, 2012.

14. Jay Yuenger, "Misfits Arrested in New Orleans," Jyuenger.com, http://www.jyuenger.com/?p=4365.

15. Williams, telephone interview.

16. "Punk-Rock Musicans Arrested in Cemetery." *The Times-Picayune* (New Orleans, LA), October 19, 1982.

17. Yuenger, "Misfits Arrested in New Orleans." Williams, telephone interview.

18. "Misfits Time Line," Misfits Central.

19. The Misfits, *Evilive*, Plan 9 Records, 1982, seven-inch vinyl record.

20. Mike Stax, telephone interview with the author, March 29, 2011.

21. "Misfits—Santa Monica Civic 1983."

22. "Misfits Time Line," Misfits Central.

23. "Samhain: 'We Don't Want to Be Called a Hardcore Band,'" *Hard Times* 1, no. 1 (August 1984): 1–4. Stephen Blush, "Glenn Danzig," *Seconds*, no. 44 (October 1997): 34–44.

24. "Samhain," *Hard Times,* 1–4.

25. Mike Stax, "All Hell Breaks Loose: The Jerry Only Interview," *Ugly Things*, no. 12 (Summer 1993): 23–24.

26. James Greene Jr., "Lyle Preslar Sets the Record Straight about U2, MTV, and Tesco Vee," Crawdaddy.com, April 16, 2010, http://www.crawdaddyarchive.com/index.php/2010/04/16/minor-threat-s-lyle-preslar-sets-the-record-straight-about-u2-mtv-and-tesco-vee.

27. "Misfits Time Line," Misfits Central.

28. Stax, "All Hell Breaks Loose," 24. "Samhain," *Hard Times,* 1–4.

29. "Brian Keats Drummer, Near Death," *Rayon's Blog*, January 12, 2010, http://www.myspace.com/rayon/blog/524678595.

30. Todd Swalla, e-mail interview with the author, September 2010.

31. "Brian Keats Drummer, Near Death."

32. "The Misfits—Live at the Graystone Hall," posted by Honkofthewall, September 6, 2010, http://www.youtube.com/watch?v=m7O8jBUABjw.

33. "Back Porch Video: The Misfits Play Greystone Hall and Meet Mrs. Gibb," Fourwaymirror.com, July 7, 2009, http://www.fourwaymirror.com/2009/07/back-porch-video-misfitsplay-greystone.html.

34. "Brian Keats Drummer, Near Death."

35. Sal Cannestra, "Kryst the Conqueror: Ex-Misfits Metal Meltdown," *Jersey Beat*, no. 40 (Summer 1990).

36. The Misfits, *Earth A.D./Wolfs Blood*, Plan 9 Records, 1983, vinyl record. D. X. Ferris, "Danzig's Blackest of the Black Tour Promises to Melt Your Face Off," *The Dallas Observer*, October 30, 2008, http://www.dallasobserver.com/2008-10-30/music/danzig-s-blackest-of-the-black-tour-promises-to-melt-your-face-off.

37. MacKaye, telephone interview.

38. "Horror Film: 1970s–1980s," Wikipedia, http://en.wikipedia.org/wiki/Horror_film#1970s.E2.80.931980s.

39. "Misfits Time Line," Misfits Central.

6. GREEN HELL

1. The Misfits, "Die, Die My Darling," Plan 9 Records, 1984, vinyl record.

2. "Samhain Time Line," Misfits Central, http://misfitscentral.com/samhain/timeline.php.

3. James Greene Jr., "Lyle Preslar Sets the Record Straight about U2, MTV, and Tesco Vee," Crawdaddy.com, April 16, 2010, http://www.crawdaddyarchive.com/index.php/2010/04/16/minor-threat-s-lyle-preslar-sets-the-record-straight-about-u2-mtv-and-tesco-vee.

4. "Samhain Time Line," Misfits Central.

5. "Samhain: 'We Don't Want to Be Called a Hardcore Band,'" *Hard Times* 1, no. 1 (August 1984): 1–4.

6. Pete Marshall, interview with the author, February 10, 2011.

7. Eerie Von and Steve Zing, "Liner Notes," *Box Set*, Samhain, Evilive Records, 2000, compact disc set.

8. Robert O'Driscoll, ed., *The Celtic Consciousness* (New York: Braziller, 1981); Anne Ross, "Material Culture, Myth and Folk Memory," in *Celtic Consciousness,* 197–216; Kevin Danaher, "Irish Folk Tradition and the Celtic Calendar," in *Celtic Consciousness,* 217–242.

9. Marshall, interview.

10. Glenn Danzig, "Liner Notes," *Box Set*, Samhain, Evilive Records, 2000, compact disc set.

11. Samhain, *Initium*, Plan 9 Records, 1984, vinyl record. Samhain, *Unholy Passion*, Plan 9 Records, 1985, vinyl record.

12. Samhain, *Initium*. Steve Zing, telephone interview with the author, March 15, 2003.

13. "Samhain 'Initium,'" *Flipside,* no. 44 (Fall 1984): 31.

14. Marshall, interview.

15. *Kaufhold et al v. Caiafa et al*, Case No. 11-cv-01460-WJM-MF, originally filed June 11, 2010, 7.

16. "Samhain," *Your Flesh*, vol. 1 (Spring 1986).

17. Martin Eric Ain, e-mail interview with the author, March 2012.

18. Marshall, interview.

19. Mark Kennedy, telephone interview with the author, October 20, 2011.

20. "Glenn D," *Black Market*, no. 6 (Fall 1986).

21. Christy Marx, e-mail interview with the author, September 2010.

22. Tim Bunch, telephone interview with the author, April 2, 2011.

23. Harald Olmoen, personal interview with Cliff Burton, transcribed by Corrine Lynn, 1986. Pushead, "James Hetfield and Kirk Hammet," *Thrasher* (August 1986): 69.

24. "The $5.98 E.P. Garage Days Re-Revisited: Awards" AllMusic, http://www.allmusic.com/album/the-598-ep-garage-days-re-revisited-mw0000196847/awards. "Master of Puppets: Awards," AllMusic, http://www.allmusic.com/album/master-of-puppetsmw0000667490/awards.

25. "Jerry Only Interview," *YesZista* (Spring 1989).

26. The Misfits, *Misfits*, Caroline Records, 1987, compact disc.

27. The Misfits, *Evilive*, Caroline Records, 1987, compact disc.

28. "Jerry Only Interview," *YesZista*.

29. Kryst the Conqueror, *Deliver Us from Evil*, Cycoplian Music, 1989, cassette tape.

30. "Kryst the Conqueror," *Doyle Fan Club*, no. 6 (1989).

31. "Jerry Only Interview," *YesZista*.

32. Geoffrey Tilander, "Bobby Steele Interview," *MaximumRockNRoll* (1992).

33. Bunch, telephone interview.

34. "Jerry Only Interview," *YesZista*.

35. Sal Cannestra, "Kryst the Conqueror: Ex-Misfits Metal Meltdown," *Jersey Beat,* no. 40 (Summer 1990).

36. "Letter #10," *Doyle Fan Club*, no. 10 (January 1990).

37. Kim Neely, "Danzig—Danzig," *Rolling Stone*, November 17, 1988. 152. Mick Mercer, "The Dead Zone," *Melody Maker* (October 22, 1988).

38. "Discography of Official Misfits Releases," MisfitsCentral, http://misfitscentral.com/misfits/discog.php.

39. Robert Palmer, "Danzig III: How the Gods Kill," *Rolling Stone*, July 9, 1992.

40. Danzig, *Danzig III: How the Gods Kill*, Def American, 1992, compact disc.

41. Jeff Kitts, "The Dark Knight Returns," *Fluz*, no. 1 (September 1994): 50.

42. "Glenn Danzig Says He Oughta Be in Pictures," MTV.com, June 3, 1997, http://www.mtv.com/news/articles/1427843/glenn-danzig-oughta-be-in-pictures.jhtml.

43. Danielle Bacher, "Danzig Says He Would Have Played Wolverine Less 'Gay' Than Hugh Jackman," *L.A. Weekly*, May 25, 2012, http://blogs.laweekly.com/westcoastsound/2012/05/danzig_legacy_wolverine_stalker_misfits.php.

44. Scott, "A Scary Short Guy Takes on a Dead Alcoholic, a One-Armed Drummer, and Four Other Clowns," *Genetic Disorder,* no. 10 (1994).

45. Nardwuar, "Nardwuar the Human Serviette versus Glenn Danzig," Nardwuar.com, December 1999, http://nardwuar.com/vs/glenn_danzig/index.html.

46. Danzig, *4p*, Def American Records, 1994, compact disc.

47. "Discography of Official Danzig Releases," Misfits Central, http://misfitscentral.com/danzig/discog.php.

48. Joel Whitburn, *Joel Whitburn Presents The Billboard Albums,* 6th ed. (Menomonee Falls, WI: Record Research, 2007), 265.

49. Mick Mercer, "The Dead Zone," *Melody Maker* (October 22, 1988).

50. Maria Ma, "Danzig: Def New Music," *Concrete Foundations*, December 10, 1988, http://www.misfitscentral.com/display.php?t=darticle&f=concrete.88.

51. *Caiafa et al v. Anzalone et al*, Case No. 1:92-v-06908-LAP, originally filed September 18, 1992.

7. NIGHT OF THE LIVING DEAD

1. Brian Baker, telephone interview with the author, January 3, 2011.

2. "What Happened to Axl Rose—The Inside Story of Rock's Most Famous Recluse," *Rolling Stone,* May 11, 2000, reprinted at HereTodayGoneToHell.com, http://www.heretodaygonetohell.com/articles/showarticle.php?articleid=32.

3. "Guns n' Roses Discography," Wikipedia, http://en.wikipedia.org/wiki/Guns_N%27_Roses_discography.

4. Mike Stax, telephone interview with author, March 29, 2011.

5. Mike Stax, "All Hell Breaks Loose: The Jerry Only Interview," *Ugly Things,* no. 12 (Summer 1993): 22.

6. Lyle Preslar, e-mail interview with the author, June 2012.

7. "Why Do Fools Fall in Love (Song): Writing Credits," Wikipedia, http://en.wikipedia.org/wiki/Why_Do_Fools_Fall_in_Love_(song)#Writing_credits.

8. "Company Town: Beach Boys' Mike Love Wins His Case, Stands to Collect Millions," *Los Angeles Times,* December 13, 1994, http://articles.latimes.com/1994-12-13/business/fi-8511_1_beach-boys-lead-singer.

9. "Exhibit C," *Kaufhold et al v. Caiafa et al,* Case No. 11-cv-01460-WJM-MF, filed July 22, 2011, 1–9.

10. "Exhibit D," *Kaufhold et al v. Caiafa et al,* Case No. 11-cv-01460-WJM-MF, filed July 22, 2011, 1–4.

11. Mark Kennedy, telephone interview with the author, October 20, 2011.

12. Tim Bunch, telephone interview with the author, April 2, 2011.

13. David MacIntyre, "Dr. Chud Interview," June 17, 2007, http://www.angelfire.com/divozz/chud.html.

14. Kennedy, telephone interview; Stax, telephone interview.

15. Michale Graves, telephone interview with the author, September 6, 2011.

16. Bunch, telephone interview. "Misfits Time Line," Misfits Central, http://misfitscentral.com/misfits95/timeline.php.

17. Kennedy, telephone interview.

18. "Misfits Time Line," Misfits Central.

19. *Animal Room,* directed by Craig Singer (1995; Los Angeles, ViewCave), DVD.

20. Mike Stax, "Coming Soon to a Cemetery Near You . . . The Return of the Misfits," *Ugly Things,* no. 14 (Fall 1995): 44–45.

21. William F. Powers, "Signs of Intelligent Life—Cult Favorite Gains a Following among the Masses," *Washington Post,* September 17, 1995.

22. "Wes Craven: Directing and Writing Career," Wikipedia, http://en.wikipedia.org/wiki/Wes_Craven#Directing_and_writing_career.

23. Albert Kim, "Pulp Nonfiction," *Entertainment Weekly,* July 8, 1994, http://www.ew.com/ew/article/0,,302832,00.html; Janice E. Shuetz and Lin S. Lilley, *The O. J. Simpson Trials: Rhetoric, Media, and the Law* (Carbondale; Southern Illinois University Press, 1999).

24. Graves, telephone interview.

25. Richard Abowitz, "The Misfits—American Psycho," *Rolling Stone,* May 15, 1997, 115.

26. Stephen Thompson, "American Psycho," review, The Onion A.V. Club, http://www.avclub.com/articles/misfits-american-psycho,21093.

27. David Grad, "Misfits, American Psycho," review, *Entertainment Weekly,* May 16, 1997, http://www.ew.com/ew/article/0,,287893,00.html.

28. The Misfits, *American Psycho,* Geffen Records, 1997, compact disc.

29. Graves, telephone interview.

30. Bunch, telephone interview.

31. Preslar, e-mail interview.

32. Bunch, telephone interview.

33. "Discography of Official Misfits Releases," MisfitsCentral.com, http://www.misfitscentral.com/misfits/discog.php.

34. Bunch, telephone interview.

35. Graves, telephone interview; Bunch, telephone interview.

36. Jerry Only, "Untitled Press Release," Misfits Central, May 27, 1998, http://misfitscentral.com/display.php?t=marticle&f=mfc_sing.98.

37. "Myke Hideous Interview," TVCasualty.com, http://tvcasualty.com/articles/a_mykeh.html.

38. Moe Wyoming, "Myke Hideous," *MK Magazine,* November 1, 2003, http://www.mkmagazine.com/interviews/archives/000118.php.

39. Graves, telephone interview.

8. HATE BREEDERS

1. Peter Berger, *The Social Construction of Reality* (New York: Anchor, 1966), 109.
2. Vinnie Apicella, "Misfits—Never Say Die," *The Aquarian Weekly* (June 17, 1998).
3. The Misfits, *Famous Monsters*, Roadrunner Records, 1999, compact disc.
4. "Discography of Official Misfits Releases," Misfits Central, http://misfitscentral.com/misfits95/discog.php.
5. The Misfits, "Scream," directed by George Romero, Roadrunner Records, 1999, music video.
6. The Misfits, "Cuts from the Crypt," Roadrunner Records, 2001, compact disc.
7. "Jerry Only Interview," MTV.com, June 22, 1999, http://www.mtv.com/bands/archive/m/misfits/misfitsfeature99_1.jhtml.
8. "SuperBrawl V Results," ProWrestlingHistory.com, http://www.prowrestlinghistory.com/supercards/usa/wcw/s-brawl.html#V.
9. "Gorgeous George (Stephanie Bellars)," *Adam's Wrestling Blog*, March 26, 2012, http://adamswrestling.blogspot.com/2012/03/gorgeous-george-stephanie-bellars.
10. Michale Graves, telephone interview with the author, September 6, 2011.
11. Tim Bunch, telephone interview with the author, April 2, 2011.
12. *Big Money Hustlas*, directed by John Cafiero (2000; Psychopathic Films), DVD.
13. *John Cafiero v. Doug Custer*, Case Number 3:08-CV-00202, originally filed August 2008.
14. Bunch, telephone interview.
15. *John Cafiero v. Doug Custer*.
16. Joseph Bruce and Hobey Echlin, "Big Money Hustlas," *Behind the Paint* (Royal Oak, MI: Psychopathic Records, 2003): 424–432.
17. *Big Money Hustlas*, DVD.
18. Bruce and Echlin, "Big Money Hustlas," 424–32.
19. Graves, telephone interview; Bunch, telephone interview.
20. "Misfits Tour Dates," Misfits Central, http://misfitscentral.com/misfits95/tourdates.php.
21. Graves, telephone interview.
22. Bunch, telephone interview.
23. Dave Brockie, telephone interview with the author, March 14, 2011.
24. Graves, *Web of Dharma*, GUB Records, 2002, compact disc.
25. Moe Wyoming, "Ex Misfit Michale Graves," *MK Magazine*, November 1, 2003, http://www.mk-magazine.com/interviews/archives/000113.php.
26. "The Clash," segment on *The Daily Show with Jon Stewart*, Comedy Central, originally aired June 23, 2004.
27. "Michale Graves: Three Chords and the Truth," Live-Metal.net, September 7, 2008, http://www.live-metal.net/interviews_michalegraves.html.
28. Danzig, *Blackacidevil*, Hollywood Records, 1996, compact disc.
29. Danzig, *4*, Def American Records, 1994, compact disc.
30. Danzig, *Blackacidevil*.
31. Jeff Stratton, "The Devil Inside," *Miami New Times*, April 20, 2000, http://www.miaminewtimes.com/2000-04-20/music/the-devil-inside/1.
32. Bruce McCulloch, telephone interview with the author, February 16, 2012.
33. *Kids in the Hall: Brain Candy*, directed by Kelly Makin (1996; Paramount Pictures), DVD.
34. Danzig, *6:66: Satan's Child*, E-Magazine, 1999, compact disc.
35. Chris Norris, "Moonwalking in L.A.," *Spin*, December 1999, 124.
36. Nardwuar, "Nardwuar the Human Serviette Versus Glenn Danzig," Nardwuar.com, December 1999, http://nardwuar.com/vs/glenn_danzig/index.html.
37. Pete Marshall, interview with the author, February 10, 2011.
38. Danzig, *I Luciferi*, Spitfire Records, 2002, compact disc.
39. "Cybernetic Ghost of Christmas Past from the Future," episode of *Aqua Teen Hunger Force*, Cartoon Network, originally aired December 29, 2002.

40. Bunch, telephone interview; Bobby Gorman, telephone interview with the author, March 15, 2011; Brockie, telephone interview.

41. Annie Zaleski, "Misfits Reunion Allegedly Scuttled by New Leader Jerry Only," *Riverfront Times*, September 11, 2008, http://blogs.riverfronttimes.com/rftmusic/2008/09/misfits_reunion_jerry_only_danzig_misfits_gorgeous_frankenstein_doyle.php.

42. Chris Alo, "Glenn Danzig—Finally Some Words about 'The Misfits,' Movies and Dolls," *Rock Brigade* (October 1994).

43. Bunch, telephone interview.

44. Mark Prindle, "Jerry Only—2003," MarkPrindle.com, http://www.markprindle.com/only-i.htm.

45. "Misfits Tour Dates," Misfits Central, http://misfitscentral.com/misfits95/tourdates.php.

46. The Misfits, "The Day the Earth Caught Fire," Misfits Records, 2002, compact disc single.

47. The Misfits, *Project 1950*, Misfits Records, 2003, compact disc.

48. Congruent Machine Company, Inc., CongruentMachine.com.

49. Holly Day, "A Ghoulish Conversation with Jerry Only," *Maximum Ink*, http://www.maximum-ink.com/archive/99/nov/html/feature.html.

50. "Doyle Interview," Reign in Blood (blog), http://www.myspace.com/rib333/blog/429817046.

9. VIOLENT WORLD

1. Nigel Goodall, "Transcript of Elvis's 1972 Press Conference," June 8, 2011, http://www.elvis.com.au/presley/interview_with_elvis_presley_the_1972_press_conference.shtml.

2. Dave Kim, "Ryan Adams Performs Acoustic Version of Danzig's 'Mother,'" Diffuser.fm, May 16, 2012, http://diffuser.fm/ryan-adams-danzig-mother.

3. Dave Maher, "My Morning Jacket, Pajo Cover Misfits on Comp," Pitchfork Media, October 18, 2007, http://web.archive.org/web/20080208192044/http://www.pitchforkmedia.com/article/news/46478-my-morning-jacket-pajo-cover-misfits-on-comp.

4. Jon DeRosa, "Stuck in Lodi," Pitchfork Media, March 7, 2005, http://pitchfork.com/features/articles/5982-stuck-in-lodi.

5. AFI, *A Fire Inside*, Adeline Records, 1999, compact disc.

6. Various Artists, *Tony Hawk's American Wasteland*, Vagrant Records, 2005, compact disc.

7. The Network, *Money Money 2020*, Adeline Records, 2003, compact disc.

8. Steve Huey, "Slipknot Biography," AllMusic, http://www.allmusic.com/artist/slipknotmn0000750742.

9. "What Caused Glenn Danzig to Lose His Temper in North Side Kings Altercation?" Blabbermouth.net, December 23, 2004, http://www.blabbermouth.net/news.aspx?mode=Article&newsitemID=30705.

10. "Glenn Danzig: North Side Kings Punchout Was a 'Setup,'" Blabbermouth.net, August 20, 2004, http://www.blabbermouth.net/news.aspx?mode=Article&newsitemID=26000.

11. "Blackest of the Black Tour Cancelled," Blabbermouth.net, September 15, 2004, http://www.blabbermouth.net/news.aspx?mode=Article&newsitemID=26924.

12. "Danzig to Team Up with Doyle for Two Shows in December," Blabbermouth.net, October 30, 2004, http://www.blabbermouth.net/news.aspx?mode=Article&newsitemID=28565.

13. "Doyle Interview," Reign In Blood (blog), http://www.myspace.com/rib333/blog/429817046.

14. "Gorgeous Frankenstein: The Band," GorgeousFrankenstein.com, http://www.gorgeousfrankenstein.com.

15. "News: October 19, 2012," DrChud.com, http://www.drchud.com/index.html.

16. DJ Troll, "Gorgeous Frankenstein Exclusive Phone Interview," Yahoo! Voices, May 6, 2009, http://voices.yahoo.com/gorgeous-frankenstein-exclusive-phone-interview-3242649. html.

17. "About Doyle's Made in Hell Hot Sauce," DoylesMadeInHell.com, http://www. doylesmadeinhell.com.

18. *Kaufhold et al v. Caiafa et al*, Case No. 11-cv-01460-WJM-MF, originally filed June 11, 2010, 1–19.

19. "Ex-Misfits Guitarist Releases Own Version of Band's Controversial 'Lost' Album," Blabbermouth.net, December 11, 2007, http://blabbermouth.net/news.aspx?mode=Article& newsitemID=86588.

20. Ashley Warren, "7th House Message Board Posting," Misfits Central, October 22, 2001, http://misfitscentral.com/hits.php.

21. "Ex-Misfits Guitarist Releases Own Version."

22. "Ex-Misfits Guitarist Releases Own Version."

23. "Exclusive Coverage!—2011 Chiller Theatre Expo—Part 2!" RadioDeadly.net, http:// www.radiodeadly.net/2011/05/08/chiller-part-2.

24. Bloodfeast (August 1, 2012), "The Undead and Post Mortem Records Websites Are Down [Msg 24250]", message posted to http://www.misfitscentral.com/forum/viewtopic.php? f=2&t=1704&start=20.

25. Ian MacKaye, telephone interview with the author, January 28, 2011.

26. The Misfits, "Land of the Dead," Misfits Records, 2009, compact disc single.

27. "Marky Ramone: The Hellbound Interview," Hellbound.ca, September 1, 2010, http:// www.hellbound.ca/2010/09/marky-ramones-the-hellbound-interview.

28. Mike IX Williams, telephone interview with author, October 2, 2012.

29. "Misfits Replace Robo, Title New Album," Punknews.org, November 24, 2010, http:// www.punknews.org/article/40723/misfits-replace-robo-title-new-album.

30. The Misfits, *The Devil's Rain*, Misfits Records, 2011, compact disc.

31. Michael Christopher, "Rock Music Menu: The Misfits Are Short on Scary," *Delaware County Times*, October 13, 2011, http://delcotimes.com/articles/2011/10/13/entertainment/ doc4e976b083411d673653143.txt?viewmode=fullstory.

32. Mark Prindle, "The Devil's Rain," MarkPrindle.com, http://markprindle.com/misfitsa. htm#devils.

33. "Misfits Concert Setlists and Tour Dates," Setlist.fm, http://www.setlist.fm/setlists/ misfits-73d68ed5.html.

34. Benjy Eisen, "Inside the Misfits' First Album in 12 Years," RollingStone.com, August 19, 2011, http://www.rollingstone.com/music/news/inside-the-misfits-first-album-in-12-years-20110819.

35. "Glenn Danzig House Profile Los Angeles, CA," Celebrity Detective, http://www. celebritydetective.com/Celebrity_Homes_Glenn-Danzig-house-Los-Angeles-CA.html.

36. Alex Distefano, "The Craziest Danzig Stalker of Them All," *LA Weekly* blog, October 27, 2011, http://blogs.laweekly.com/westcoastsound/2011/10/danzig_stalker.php.

37. Lonny Knapp, "Glenn Danzig Duets with Melissa Auf der Maur," Spinner, June 29, 2010, http://www.spinner.com/2010/06/29/glenn-danzig-melissa-auf-der-maur-duet.

38. Sean Cannon, "Danzig Watch 2010: In Which I Talk to Danzig Himself," Buzzgrinder, October 28, 2010, http://www.buzzgrinder.com/2010/danzig-interview.

39. "Danzig Legacy Show Coming to NYC & CA," Brooklyn Vegan, August 12, 2011, http://www.brooklynvegan.com/archives/2011/08/danzig_legacy_s.html.

40. "Kitty Litter," Posting on Fun Fun Fun Fest's Facebook page, November 5, 2011, https:/ /www.facebook.com/funfunfunfest/posts/10150920539195381.

41. Dave Maher, "My Morning Jacket, Pajo Cover Misfits on Comp," Pitchfork Media, October 18, 2007, http://web.archive.org/web/20080208192044/http://www.pitchforkmedia. com/article/news/46478-my-morning-jacket-pajo-cover-misfits-on-comp.

42. Seth Graves, "Bonnaroo 2012, Gravy Style Day Three: Glenn Danzig vs. Nashville Cream," Nashville Scene, June 10, 2012, http://www.nashvillescene.com/nashvillecream/ archives/2012/06/10/bonnaroo-2012-gravy-style-day-three-glenn-danzig-vs-nashville-cream.

43. "Danzig: 'Devil's Angels' Cover Available for Streaming," Blabbermouth.net, May 8, 2012, http://www.blabbermouth.net/news.aspx?mode=Article&newsitemID=173726.

44. MacKaye, telephone interview.

45. Bruce McCulloch, telephone interview with the author, February 16, 2011.

46. JR, telephone interview with the author, June 12, 2012.

Bibliography

"The $5.98 E.P. Garage Days Re-Revisited: Awards." *AllMusic*. http://www.allmusic.com/ album/the-598-ep-garage-days-re-revisited-mw0000196847/awards.

"About Doyle's Made in Hell Hot Sauce." *DoylesMadeInHell.com*. http://www. doylesmadeinhell.com.

Abowitz, Richard. "The Misfits—American Psycho." *Rolling Stone*, no. 790, May 15, 1997.

Allison, Andrea. "The Devil's Tree." *Paranormalstories*, February 26, 2010. http:// paranormalstories.blogspot.com/2010/02/devils-tree.html.

Alo, Chris. "Glenn Danzig—Finally Some Words about 'The Misfits,' Movies and Dolls." *Rock Brigade*, October 1994.

Apicella, Vinnie. "Misfits—Never Say Die." *The Aquarian Weekly*, June 17, 1998.

Asch, Andrew. "Cancer: Survivor." *OC Weekly*, November 9, 2001. http://www.ocweekly. com/2001-12-06/music/cancer-survivor.

Azerrad, Michael. *Our Band Could Be Your Life: Scenes from the American Indie Underground: 1981–1991*. New York: Back Bay, 2002.

Berger, Peter. *The Social Construction of Reality*. New York: Anchor, 1966.

Bernstein, Adam. "Les Paul, 94, 'Wizard of Waukesha' Invented Guitars That Changed Popular Music." *The Washington Post*, August 14, 2009. http://www.washingtonpost.com/ wpdyn/content/article/2009/08/13/AR2009081301768.html.

Bessy, Claude. "The Misfits." *Slash*, November 1978, 28.

"Blackest of The Black Tour Cancelled." Blabbermouth.net, September 15, 2004. http://www. blabbermouth.net/news.aspx?mode=Article&newsitemID=26924.

"Blue Cheer." AllMusic. http://www.allmusic.com/artist/blue-cheer-mn0000059537.

Blush, Stephen. *American Hardcore: A Tribal History*. Port Townsend, WA: Feral House, 2010.

———. "Glenn Danzig." *Seconds*, no. 44 (October 1997): 34–44. "Bobby Steele Interview." *Punk Floyd*, October 1993.

"Bobby Steele Interview." TV Casualty, April 25, 1998. http://www.tvcasualty.com/articles/a_ bobby.html.

Boluk, Stephanie, and Wylie Lenz. *Generation Zombie: Essays on the Living Dead in Modern Culture*. Jefferson, NC: McFarland, 2011.

Brinkman, Tom. "It's a Violent, Violent, Violent, Violent World." BadMags.com. http://www. badmags.com/bmviolent.html.

"Brian Keats Drummer, Near Death." *Rayon's Blog*, January 12, 2010. http://www.myspace. com/rayon/blog/524678595.

Brubaker, Paul. "Bada Bing Club Is Auctioning 'Sopranos' Memorabilia Online." *Herald News*, August 25, 2007. http://www.northjersey.com/page.php?qstr=eXJpcnk3ZjcxN2Y3dn FlZUVFeXk3JmZnYmVsN2Y3dnFlZUVFeXk3MTg2MTAy.

"Bruce Springsteen." *Biography*. http://www.biography.com/people/bruce-springsteen-9491214.

"Bud Geary." The Files of Jerry Blake. http://filesofjerryblake.netfirms.com/html/bud_geary. html.

Caiafa et al v. Anzalone et al, Case No. 1:92-cv-06908-LAP. Originally filed September 18, 1992.

Cannestra, Sal. "Kryst the Conqueror: Ex-Misfits Metal Meltdown." *Jersey Beat*, no. 40 (Summer 1990): 9–11.

Cashmore, Steven. "Northland Rock: Part Four—The Beat Goes On." *Highland Archives*, 1998. http://www.internetpromotions.co.uk/archives/northlands/north4.htm.

Chute, David. "Misfits Make a Joke of Hard-Core Punk." *Los Angeles Herald-Examiner*, April 15, 1982.

Cipriani, Frank D. "Welcome to the Gatherer Institute." Gatherer.org. http://www.gatherer.org.

Clark, Randall. *At a Theater or Drive-In Near You: The History, Culture and Politics of the American Exploitation Film*. New York: Routledge, 1995.

The Crimson Ghost. IMDb. http://www.imdb.com/title/tt0038435.

"Danzig to Team Up with Doyle for Two Shows in December." Blabbermouth.net, October 30, 2004. http://www.blabbermouth.net/news.aspx?mode=Article&newsitemID=28565.

"Discography of Official Danzig Releases." Misfits Central. http://misfitscentral.com/danzig/discog.php.

"Discography of Official Misfits Releases." Misfits Central. http://misfitscentral.com/misfits/discog.php.

Donohue, Jeanne. "Family/Boardwalk Tradition: Salt Water Taffy." *The Press of Atlantic City*, June 8, 2006. http://nl.newsbank.com/nl-search/we/Archives?p_product=AC&p_theme= ac&p_action=search&p_maxdocs=200&p_topdoc=1&p_text_direct-0=11224176B7C4EA A0&p_field_direct-0=document_id&p_perpage=10&p_sort=YMD_date:D&s_trackval= GooglePM.

Dotson, Kelleigh. "New Jersey's Devils Tower Is Haunted." Suite101, June 13, 2009. http:// suite101.com/article/newjerseys-devils-tower-is-haunted-a124961.

End of the Century. Directed by Jim Fields and Michael Gramaglia. Los Angeles, CA: Magnolia Pictures, 2003. DVD.

"Ex-Misfits Guitarist Releases Own Version of Band's Controversial 'Lost' Album." Blabbermouth.net, December 11, 2007. http://blabbermouth.net/news.aspx?mode=Article& newsitemID=86588.

"Exhibit C." *Kaufhold et al v. Caiafa et al*, Case No. 11-cv-01460-WJM-MF. Filed July 22, 2011.

"Exhibit D." *Kaufhold et al v. Caiafa et al*, Case No. 11-cv-01460-WJM-MF. Filed July 22, 2011.

Ferris, D. X. "Danzig's Blackest of the Black Tour Promises to Melt Your Face Off." *The Dallas Observer*, October 30, 2008. http://www.dallasobserver.com/2008-10-30/music/danzig-s-blackest-of-the-black-tour-promises-to-melt-your-face-off.

The Filth and the Fury, Directed by Julien Temple. London: FilmFour, 2000. DVD.

"Frank Sinatra Obituary." *BBC News*, May 16, 1998. http://news.bbc.co.uk/2/hi/special_report/1998/05/98/sinatra/67911.stm.

Fybush, Scott. "77 WABC, Lodi, N.J." Fybush.com. May 27, 2005. http://www.fybush.com/sites/2005/site-050527.html.

Gill, Barbara. "Lindbergh Kidnapping Rocked the World 50 Years Ago." *Hunterdon County Democrat*, 1981. http://www.nj.com/lindbergh/hunterdon/index.ssf?/lindbergh/stories/demcovr.html.

"Glenn D." *Black Market*, no. 6 (Fall 1986).

"Glenn Danzig: North Side Kings Punchout Was a 'Setup.'" Blabbermouth.net, August 20, 2004. http://www.blabbermouth.net/news.aspx?mode=Article&newsitemID=26000.

"Glenn Danzig Interview." Pennyblood.com, January 30, 2010. http://www.pennyblood.com/danzig.html.

Goodall, Nigel. "Transcript of Elvis's 1972 Press Conference." June 8, 2011. http://www.elvis.com.au/presley/interview_with_elvis_presley_the_1972_press_conference.shtml.

"Gorgeous Frankenstein: The Band." GorgeousFrankenstein.com. http://www.gorgeousfrankenstein.com.

Greenberg, Peter S. "Saints and Stinkers." *Rolling Stone*, February 19, 1981.

Grondahl, Paul. "Remembering Bob Gori, Punk Rocker." *The Times Union*, April 22, 2011. http://www.timesunion.com/local/article/Remembering-Bob-Gori-punk-rocker-1347843.php.

"Guns n' Roses Discography." Wikipedia. http://en.wikipedia.org/wiki/Guns_N%27_Roses_discography.

"The Hindenburg Disaster." Airships.net. http://www.airships.net/hindenburg/disaster.

"History." KoolAndTheGang.com. http://www.koolandthegang.com/history.

"History of the Campbell's Soup Company." CampbellSoup.com.au. http://www.campbellsoup.com.au/about-campbells/our-history.aspx.

Juliano, Dave. "The Jersey Devil." Shadowlands.net, Accessed August 1, 2012. http://theshadowlands.net/jd.htm.

Kaufhold et al v. Caiafa et al, Case No. 11-cv-01460-WJM-MF. Originally filed June 11, 2010, 12.

Kids in the Hall: Brain Candy. Directed by Kelly Makin. Los Angeles, CA: Paramount Pictures, 1996. DVD.

Kit, Chas. "Lost and Found." Garage Hangover, August 28, 2007. http://www.garagehangover.com/?q=lostandfound.

Kitts, Jeff. "The Dark Knight Returns." *Flux*, no. 1 (September 1994).

Klett, Joseph R. "Using the Records of East & West Jersey Proprietors." NJ.gov, 2008. http://www.nj.gov/state/darm/pdf/proprietors.pdf.

"Kryst the Conqueror." *Doyle Fan Club*, no. 6 (1989).

Lee, Craig. "Horror-Movie Rock from The Misfits." *Los Angeles Times*, April 15, 1982.

Leibrock, Rachel. "Cramps Singer Lux Interior Dies at 60." *Sacramento Bee*, February 4, 2009. http://www.sacbee.com/static/weblogs/ticket/archives/019288.html.

"Making The Misfits." *Great Performances*. PBS, 2001.

Marcus, Greil. *Stranded: Rock and Roll for a Desert Island*. New York: Knopf, 1979.

"Master of Puppets: Awards." AllMusic. http://www.allmusic.com/album/master-of-puppetsmw0000667490/awards.

Mercer, Mick. "The Dead Zone." *Melody Maker*, October 22, 1988.

"Misfits, American Psycho." *Entertainment Weekly*, May 16, 1997. http://www.ew.com/ew/article/0,,287893,00.html.

"The Misfits—3 Hits From Hell"; "The Misfits—Halloween." *Wave Sector* (1981).

"Misfits Concert Setlists and Tour Dates." Setlist.fm. http://www.setlist.fm/setlists/misfits-73d68ed5.html.

"Misfits Interview." *Flipside*, no. 36 (December 1982). "Misfits Interview." *Touch & Go*, no. 18 (Fall 1981).

"The Misfits—Live at the Graystone Hall." Posted by Honkofthewall, September 6, 2010. http://www.youtube.com/watch?v=m7O8jBUABjw.

"Misfits—Santa Monica Civic 1983." Posted by drinkyeflaggons, December 3, 2011. http://www.youtube.com/watch? v=EdUcVbiAiU4.

"Misfits Time Line." Misfits Central. http://misfitscentral.com/misfits/timeline.php.

"Misfits Tour Dates." Misfits Central. http://misfitscentral.com/misfits95/tourdates.php.

"Misfits—'Walk Among Us.'" *Forced Exposure* (March 1982).

"Misfits—'Walk Among Us.'" *Terror Times* (March 1982).

"Myke Hideous Interview." TVCasualty.com. http://tvcasualty.com/articles/a_mykeh.html.

McCann, Graham. *Rebel Males: Clift, Brando and Dean*. London: Hamish Hamilton Ltd, 1991.

Nardwuar. "Nardwuar the Human Serviette versus Glenn Danzig." Nardwuar.com, December 1999. http://nardwuar.com/vs/glenn_danzig/index.html.

Neely, Kim. "Danzig—Danzig." *Rolling Stone*, November 17, 1988.

Nible, Geri. "Jerry Only Interview." *Feh*, no. 12 (September/October 1994).

Ogg, Alex. "Everything Went Black." AllMusic. http://www.allmusic.com/album/everythingwent-black-mw0000192996.

Olver, Lynne. "Mcdonald's Hamburger Prices." FoodTimeline.org. http://www.foodtimeline.org/foodfaq5.html.

Only, Jerry. "Untitled Press Release." Misfits Central, May 27, 1998. http://misfitscentral.com/display.php?t=marticle&f=mfc_sing.98.

Palmer, Robert. "Danzig III: How the Gods Kill." *Rolling Stone*, July 9, 1992.

Patrick, Maggy. "Summit High Hosted Velvet Underground's First Show." SummitPatch.com, January 28, 2010. http://summit.patch.com/articles/summit-high-hosted-velvet-undergrounds-first-show.

Prindle, Mark. "Jerry Only—2003." MarkPrindle.com. http://www.markprindle.com/onlyi.htm.

———. "John Stabb—2008." MarkPrindle.com, 2008. http://markprindle.com/stabb-i.htm.

Pushead. "James Hetfield and Kirk Hammet." *Thrasher*, August 1986.

"Punk-Rock Musicians Arrested in Cemetery." *New Orleans Times-Picayune*, October 18, 1982.

"Radio Listeners in Panic, Taking War Drama as Fact." *New York Times*, October 31, 1938. http://select.nytimes.com/gst/abstract.html?res=F70A17FB3D5F1B7A93C3AA178BD95F4C8385F9.

Raggett, Ned. "The Damned." AllMusic. http://www.allmusic.com/artist/the-damnedmn0000138520.

———. "Walk Among Us." AllMusic. http://www.allmusic.com/album/walk-among-usmw0000197473.

Ralph, Randy D. "Ramapough Mountain People 'The Jackson Whites.'" Netsrider.com, January 2, 2001. http://www.netstrider.com/documents/whites.

Rollins, Henry. *Get in the Van: On the Road with Black Flag*. Los Angeles: 2.12.61, 2004.

Rosenfeld, Everett. "Jersey Shore Attacks, 1916." *Time*, August 1, 2011. http://www.time.com/time/specials/packages/article/0,28804,2085822_2085823_2085948,00.html.

Ryan, A. J., and Pamela Hazelton. "I Am Misfit." *Lucanae*, no. 7 (April 1996).

"Samhain Time Line." Misfits Central. http://misfitscentral.com/samhain/timeline.php.

"Samhain: 'We Don't Want to Be Called a Hardcore Band.'" *Hard Times* 1, no. 1 (August 1984).

Snyder, John P. "The Story of New Jersey's Civil Boundaries: 1606–1968." Bureau of Geology and Topography, 1969.

Sokolic, William H. "Underdog Gives Woman New Leash on Life." *Courier Post* (New Jersey), April 17, 1999.

Sommer, Tim. "New York Noos." *Sounds*, May 1, 1982.

"Song and Name Information." Misfits Central. http://misfitscentral.com/misfits/timeline.php.

Stasi, Linda. "Story Behind The Real 'Sopranos.'" *New York Post*, June 23, 2010. http://www.nypost.com/p/entertainment/tv/story_behind_the_real_sopranos_6WwWzB3HbtEfL63vKrxrFN.

State of New Jersey Commission of Investigation. "The Changing Face of Organized Crime in New Jersey: A Status Report." May 2004.

Stax, Mike. "All Hell Breaks Loose: The Jerry Only Interview." *Ugly Things*, no. 12 (Summer 1993).

———. "Image of a Misfit: An Interview with Joey Image." *Ugly Things*, no. 13 (1994).

Stewart, Jocelyn Y. "Actress, TV Horror Hostess Vampira." *Los Angeles Times*, January 16, 2008. http://articles.latimes.com/2008/jan/16/local/me-nurmi16.

Stratton, Jeff. "The Devil Inside." *Miami New Times*, April 20, 2000. http://www.miaminewtimes.com/2000-0420/music/the-devil-inside/1.

Taylor, Steven. *False Prophet: Field Notes from the Punk Underground*. Middletown, CT: Wesleyan University Press, 2003.

Thompson, Stephen. "American Psycho." Onion A.V. Club. http://www.avclub.com/articles/misfits-american-psycho,21093.

———. "New York Dolls." AllMusic. http://www.allmusic.com/artist/new-york-dolls-p5019.

Thorn, Steve. "The History of San Diego Rock 'n' Roll, Part One: A Sleeping Town Wakes Up." *Kicks*, no. 3 (November 1979).

Tilander, Geoffrey. "Bobby Steele Interview." *MaximumRockNRoll* (1992).

"Tour Dates." Misfits Central. http://misfitscentral.com/misfits/timeline.php.

Von, Eerie. "Liner Notes." *The Misfits*. Caroline Records, 1996. Compact disc set.

Walsh, Bryan. "The Electrifying Edison." *Time*, July 5, 2010. http://www.time.com/time/specials/packages/article/0,28804,1910417_1910419_1910460,00.html.

Warburton, Nick. "Them." Garage Hangover, May 17, 2010. http://www.garagehangover.com/?q=taxonomy/term/1638.

Waters, John. *Crackpot: The Obsessions of John Waters*, New York: Macmillan, 1983.

Watson, Elena M. *Television Horror Movie Hosts: 68 Vampires, Mad Scientists and Other Denizens of the Late Night Airwaves Examined and Interviewed*. Jefferson, NC: MacFarland, 2000.

"Welcome to Satin Dolls, The Original 'Bada Bing!' Club." SatinDollsNJ.com. http://www.satindollsnj.com/satindollshome.html.

"What Caused Glenn Danzig to Lose His Temper in North Side Kings Altercation?" Blabbermouth.net, December 23, 2004. http://www.blabbermouth.net/news.aspx?mode=Article&newsitemID=30705.

Whitburn, Joel. *Joel Whitburn Presents the Billboard Albums*. Menomonee Falls, WI: Record Research, 2007.

Wright, Kevin W. "The Indigenous Population of Bergen County." BergenCountyHistory.org. http://www.bergencountyhistory.org/Pages/indians.html.

Wyoming, Moe. "Myke Hideous." *MK Magazine*, November 1, 2003. http://www.mk-magazine.com/interviews/archives/000118.php.

Unterberger, Richie. "The Four Seasons." VocalGroup.org. http://www.vocalgroup.org/inductees/the_four_seasons.html.

Yuenger, Jay. "Misfits Arrested in New Orleans." Jyuenger.com. http://www.jyuenger.com/?P=4365.

Zaleski, Annie. "Misfits Reunion Allegedly Scuttled by New Leader Jerry Only." *Riverfront Times*, September 11, 2008. http://blogs.riverfronttimes.com/rftmusic/2008/09/misfits_reunion_jerry_only_danzig_misfits_gorgeous_frankenstein_doyle.php.

Zanni, Ian. "10 More Roads That Will Scare You Stupid." ListVerse.com, February 6, 2011. http://listverse.com/2011/02/06/10-more-roads-that-will-scare-you-stupid.

Zogbi, Mariana. "Danzig on Thin Ice." *Metal Mania*, Spring 1989.

Index

About the Author

James Greene Jr. is a freelance writer who has contributed to *Crawdaddy!*, *New York Press*, *Splitsider*, *PopMatters*, *Geek Monthly*, and *Uncle John's Bathroom Reader*. He graduated from the University of Central Florida with a BA in organizational communication (the only thing he really learned during that matriculation is the plural of communication is communication). James Greene Jr. is not ambidextrous and currently lives somewhere in New York.